LET MY PEOPLE GO

LET MY PEOPLE GO

The untold story of Australia and the Soviet Jews 1959-89

SAM LIPSKI AND SUZANNE D. RUTLAND

HYBRID
PUBLISHERS

Published by Hybrid Publishers
Melbourne Victoria Australia

© Sam Lipski 2015

First published 2015

National Library of Australia Cataloguing-in-Publication entry
Author: Lipski, Sam, 1938– author.
Title: Let my people go: The untold story of Australia and the
Soviet Jews 1959–89 / Sam Lipski
Suzanne D Rutland.

ISBN: 9781925000856 (paperback)

Notes: Includes index.
Subjects: Leibler, I. J. (Isi J.)
Jews – Persecutions – Soviet Union.
Refuseniks.
Jews – Soviet Union – History – 20th century.
Jews, Soviet – Australia – History.
Soviet Union – Emigration and immigration – Political aspects.
Soviet Union – Politics and government – 1953–1985.
Australia – Emigration and immigration – Political aspects.
Australia – Politics and government – 1945–

Other Authors/Contributors:
Rutland, Suzanne D. (Suzanne Dorothy), 1946–

Dewey Number: 305.8924094

Cover design by Art on Order
Typeset in 12/15.5 pt Minion Pro

FOREWORD

The Soviet Jewry movement gave me my first serious experience as a journalist and editor; my first taste of Zionist activism; and my first exposure to Cold War politics, Australian style.

I had wanted to write a book about it ever since I spent an unforgettable ten days in Moscow in September 1987. That is when I met the heroic refuseniks, came up against the Soviet totalitarian system and, as an Australian Jew, felt grateful and proud that the Australian government and its diplomats had supported a just and righteous cause.

My well-intentioned plans to write the book lay dormant for the next fifteen years. They almost certainly would have stayed that way had it not been for Isi Leibler and Suzanne Rutland.

During meetings in Jerusalem in 2004, I mentioned to Isi that I had started some initial research on the Soviet Jewry story at the National Archives in Canberra. I did not know, however, that during her visits to Jerusalem, Suzanne Rutland, a Professor of History at the University of Sydney, and the long-time Head of the Department of Jewish Studies there, had been doing her own research on Australia and Soviet Jewry in the extensive Leibler archive.

When Isi suggested that Suzanne and I collaborate to write a book, and when Suzanne agreed, I was delighted. Not only did I admire her many defining contributions to Australian Jewish history as a pioneering academic in the field, but we had worked together on some of the chapters in *Pages of History,* her history of the Australian Jewish press.

A declaration of interest: I had known Isi since he had been my Zionist youth movement leader in Melbourne in the 1950s. We had been friends who worked together in the Soviet Jewry campaign for some 30 years. And it was he and his wife Naomi who had invited me and my wife Aura to join them in Moscow in 1987. I had also worked professionally for him during the 1980s as a consultant, speech-writer and media adviser. The professional relationship ended in 1987 when I became the editor and publisher of the *Australian Jewish News*, but our friendship has continued. So in writing about Isi, I do not claim total objectivity. But I hope I have been fair, and respected the record.

Although this book has been a collaborative venture with Suzanne, it would not have happened without her indispensable and foundational research in Jerusalem, Sydney and Canberra. In addition to mining the vast Leibler collection, which is the world's most comprehensive private Soviet Jewry archive, Suzanne undertook ground-breaking research at the National Archives in Canberra.

Awarded a prestigious Prime Minister's research grant in 2009–10, she was given unprecedented access to Prime Ministers' and Cabinet papers, previously unavailable Foreign Affairs cables and records, and Australian Security Intelligence Organisation (ASIO) wiretap transcripts.

Nor would the book have happened unless Suzanne had undertaken the initial drafting of all but two of the book's 23 chapters. I owe her a co-author's debt of special gratitude for the heavy lifting, her unmatched knowledge of the subject material, and persistent and patient encouragement.

After planning the book's structure together in 2009, it unfolded in three stages. In the first stage, Suzanne drafted each chapter and we edited the first six chapters together. In the second stage, working with the edited chapters and Suzanne's drafts, I rewrote all the chapters, added new research and interview material, and reorganised the book's structure. I also wrote a new opening chapter and chapter 11 about my Washington experience.

During this stage, I also introduced the first-person voice where I had been directly involved in some of the events described, as in Chapter 5 on "The Cohen Affair". In the third and final stage, Suzanne drafted Chapters 21 and 22, which I then edited and rewrote, again adding the first-person voice where appropriate.

Although Suzanne and I worked closely throughout all the editing and rewriting stages, and while I incorporated most of her suggestions for changes, we agreed that I would take the writer's responsibility for the book's final version.

In a separate section I have expressed my thanks and acknowledgments to some of the many people who helped me in thinking about the book and during the course of writing. This foreword, however, is dedicated in gratitude to my co-author, Suzanne Rutland.

Sam Lipski
Melbourne
January 2015

CONTENTS

Foreword   v

Abbreviations   xi

Glossary   xiii

Acknowledgements   xv

Introduction   xiii

1. From Russia with Thanks   1

2. The Spymaster and the Recruit   15

3. Three Leaders, Three Voices   24

4. Wentworth Asks, Barwick Answers   34

5. The Cohen Affair   47

6. Channels of Communication   60

7. From Right to Left   67

8. Italian liners and the Party   79

9. Exodus via *Samizdat*   90

10. Prisoners of Zion   104

11. Henry J and Henry K   115

12. "You people are hard to please"   123

13. Freedom Ride to Canberra   133

14. From Melbourne to Moscow   146

15. The Games Russians Play   155

16. Hawke's Mission Impossible   163

17. Hope against Hope   170

18. Some of my Closest Friends are KGB   179

19. It's About the Refuseniks   189

20. Gorbachev, Geneva and *Glasnost*   199

21. Ten Days in Moscow   207

22. The Full Circle   220
About the Authors   231
Endnotes   233
Index   265

ABBREVIATIONS

ACRSJ	Australian Campaign for the Rescue of Soviet Jewry
ACSJ	Australian Conference on Soviet Jewry
ACTU	Australian Council of Trade Unions
AJH	Australian Jewish Herald
ALP	Australian Labor Party
AOF	Australian Olympic Federation
ASIO	Australian Security Intelligence Organisation
AUCTU	All Union Council of Trade Unions (Soviet)
CCCR	the Union of Soviet Socialist Republics
CIA	Central Intelligence Agency
CIS	Commonwealth Investigation Services (ASIO's predecessor)
CPA	Communist Party of Australia
CPSU	Communist Party of the Soviet Union
DLP	Democratic Labor Party
ECAJ	Executive Council of Australian Jewry
ILO	International Labor Organisation
IOC	International Olympic Federation
JCFAD	Joint Committee on Foreign Affairs and Defence (Parliament of Australia)
JUA	Jewish Unity Association
KGB	Soviet Union's main security agency and secret police 1954–91
LCP	Liberal Country Party
MAOZ	Israel's Soviet Jewry campaign
MFN	Most Favoured Nation
MHR	Member, House of Representatives (Parliament of Australia)
MP	Member of Parliament
NATO	North American Treaty Organisation
NCSJ	National Conference on Soviet Jewry (United States)

NKVD	KGB's secret police predecessor
NSW	New South Wales
OVIR	Soviet passport and visa office
PATA	Pacific Asia Travel Association
PLO	Palestine Liberation Organisation
RAAF	Royal Australian Air Force
SALT	Strategic Arms Limitation Talks
SPA	Socialist Party of Australia
VJBD	Victorian Jewish Board of Deputies
WJC	World Jewish Congress

GLOSSARY

Anachnu V'Atem (Hebrew): "We and You", title of a popular song in the Soviet Jewry campaign.

aliyah (Hebrew, literally "going up"): migration to Israel.

bar mitzvah (Hebrew, literally "son of the commandments"): religious ceremony to mark a Jewish boy's religious maturity at the age of thirteen.

Beth Din (Hebrew, literally "House of Judgement"): rabbinical court.

chutzpah (Hebrew and Yiddish): insolence, cheek or audacity.

diaspora (Greek): a term for Jews and Jewish communities outside Israel.

glasnost (Russian): Mikhail Gorbachev's efforts in the 1980s to provide more freedom of expression and openness in the Soviet Union.

Hatikvah (Hebrew): "The Hope", Israel's national anthem.

kosher (Hebrew *kasher*): complying with the Jewish dietary laws.

Lishkat Hakesher (*Lishkah*): The Liaison Bureau.

madrich (Hebrew): youth leader.

matza (*matzot*) (Hebrew): unleavened bread singular (plural).

Nativ (Hebrew): literally "path" – code name for Lishkat Hakesher.

neshira (Hebrew): the "drop-out" factor.

noshrim (Hebrew): drop-outs.

perestroika (Russian): Mikhail Gorbachev's efforts to reform the Soviet Communist Party.

pogrom a term first used in Tsarist Russia for organised violent mob attacks especially directed against Jews.

refusenik (Russian): a term referring to Soviet Jews who applied to emigrate to Israel, but who were refused permission to do so.

samizdat (Russian): clandestine literature and documentation which circulated secretly in the Soviet Union.

shtadlonus (Yiddish): historically it referred to "intercession" with authorities by Jewish leaders on behalf of their communities; more recently used as a derogatory term for leaders reluctant to represent Jewish interests vigorously.

simchah (Hebrew): (literally "happiness") rejoicing on a special occasion, such as a wedding.

Simchat Torah (Hebrew): Jewish festival, "Rejoicing of the Law", when the cycle of the reading of the Torah (Five Books of Moses) is completed and then recommenced each year.

Talmudic (from Hebrew, *Talmud*, literally "study"): adjective for a student of the classical work of rabbinic law and literature.

Yeshivah (Hebrew): College and seminary for Talmudic studies.

Yom Kippur (Hebrew): Day of Atonement, the most solemn day in the Jewish calendar.

ACKNOWLEDGEMENTS

Sam Lipski

My idea for this book began in the refuseniks' homes in Moscow in 1987, and I thank all of them, whether named or not.

For their special insights into the Soviet Jewry campaign I am grateful to David Harris in New York, Richard Perle, Elliot Abrams and Charles Horner in Washington DC, and former Prisoner of Zion, now Speaker of Israel's Knesset, Yuli Edelstein. My thanks, too, to former Prisoner of Zion, Natan Sharansky, now Chairman of the Jewish Agency, for an illuminating conversation during his visit to Melbourne in 2014.

For helping with my own research I am grateful to the staff at the Australian National Archives, the National Library of Australia, the Parliamentary Library, Canberra, the State Library of Victoria, the State Library of New South Wales, the Baillieu Library, University of Melbourne, and the Fisher Library, University of Sydney. As the end notes demonstrate, in addition to the primary source materials which provided the main documentation, Suzanne and I read and consulted a wide range of secondary sources. We are grateful to all the authors and their publishers.

More than 25 years after the main events in which he was so deeply involved, I interviewed Bob Hawke in his Sydney office. The former Australian Prime Minister was generous with his time and open with his views. I am grateful for both responses. Among friends and colleagues, Michael Gawenda was supportive, encouraging, and an objective editor whose advice after reading the first draft was invaluable. Writing about a cause which the late Richard Pratt supported vigorously, added yet another reason to thank the Pratt family for their ongoing support.

In the Hebrew phrase, "The very last is the most beloved", I give thanks to – and for – my own family: to Ilana and Ahron, who are old enough to understand the Soviet Jewish story; to Avital, named after a heroine of the Jewish people, Avital Sharansky; to Ezra who was born in the year that the Soviet empire fell; and to my grandson Nadav, who will one day read this story.

Suzanne Rutland and I are both grateful to Hybrid's publishers Louis de Vries and Anna Blay for their guidance, patience, and professionalism in enabling our manuscript to become a book. Their empathy and understanding for the story we had told, and their guidance at every stage were deeply encouraging and warmly appreciated.

When it comes to thanks, however, my loving wife Aura is in a special category. Not just for accepting the endless "Never on Sunday" excuses as I grappled to find time to write, but for caring deeply about the story. We had been to the Soviet Union together, and she had sung secretly in the refuseniks' homes. And then she had come again with her mother Vera to sing publicly in Moscow and Leningrad when the refuseniks were free. She was there for me as I wrote. As always.

Suzanne D Rutland

I wish to thank the Australian Prime Ministers Centre for their Fellowship, 2008–09, to undertake archival research for this project in Canberra and Israel.

I am also grateful to:

- The staff at the National Archives of Australia, Canberra, and in particular to Carolyn Connor, who provided constant assistance;
- Dr David Lee, Director of Historical Publications and Information Section, Department of Foreign Affairs and Trade, for his assistance in 2009 in gaining access to the materials in the National Archives for the relevant closed period, 1979–92;

- Professor Jeffrey Riegel, Head of the School of Languages and Cultures, and the Faculty of Arts, University of Sydney, for their support of this project;
- Stanley Green, who helped type up my notes in the Leibler Archive in Jerusalem.

And a special thanks to Isi Leibler for granting access since 2000 to his extensive materials on the Campaign for Soviet Jewry, without which the book could not have been written.

INTRODUCTION

The Berlin Wall fell on 9 November 1989. In 2009, a few days before the event's 20th anniversary, I listened to Natan Sharansky address a conference of Jewish philanthropists in Rome. Sharansky was speaking as the Jewish Agency's Chairman and a former minister in the Israeli government. But for me, and everyone in the audience, Sharansky had earned his moment in history some three years before the Wall fell. That was when he had walked across a Berlin bridge, from East to West, free at last, as the most famous Soviet refusenik and Prisoner of Zion.

The human rights campaigner had been imprisoned on a false charge of treason, but his only "crimes" had been to apply for emigration to Israel and to campaign for his fellow Soviet dissidents. On 11 February 1986, after nine years in a Siberian Gulag, often in solitary confinement, Sharansky was the first high-profile political prisoner whom Mikhail Gorbachev released, in response to international pressure.

So for Sharansky and his Rome audience there was every reason to remember the Berlin Wall's destruction. He noted that November 9 marked two great victories: freedom's victory over tyranny, and the Jewish people's victory over oppression. But Sharansky, ever the human rights activist, saw a connection between the two victories. He insisted that Soviet Jewry's successful struggle for freedom had mattered far beyond the latter-day Exodus of more than a million Jews to Israel. In his words: "The liberation of Soviet Jewry ... tore a gaping hole in the Iron Curtain, one that would eventually spell the end of the Soviet Empire."

Most historians and commentators disagree with Sharansky. Some might concede that the Soviet Jewry campaign contributed to the Soviet Empire's downfall, but history's verdict, at least in the short term, is that the Cold War's inexorable pressures, and Moscow's own economic and geo-political fault lines, were far more important.

I believe that, in the longer term, history's judgment will come closer to Sharansky's. But even if his view is too sweeping, Soviet Jewry's triumph was a monumental one. Chronologically, it came after the Holocaust and the State of Israel. But it ranks alongside them as one of the Jewish people's three Himalayan peaks in the 20th century. And in a resounding echo of recurring themes in the Jewish story, it was a victory of the few against the many, ultimately won not by power, but by the spirit.

Yet awareness of this epic saga, barely 25 years later, seems paradoxically to have receded from world Jewry's collective historical memory. After all, there is no lack of books, documentary films, newly available Soviet archives, and oral histories which continue to show the Soviet Jewry movement's widespread and transformative impact.

To consider just some of it: the emigration of over a million Jews to Israel, after an international campaign lasting more than three decades, redefined the notion of human rights. Indeed, Sharansky claims it as the 20th century's most successful human rights movement. Reflecting in 2007 on the movement's triumph, George Shultz, the former United States Secretary of State, summed up its lasting significance: "So the best of all reasons to record and remember how the Soviet Jews were saved is to be prepared to act again when the need arises ... We must not only preach the doctrine of human rights; we must also learn how to be our brothers' keeper."

As Shultz also pointed out in the early 1990s, the arrival of the Soviet Jewish émigrés, many with advanced academic qualifications, was better for Israel than if it had struck oil. Indeed, the emigration was the largest human knowledge transfer in the 20th century. It even eclipsed the migration of Jewish scientists and intellectuals in the 1930s from Nazi Germany to the United States. The Soviet arrivals not only helped Israel become the Start-up Nation economically and scientifically; they changed the country's politics and thus shaped events in the Middle East.

As for American Jews, the largest Diaspora community, they

are rightly credited with helping to save Soviet Jewry. They lobbied the Congress and the White House. They demonstrated, marched and organised. But it is just as relevant to say that the Soviet Jewry campaign helped to save many American Jews from assimilation and premature loss of identity. Whatever concerns there may be in the 21st century about the future of American Jews, the campaign for Soviet Jewry gave many a rallying point in the 20th.

Inevitably, this book refers to the wider story, inside the Soviet Union and internationally. But it has a more specific Australian focus. For the three critical decades, between 1959 and 1989, Australian Jews and their community leaders were deeply involved in the international Soviet Jewry movement. Australian governments, parliamentarians, diplomats, human rights activists and opinion leaders also contributed significantly. By any measure, Australia played a role above and beyond what might be expected from a middle-ranking nation with limited international influence.

In the pages ahead, Suzanne Rutland and I have set out to tell this Australian story. We believe it deserves telling. It chronicles a largely unknown, but important and interesting aspect of 20th century Australian political history during the Cold War. It highlights the distinctive contribution to international affairs made by some leading Australians, including Bob Hawke, Garfield Barwick, Malcolm Fraser, William Wentworth and John Wheeldon. But the lead actor was Isi Leibler, and this is very much also his story. Widely recognised and honoured internationally, his involvement and leadership – his "magnificent obsession" – with the refuseniks and Soviet Jews, merit a full account and an Australian Jewish perspective.

For me, that perspective has changed dramatically in my lifetime. In the 1940s, as destruction and tragedy enveloped Europe's Jews, demographers were predicting the disappearance of Australian Jews through assimilation. In the 1960s when I first became actively involved in the Soviet Jewish story, there were 60,000 Jews in Australia, many of them Holocaust survivors and their children. Today there are over 120,000 Jews, the majority born in Australia. They represent the eighth largest community outside Israel and the only Jewish community of stature in the Asia Pacific region. So most of all, we hope the Soviet Jewish story adds to the understanding of the Australian Jewish story – from the post-war community of mostly immigrants and survivors to the grateful participants in a pluralist society.

CHAPTER 1

FROM RUSSIA WITH THANKS

For the Jews of Australia, it was a night to remember. On 17 May 1988, some 3000 of them came to the Concert Hall at Melbourne's Arts Centre to celebrate, to pay tribute and to give thanks. On stage were fifteen former Soviet refuseniks. Just months earlier, after some had waited "in refusal" for as long as seventeen years, Mikhail Gorbachev had let them leave for Israel. Just days earlier, they had landed at Melbourne Airport to a heroes' welcome from the Jewish community.

The event at the Concert Hall was billed as "From Russia With Thanks", and began as a festival. But it did not quite end like that. For the first two hours, however, it was a night for the heart, a family *simchah*. A joyous celebration akin to a bar mitzvah or wedding. Choirs from the Jewish day schools led the audience in "Advance Australia Fair" and "Hatikvah", the Israeli national anthem.

Isi Leibler, who had driven Australia's Soviet Jewry campaign for 30 years, and had been deeply involved with the refuseniks and their families, began with the mantra from modern Zionism's founder, Theodor Herzl: "If you will it, it is no dream". When he said: "For all my joy I cannot rest, and none of us will rest, until all those Jews who wish to leave the Soviet Union can do so ..." the applause swept the auditorium. And when Aura Levin, who had met the refuseniks in Moscow just a few months earlier, sang *"Anachnu V'Atem"* – "We and You", the Soviet Jewry campaign hymn, the crowd's rhythmic clapping enveloped everybody. Writing more than 25 years later, I still recall clearly the pride, elation and tears, as each of the refuseniks spoke.

But later in the evening, Prime Minister Bob Hawke punctured the air of celebration. In an otherwise powerful and uplifting speech,

Hawke included just one unsettling sentence. In it he drew comparisons between Soviet Jews, and the Palestinians and black Africans under apartheid. There was an audible drawing in of collective breath. Then a turning of heads in disbelief. The remarks distressed the refuseniks, disappointed many of Hawke's admirers, and marked a turning point in Hawke's public views on Israel. With a few words, his public persona changed from the Jewish state's most passionate admirer in Australia to its sorely troubled critic.

Hawke's unexpected but deliberately chosen remarks also ended more than a decade of friendship, business partnership and collaboration on Soviet Jewry between him and Leibler. A great human rights cause had brought together these two dominant yet contrasting personalities from completely different backgrounds. What should have been their time of mutual joy, deteriorated into acrimony.

Yet although Hawke's surprise sentence marred the event, it could not detract from its historic significance. "From Russia With Thanks" marked a watershed in Australian Jewish history. It had its symbolic moments, but it was about more than symbolism. It had its emotional dramas, but it was about more than emotional identification. It was, above all, a political graduation ceremony.

The Soviet Jewry campaign had been at the centre of the Australian Jewish political and communal experience for three decades. In some ways, it had loomed even larger than the community's political activism for Israel. There was a clarity and simplicity about Soviet Jewry's compelling human rights story. "Let My People Go" resonated – as a slogan, but also as a call to involvement.

The refuseniks' human stories and the even more poignant cases of the Prisoners of Zion, those refuseniks who had been jailed, gave the larger campaign for free emigration a personalised narrative, and an additional edge. As a result, the Soviet Jewry cause in Australia, as happened internationally, often captured a wider cross-section of activists than Israel: left and right, Zionist and non-Zionist, religious and secular, old and young.

The campaign's leaders, however, and many of the cadres, were nearly always also strong Israel supporters. This meant that the

Australian campaign enhanced the community's pro-Israel activities, while providing much of the training ground for its post-war political development. Moreover, in making the case for Soviet Jewry, Australian Jews also learned how to advocate more effectively for its local needs in immigration, education and welfare. Most tellingly, the campaign helped a post-war migrant minority, somewhat uncertain of its place in Australia, and emerging from the post-Holocaust shadow, to become a mainstream participant in the open society.

Indeed, by the late 1980s, Jews had come to regard Australia as the latter-day "Goldeneh Medineh", the "Golden Kingdom". It was the title which American Jews had bestowed on the United States in the early 20th century. But it was the more recent "Goldeneh Medineh", an Australia where Jews had found refuge and been a success story, which provided the backdrop for the gratitude on open display in the Concert Hall.

In particular, there were thanks to Hawke and to his immediate predecessor, former Liberal Prime Minister Malcolm Fraser. Serendipitously, Fraser happened to be visiting the Soviet Union. He was waiting in the Australian embassy in Moscow to speak to the Concert Hall via a telephone hook-up. With him was a group of refuseniks who, determined and hopeful, were still waiting for their freedom.

The Concert Hall audience was there, too, to thank the Liberals' John Howard, who joined Hawke on stage to proclaim the refuseniks' "victory of the human spirit". And there were cheers for the Speaker of the House of Representatives, Labor's Joan Child, when she walked on stage. Child had led a bipartisan delegation of Australian parliamentarians to Moscow in 1986 where, on the refuseniks' behalf, she had spoken out boldly in the Kremlin.

A Labor Prime Minister, a former Liberal Prime Minister, a Liberal Leader of the Opposition – who would one day also be Prime Minister – and the parliament's Labor Speaker, all united by their solidarity with Soviet Jewry and their support for Australian Jewry. For 30 years, the "grassroots" campaign for Soviet Jewry had underpinned the more targeted political campaign directed at governments, parliamentarians and opinion makers. Many at the Concert Hall, together with Jews in Sydney, Perth, Brisbane and Adelaide, had not directly lobbied prime ministers. But they had demonstrated outside Russian circuses and held candlelight vigils whenever the Bolshoi Ballet toured. They had stood on flat-bed trucks outside the Soviet consulate singing Hebrew protest songs. And they had travelled to Canberra on "Freedom Buses" to protest outside the Soviet embassy.

Youth movement members had sent New Year cards to clandestine Hebrew teachers. Rabbis had organised prayer-vigils. University students had dressed in Gulag uniforms and chained themselves to town halls. University academics had signed petitions and written to Leonid Brezhnev. Doctors had protested against the Soviet abuse of psychiatry to silence dissidents and refuseniks. Women's organisations had adopted refusenik families and sent jeans to be used as currency. Bar mitzvah boys in Perth had twinned with their thirteen-year-old counterparts in Leningrad. Synagogue congregations had written letters to Prisoners of Zion in Siberia. And communal leaders had phoned Moscow knowing the KGB recorded their conversations.

At various times, depending on how dark the prospects were for Soviet Jews, the grassroots campaign had waxed and waned, but it had never died. Australian Jews had consistently contributed to the international campaign. Some communities, most notably American Jews, were much larger and more influential. But Australian Jews had taken up the issue before the Americans, and many at the Concert Hall were proud of their own distinctive contribution. They knew, however, that they had succeeded only because Australian political leaders and opinion makers across the ideological spectrum had also supported their cause. In 1988 this awareness resonated. The memories of surviving genocide and totalitarian regimes were still vivid. The majority of Melbourne's Jewish families were survivors, refugees, or immigrants. Or their children. Australia had been good to them, and for them, and this was yet another reason to be grateful to Australia. To borrow a phrase from Australian political lore, it was a night for "the true believers".

Leibler captured this sense of gratitude in his remarks directed to Hawke.

All honour is due to you for your personal commitment …
going back to your first meetings with Golda Meir … I know of
none who have combined the demands of statesmanship and
personal commitment with such dedication, understanding,
earthy passion, colourful language, and unabashed personal
involvement.[1]

The fifteen refuseniks on stage were a mixed bunch. Some were
Orthodox; some were secular Zionists. Some were Hebrew scholars;
some barely spoke a few words. Some came from formerly leading
communist families; others had been anti-communists from their
youth. Out of respect for his intellectual stature, gravitas and a
benevolent uncle's concern for his "family" of dissidents, Alexander
Lerner had emerged early as the Moscow refuseniks' natural leader.
A distinguished cyberneticist with an international reputation,
Lerner had waited seventeen years for his exit visa. Despite regular
raids, threats and arrests by the KGB, Lerner continued to conduct
his weekly seminars for refusenik scientists in his apartment.

Vladimir Slepak, with his wife Maria, had also waited for seventeen years. A radio engineer, whom the KGB arrested ten times and
exiled to Siberia for five years, had become one of the best-known
activists. Beginning in 1969, he was one of the first Soviet Jews to
address petitions to the United Nations. A decade after leaving the
Soviet Union, the prominent American Jewish writer, Chaim Potok,
told the Slepaks' story in *The Gates of November* (1997).

Yosef Begun had been a mathematician but had lost his job in
1971 when he applied for a visa. A former Prisoner of Zion, he had
been jailed for ten years on charges of "parasitism" for trying to teach
Hebrew. His wife Inna was only rarely allowed to hear from him
during his prison years, many spent in solitary confinement.

Their refusenik colleagues who had travelled with them from
Israel to Australia each had their own heroic stories. Pavel and Marta
Abramovich; Alexander and Rosa Ioffe; Alexander Kholmianksy,
who had been another Prisoner of Zion, and Anna Kholmyansky;
Vladimir Prestin, a leader in the struggle to teach Hebrew, and
Elena Prestin; Leonid Volkovsky, who spent three years in a labour
camp, and Ludmilla Volkovsky – each had waited twelve, fourteen,

or seventeen years to leave. Each had lost their jobs; each had been harassed, arrested and repeatedly threatened. The KGB had tapped their phones, interrogated them, and denounced them as enemies of the state.

But tonight, when each spoke briefly, some in fluent English, others haltingly, there was no bitterness or anger. Each expressed gratitude to Hawke, to the Australian people who, in Prestin's words, had given their Prime Minister "the moral mandate" to work for Soviet Jewry's freedom, to Leibler, and to Australia's Jews. Abramovich provoked laughter and applause when he said: "I am a free man. Hawke is a free man. Now we are equal."

The laughter and applause that followed had a double edge. For the Jewish audience, Hawke shared something else with Abramovich. He too was both a hero, and a folk-hero, on Israel as well as on Soviet Jewry. Even though some of his views on Israel since winning government in 1983 had become less positive, Jewish audiences still welcomed him with a familial affection. After all, he was the Australian leader who had once said: "I'm an Israeli. If I were to have my life again, I would want to be born a Jew."[2]

As he entered the Concert Hall with his wife Hazel, a standing ovation hailed Hawke as the great friend and defender. He was the outspoken Labor Party leader who, as the ALP President, had fought vigorously, passionately, and often almost alone, against his own party when Gough Whitlam had been Prime Minister in the early 1970s.

At a time when the anti-Israel, anti-American Left had helped to shape foreign policy on the Middle East conflict, Hawke was Australian Jewry's champion who brought intellect and emotion to the case for Israel. Many in the audience knew that Hawke had paid a price for his pro-Israel advocacy, and that he and his family had had to deal with abuse and threats to his life from Palestinian terror groups and their Australian sympathisers. Hawke's active involvement with Soviet Jewry, and especially with the refuseniks, had endeared him even more.

But the refuseniks' night also celebrated the bipartisan support which most Australian leaders and governments had given the Soviet Jewry cause for some 30 years, dating back to the Robert Menzies government. John Howard, who had lost the 1987 federal election to Hawke, spoke impressively, and generously acknowledged Hawke's role. The Liberal leader lauded the refuseniks, described their release as a small but important defeat for totalitarianism, and spoke with pride of his party's record on Soviet Jewry, Israel and the Jewish community.

In retrospect, Howard's brief but carefully nuanced words marked the beginning of a much stronger connection to the Melbourne Jewish leadership and to Australian Jews generally. After the event, when the audience contrasted his remarks with Hawke's, Howard grew in stature. A decade later, when Howard was in government and became known as Australia's most pro-Israel Prime Minister, he would recall the refuseniks' night in fine detail.

But "From Russia with Thanks" was always meant to be Hawke's night. In recognition for his dedication to Soviet Jewry, Hawke received two awards. World Jewish Congress President, Edgar Bronfman, who had flown in to Melbourne in his private jet direct from meetings with the Soviet leaders in Moscow, presented the first: the Australian Institute of Jewish Affairs' Human Rights Award. But it was the second, a specially commissioned silver sculpture which Lerner presented on behalf of the refuseniks, which visibly moved Hawke. He read the inscription and then handed it to Hazel.

Lerner addressed him directly.

> Through your strength, you have saved the Jewish community of Russia from a loss of dignity and from death. Your name will be remembered forever … I thank you with all my heart.[3]

As the two men embraced and kissed, the applause, punctuated by shouting and whistling from the youth movements, rolled on. When it subsided, Hawke began by recalling the message he had received from President Mikhail Gorbachev after he had met the Soviet leader in Moscow some six months earlier.

> Perhaps you can begin to imagine the emotion I felt when the messenger told me that Mr Gorbachev personally authorised

him to say that ... Rosa and Alex Ioffe and their daughter
Anna and Marta and Pavel Abramovich – five on the list I had
presented ... were to be allowed to leave ...

Naturally my thoughts flashed back nine years, to 1979, to
the time of high hopes at the end of my previous visit followed
by the agonising despair of dashed expectations.

And perhaps you can understand that I allowed myself the
luxury of a little exultation at a mission, long frustrated, now
partly accomplished.[4]

Speaking of his "unqualified joy for the bravest of people," he
turned to Professor Lerner:

Even though nine years have passed since I first believed you
would be free, it is still a precious pleasure to welcome you to
Australia tonight.[5]

Applause punctuated Hawke's speech every few sentences. Many
in the audience had empathised with his anguish in May 1979, eight
years earlier, almost to the day. With his wife Hazel, he had met many
of the refuseniks in Moscow. Believing that he had negotiated their
freedom, Hawke was crushed when he found that the Soviet authorities had duped him. Recalling the events in his memoirs, Hawke
wrote that "the thought of [the refuseniks'] despair tormented" him,
even to the point of taking his own life, and that the sense of responsibility for their fate haunted him until, as Prime Minister, he secured
the release for some of them eight years later.[6]

Tonight he praised "the continuing indomitable splendour of the
human spirit" which the refuseniks had displayed.

If they had given up hope, no other force would have availed.
Their strength, their courage, their determination, have been
the foundations on which everything else has been developed.[7]

Hawke also credited the world Jewish community's "sustained
and principled support", in which "the Australian Jewish community
could take great pride", and paid particular tribute to Leibler.

I venture to say, Isi, that nobody has made a greater individual
contribution than you.[8]

But then, some ten minutes into his remarks, Hawke moved
from Soviet Jewry to Israel and the Palestinians. He suggested that

the celebrations for the refuseniks were "necessarily muted to some degree" by the awareness that Israel faced major problems arising from the Intifada which had erupted in the West Bank and Gaza six months earlier. These "tragic events" had further convinced him that "the democratic, humanist principles on which Israel was built do not sit easily with the role of master of occupied territories and subject peoples".

Up to this point, Hawke's views on the Israel-Palestinian conflict were not new, although some in the audience began wondering why he was linking them to the refuseniks' celebration. And then came the surprise.

> The Palestinian in the occupied territories, as the Jew in the Soviet Union and the black in South Africa, has his aspirations to be truly free. The friends of Israel around the world are fearful that, in a real sense, we may be witnessing again, after thousands of years, a giant, eyeless in Gaza. Is there not emerging the danger of Israel being blinded to the threat to its very soul and the vision of its founders? [9]

A nervous shuffling and murmuring rippled through the audience. Leibler, his wife Naomi, and the refuseniks could not hide their dismay. Hawke's comparison of the Palestinians and black South Africans with Soviet Jews had shaken and offended his listeners. The time and place he had chosen to make it compounded the offence. Within seconds, the audience was audibly rumbling and hovered close to booing. It would have spilled over into that for any other speaker except Hawke.

Leibler's restless body-language for the rest of the evening was especially telling. From being the relatively relaxed MC, he became the nervous, tightly restrained activist, impatient to hit back. After the ceremonies concluded, Leibler hosted a reception at his home, to which he had previously invited Hawke. When the Prime Minister arrived, Leibler ushered him away from the guests and confronted him. Expletives flew freely.

Leibler angrily told Hawke he was bitterly disappointed that he was willing to exploit Soviet Jews to promote himself as "the great statesman". He claimed that Hawke was obsessed with believing that he could make history and resolve the Arab-Israeli conflict. All he had done, however, was to insult the refuseniks and the Jewish community. Just as heatedly, Hawke accused Leibler of overreacting and said that Australian Jews would accept friendly criticism from him because they trusted him. He insisted that he was indeed one of the few world leaders who could resolve the Arab-Israeli conflict, and that Leibler should be supporting him, not attacking him.

Their angry exchange over, the two men left the room. Guests could see the meeting had not gone well. What had begun as a night of celebration and mutual admiration between two men who had been bound together in close friendship and common cause for some fifteen years, ended in recrimination.

Leibler followed the confrontation at his home with a long personal letter to Hawke, which expressed his bitter disillusionment. Hawke did not reply, but asked mutual friends to act as intermediaries and explain to Leibler that he had misunderstood his remarks at the Concert Hall. Subsequently, they did not speak to each other for five months, until Hawke telephoned Leibler. The emotional conversation that ensued helped to restore some of the former relationship. But it was never the same.

Compared to his angry attack on Hawke in private, Leibler's public statement as the Executive Council of Australian Jewry (ECAJ) president was more measured. The analogies with South Africa and the Palestinians were completely "misplaced and unwarranted", and he was deeply disappointed with the one sentence which "marred an otherwise perfect evening".[10]

The refuseniks agreed with Leibler. So did every Jewish spokesman, including Isi's brother Mark, the Zionist Federation of Australia's president, who also criticised Hawke privately. The commentators in the Jewish press were universally condemnatory.[11]

Along with the criticism, there was puzzlement. The Prime Minister had rained on his own parade. Why choose that event? What could he have been thinking?

As I stood backstage that night waiting to speak to Fraser via the hook-up to the Moscow embassy, I watched the audience's surprise on the video monitor. My editorial for the *Australian Jewish News* entitled "The Prime Minister and the Jews", reflected that surprise and disappointment.

> Bob Hawke is a genuine legend in his own lifetime among Australian Jews due to his unquestioned record of support for Israel, Soviet Jewry and local Jewish interests. He has amassed such a bank of emotional credit and principled admiration that even the offensive analogy between the refuseniks and the Palestinians cannot destroy the Hawke legacy. But something has happened to tarnish it. The special relationship will never quite be the same again.[12]

It wasn't. The palpable change can be dated from his speech to the refuseniks. At the time, many of Hawke's Jewish admirers knew that he had become increasingly critical towards Israel's hard-line policies towards the Palestinians under Prime Minister Yitzhak Shamir, especially since the 1987 Intifada. Some even shared his concerns. But even Hawke's closest Jewish supporters could not understand why he had chosen the refuseniks' "night of nights" to make the invidious comparisons. Even less could they understand why, when the refuseniks offered him a graceful way to step back, he said he was sorry if he had caused distress, but that his words had been misunderstood.

In their letter to Hawke, in which they again conveyed their "love and appreciation" for his efforts, Lerner and his colleagues told him that his one sentence of comparisons had caused them distress. They added that they believed that "the way the particular sentence has been interpreted" was not how he had intended it. In his reply Hawke insisted that he was not equating Israel, the Soviet Union or South Africa, but speaking of "the feelings and emotions of individual human beings … who find their aspirations for freedom not fully realised." But he also insisted on standing by his original remarks and his "intellectually clear position".[13]

It soon became apparent that Hawke's "one sentence" was a deliberate signal, politically and personally. His views on Israel had been changing since before his visit in January 1987, when he became the first Australian Prime Minister to travel to Israel while in office. By then he had already concluded that Israel faced a profound dilemma:

it could not continue to be a Jewish state if it absorbed the Palestinians in the occupied territories and gave them citizen rights, but neither could it continue as a democracy while being the occupier and denying them those rights.

In addition, Hawke's meetings with Israeli leaders during his 1987 visit, especially with Prime Minister Yitzhak Shamir, did not go well. The Israelis were dismissive about his conflict resolution proposals. For his part Hawke was unimpressed with his interlocutors. The visit exacerbated his annoyance with Jerusalem's policies.

The Hawke government's shift towards an "even-handed" policy on Israel and the Palestinians was the very policy which he had so resolutely opposed in the Whitlam era. It gathered pace after Foreign Minister Bill Hayden retired in August 1988 to become Governor-General. Senator Gareth Evans, who succeeded Hayden in Foreign Affairs for three years under Hawke, and then for five under Paul Keating, also followed an "even-handed" policy. It was Howard and his Foreign Minister Alexander Downer who dropped the Hawke-Evans line after winning government in 1996, and introduced a strong pro-Israel policy for the next eleven years, matched again after 2013 by Prime Minister Tony Abbott and Foreign Minister Julie Bishop.

In his book on the Hawke government, Stephen Mills, who had been Hawke's speechwriter for four years, confirmed that Hawke had written the offending text himself with "great deliberation". Recalling the refuseniks' night, Mills wrote:

> This was the moment when [Hawke] was held in the highest esteem by Jews and all those who value human rights. It was at this moment that he chose to reveal his darkest fears about the future of Israel … Here was an astonishing transformation of an issue and a man … Hawke's words chilled the atmosphere of celebration …[14]

More than 20 years later, in his office in Williams Street, Sydney, I asked Hawke why he had chosen the words when he must have known they would cause distress to people whom he cared deeply about. And why mar a celebration which, by his own admission, he knew would move him deeply?

Ah, yes. I wanted my Jewish friends to know, and I wanted the world to know, that my love affair with Israel was not blind. That in my judgment … I think that Israel is sometimes almost its own worst enemy. And I just wanted to make it clear that my commitment to Israel was unshakeable, but that one needed to be objective about it. Not only in terms of one's own intellectual integrity, but in terms of Israel's interests.[15]

But why on a night about the refuseniks when nobody else was talking about Israel's conflict with the Palestinians?

Because there was a much wider context. [The evening] was going to get enormous coverage, and it did.[16]

There was indeed a wider context. The "enormous" coverage ensured that Hawke's Jewish friends understood that his "love affair" with Israel was not blind, and that it was waning, certainly while Yitzhak Shamir was its Prime Minister. Eventually, Hawke could claim some vindication. In his speech on the refuseniks' night, Hawke had proposed "an international conference and an act of simultaneous mutual recognition on acceptable conditions between Israel and the PLO".

Few of Israel's supporters in Australia supported Hawke's call at the time. But it eventually became the basis for the Oslo Accords. Yitzhak Rabin and Yasser Arafat co-signed the Accords alongside President Bill Clinton on the White House lawn in 1993. When the news broke, Hawke reminded his Jewish friends that he had been ahead of his time. Today he tells them that he supports the "people of Israel" but has long been disillusioned with their governments.

In 1988, however, his remarks meant that the refuseniks' love affair with Hawke also lost some of its rapture. They did not tell Hawke of their concerns at the Concert Hall on the night, and their letter to him explaining their distress was couched respectfully. But it was the last time they had any contact with him. Although he visited Israel after the Concert Hall evening, Hawke never again met or spoke to any of the refuseniks, and they never asked to meet or speak to him.

In his closing remarks to the Concert Hall audience, by which time many were so distracted by his earlier references to the Palestinians and black South Africans that they were not paying much attention, Hawke said:

> My friends, the story of the Soviet Jews is a human drama of
> vast proportions.[17]

In May 1988, however, it was still an unfolding drama. Ahead lay the departure of the remaining refuseniks, the fall of the Berlin Wall in November 1989, the mass exodus in the early 1990s of more than a million Jews to Israel and other countries, including Australia, and the collapse of the Soviet Union.

Australia and its Jews had played a small but active supporting role in that "human drama of vast proportions". The refuseniks' night in Melbourne did not signal the drama's end. But it was the beginning of the end.

How Australia's involvement with Soviet Jewry began; how the Jewish community became active players in the great drama; how successive Australian governments responded; why Soviet Jewry became an issue in Australian politics; how the Jewish community changed; and how it all led to the Melbourne Concert Hall in May 1988, is a story worth telling. The chapters that follow try to do that.

CHAPTER 2

THE SPYMASTER AND THE RECRUIT

In the Israeli summer of 1959, in a room overlooking the Mediterranean, Shaul Avigur met Isi Leibler at the Hotel Dan Tel Aviv, just across the street from the Soviet embassy. Avigur, Israel's legendary spymaster, was 60. Leibler, an aspiring Jewish communal leader from Melbourne, was 25.

The older man was a secular Zionist, a veteran "founding father" of the Jewish state and a self-educated, life-long member of a socialist kibbutz. The younger man was a Diaspora religious Zionist, a political science graduate and, out of family obligation, a diamond merchant. Despite the outward differences, the two men shared a binding faith: Zionism. Each believed that Israel's establishment just a decade earlier had been a transcendent event. It was not only a momentous watershed in Jewish history, but in their own lives.

The 1959 summer was just eleven years after Israel's establishment, and only fourteen years after World War II's end. Avigur and Leibler knew that the Holocaust still cast a shadow, contending with the novel experience of a sovereign Jewish state. The Cold War, in which Australia sided with the United States against the Soviet Union and its satellites, provided the background to Israel's uneasy existence in the Middle East. And although Soviet anti-Semitism was a growing concern for some Jewish leaders and Diaspora communities, Australia included, it was a marginal one.

When Leibler met Avigur, the Australian was not planning to make *aliyah*, i.e. to settle in Israel. But he certainly shared Avigur's belief that Israel's centrality was essential for Jewish continuity. An additional spur came from his grounding in religious Zionism, an ideology which he had inherited from his parents, and which he had developed in Melbourne as a *madrich*, a teenage leader in the religious

Zionist youth movement B'nei Akiva. His youth movement experience had also given him an invaluable grounding in public speaking,
organising meetings, and writing and distributing information.

In choosing Leibler the Israelis galvanised and focused an energetic, zealous and intellectually able champion for the cause. He
would become the movement's leader in Australia and win international recognition for his role. But the Avigur-Leibler meeting also
ensured that the Australian movement remained closely enmeshed
with the Israeli government's guidelines and priorities. Where the
American and British campaigns sometimes clashed with Israel's
guidelines on Soviet Jewry publicly, the Australian campaign rarely
deviated. Avigur set the pattern for this close relationship from the
first meeting at the Dan Hotel.

The former spymaster's involvement with Soviet Jewry was merely
the most recent chapter in his notable career as a pioneer nation-
builder. A select minority among Israel's founding generation were
aware of his role as the state's "grey eminence", and in 1973 he received
the Israel Prize for his "contribution to Israeli society". But for most
Israelis and Diaspora Jews, the short, nuggety and quietly-spoken
man remains an unknown player.

Which, from the limited accounts about him, is apparently how he
would have preferred it. Israel's first Ambassador to Moscow and later
Prime Minister, Golda Meir, commented on his style: "Whatever he
did, or ordered to have done, was carried out with maximum secrecy,
and every one was suspect, in his eyes, of possible indiscretion".[1]

Born in Latvia in 1899, Avigur migrated to Palestine with his
family in 1910, just after Tel Aviv was founded as a city, and became a
member of Kibbutz Kinneret in 1918. By 1959, when he met Leibler,
he headed a clandestine agency code-named Nativ (Path), and
bearing the nondescript official name of "Lishkat Hakesher" (The
Liaison Bureau), or the Lishkah, as it became more widely known to
activists in the international Soviet Jewry campaign.

Behind him, however, Avigur already had a long career as a
veteran intelligence officer and spymaster, before and after Israel's
establishment. He had organised the clandestine organisations which

facilitated illegal Jewish immigration into mandatory Palestine and had run the illegal import of weapons before Britain withdrew in May 1948. He had also been one of the founders of the Haganah's pre-state intelligence and counter-intelligence services. After Israel's creation these agencies morphed into the Israel Defence Forces (IDF) military intelligence, the Shin Bet, and Israel's famed Security Intelligence Services, the Mossad.

When Prime Minister David Ben Gurion established the Lishkah in late 1952, he appointed Avigur to report to him directly. The Lishkah's small, shadowy group of analysts and operatives was at first known only as the "Office With No Name". Its objectives, however, were clear: to establish contacts among the Soviet Union's 3,000,000 Jews, to foster Jewish education, to support Soviet Jews against the heightened anti-Semitism which Stalin had inspired and, most basically, to encourage – and prepare for – their emigration to Israel. Ben Gurion was acutely aware of Israel's demographic realities in a predominantly Arab Middle East.

Soviet Jews, the largest Diaspora Jewish community after the United States, offered a significant potential source for increasing Israel's population.[2]

History has vindicated the decision to create the Lishkah but it was a bold move fraught with risk. Writing about it nearly 50 years later, Nehemiah Levanon, one of the Lishkah's first operatives and later Avigur's successor, commented:

> Bear in mind what it meant for this small, struggling state to undertake this daring step in 1952, only four years after the Jewish state emerged from a bloody war.[3]

Avigur preferred his operatives to be affiliated with Mapai, Israel's Labor Party, or the kibbutz movement. But he chose committed Zionists from all political backgrounds. He expected a familiarity with Jewish traditions, and Nativ's official seal in Hebrew included a motto synthesised from Biblical texts: "And I shall gather you, and I shall rescue you from all places."[4]

Avigur's choice of Leibler reflected his recruitment policy. Isi Joseph Leibler was born in Antwerp, Belgium in October 1934, to

Abraham Samuel Leibler, who had come from Galicia, Poland, and to Rachel (Rachelle Akerman) born in Antwerp, a community known for the large number of Jews in the diamond industry. His parents, alert to Nazism's growing strength, migrated to Australia when he was four.

The young Leibler grew up in the suburbs where many of Melbourne's Jewish refugee community had clustered, first briefly in Elwood, and then in Caulfield. His parents were active in Jewish communal affairs: Abraham became President of the Victorian Jewish Board of Deputies, the communal roof body; Rachel was a leader in Ladies Mizrachi, the religious Zionist movement.

Educated at Melbourne High School and a First Class Honours graduate in Political Science from the University of Melbourne, Leibler expressed his Jewish leadership interests early. Among the founders of B'nei Akiva in Australia, he became the president of the National Union of Jewish Students in 1954. After completing his Arts degree in 1956, he began further studies in Israel towards a doctorate at the Hebrew University. As he recalled:

> My dream at that stage was to become an Israeli diplomat. This never eventuated because my father passed away in June 1957 … my mother insisted that I not return home but remain in Israel and then go to Antwerp … to learn the diamond trade with a view to managing my late father's business.[5]

Leibler agreed and went to Antwerp for a few months. He returned to Melbourne to help his mother care for his two brothers, Mark, thirteen, and Alan, eleven, and to manage the family's wholesale diamond business. In 1958 he married Naomi Porush, the daughter of Rabbi Dr Israel Porush, the senior rabbi at Sydney's Great Synagogue.

The couple travelled to Israel regularly in their first years of marriage. With every return to Melbourne, it became clearer that Leibler's passion did not lie in the weighing and cutting of gemstones, but in Jewish politics. He became active in the community's roof body, the Victorian Jewish Board of Deputies (VJBD), where he soon made a name as a fast-rising ambitious leader. His eyes were already set on Israel and the Jewish world beyond Melbourne.

Shortly before one of his overseas visits, Leibler heard from Israel's Ambassador to Australia, Moshe Yuval, that "someone" from the Prime Minister's office would contact him in Israel. Some 50 years later, interviewed in his apartment on Jerusalem's Ahad Ha'am Street, Leibler recalled that he was "intrigued and excited" at the prospect, but had no idea what the meeting would be about.

Leibler's first meeting was with Binyamin Eliav, one of the Lishkah's original recruits. Eliav sounded Leibler out on Soviet Jewry and his willingness to join the embryonic international network which Israel had begun to develop. A second meeting followed with Avigur, "the boss". Leibler recalled:

> Avigur's incredible role [as] the head of the Lishkah, and in many of the major events … in Israel's [creation] was unknown to me [at the time].
>
> We spoke for about an hour, and I was convinced [without too much persuasion] to take on an unofficial regional role as the lead activist in my area [for] Soviet Jewry activities.[6]

For Leibler, the meeting with Avigur was to prove life-changing. Over the next 30 years, living in Melbourne but traveling frequently and widely overseas, Leibler's political, intellectual and emotional involvement with Soviet Jewry and many of its leading figures, the refuseniks, evolved from an absorbing preoccupation to an obsession.

Among other manifestations, it was reflected in his zeal for documentation. From the beginning of his activism, Leibler kept every letter, newspaper, greeting card, magazine, news release, official statement, transcript, photograph, phone record, report, or book that in any way touched on Soviet Jewry in general, or on his own activities in particular.

By the time he moved permanently from Melbourne to Israel in 1999, Leibler had assembled a Soviet Jewry archive in his Jerusalem apartment's basement of over 40 bound volumes, each numbering some 1000 pages of documentation. In addition, his general library of over 40,000 books included hundreds of books and publications relating to Soviet Jewry. The library, with his wife Naomi's resigned agreement, overflowed into specially installed shelving in the kitchen.

In 1959, Leibler could not know how profoundly the Avigur meeting would shape his life. But he knew that he had joined a small international political network guided by an Israeli leadership that, at the highest level, regarded the fate of Soviet Jewry a matter of vital strategic interest. That strategic view had originated in the post-war period as Joseph Stalin's anti-Semitism grew. It had been signposted in January 1948 with the murder, on Stalin's personal order, of the renowned Yiddish actor and theatre director, Solomon Mykhoels. The anti-Semitic campaign continued, most notoriously with the "Night of the Murdered Poets" on 12 August 1952, when the NKVD, the KGB's precursor, tortured and executed fifteen Jewish writers and intellectuals in Moscow's Lubyanka prison.

Moscow's campaign was further highlighted in November 1952 with the show trial in Soviet-controlled Czechoslovakia of a leading Jewish communist official, Rudoph Slansky, and thirteen of his colleagues, of whom ten were Jews. They were accused of "international cosmopolitanism, Trotskyism and Zionism." The trial itself was replete with anti-Semitic denunciations. Its blatant incitement of hatred against Jews shook Israel and the Jewish world. Slansky and ten of his co-defendants were executed; three were sentenced to life imprisonment.

The widely-reported Slansky trial prompted the Israeli leadership to undertake a delicate balancing act. The Lishkah aimed "to reconcile the interest of Israel as a State – to maintain its relations with the second superpower at any cost – and its goal as the nation of the Jewish people – to help endangered Jews in the Diaspora and make sure that immigration would not be halted".[7]

Despite the growing Stalinist anti-Semitism, the Kremlin maintained the diplomatic relations it had established with Israel from 1948 until the 1967 Six-Day War, except between February and September 1953, when the Soviets withdrew their Ambassador following a bomb explosion in their Tel Aviv embassy. Thus from 1953 until 1967 the Lishkah was able to operate out of Israel's embassy in Moscow.

Its first representative there, Nehemia Levanon, was born in Latvia in 1915 and had moved to Palestine in 1938. A fluent Russian speaker, he was a founding member of Kibbutz Kfar Blum in 1943. In Moscow, from late 1953, he was officially an agricultural attaché, until he was expelled for "anti-Soviet activities". In the 1950s and 1960s, Levanon learned about Soviet anti-Semitism first-hand when he and his diplomatic colleagues travelled throughout the Soviet Union contacting Jewish communities and their leaders to encourage their connection to Israel. They distributed literature about Israel, Russian-Hebrew dictionaries and Jewish history books.[8]

In 1954, the Lishkah broadened its activities beyond the Soviet Union to include the West, naming its new policy as "Nativ-Bar" ("Open Pathway "). The aim was to inform and arouse Western public opinion about the plight of Soviet Jews, so as to "provoke … from the outside what seemed impossible from the inside".[9] Avigur began recruiting Western travellers to the Soviet Union to interest them in contacting Jews. Eliav, the multilingual diplomat whom Leibler met in 1959 at the Dan Hotel, had joined the Lishkah for the purpose.

Eliav set up offices, initially in London, Paris and New York. In London, he recruited Emanuel Litvinoff, a prominent Anglo-Jewish poet, novelist, playwright, literary critic and human rights campaigner. Litvinoff had visited Moscow in 1956 and, appalled by the Kremlin's official anti-Semitism, he became a leading advocate for Soviet Jews. For the next three decades he edited *Jews in Eastern Europe*, the British campaign's newsletter. Its carefully researched reporting and documentation became a critical resource for Leibler and his Australian colleagues. A close relationship developed between the two. Over the next three decades they were to correspond regularly, sharing frustrations and the campaign's highs and lows.

In New York, Eliav recruited American Jewish journalist Moshe Decter who, in 1960, created the small office known as Jewish Minorities Research. From there he wrote and edited hundreds of articles and reports, organised conferences and seminars, and lobbied prominent American intellectuals and human rights leaders. Decter was an ideal advocate. As the former managing editor of *The New Leader*, a left-liberal journal which the American trade union movement supported, he had already written and published widely about the persecution of Soviet Jews. *The New Leader's* special edition on Soviet Jewry in 1959 was the first of its kind in American media and intellectual circles. Although he and *The New Leader* were strongly anti-Soviet, Decter's outspoken criticism of Senator Joseph McCarthy's particular brand of anti-communist investigations during the 1950s and the "McCarthyism" of the period had established his credibility in left-liberal circles.

With the help of Jewish organisations in London and New York who provided the fronts, the Lishkah indirectly and secretly funded Litvinoff and Decter's activities. In Australia, Leibler never accepted funding from the Lishkah. He paid for campaign activities personally or through his business, and at other times through the community organisations which he led.

Although the Lishkah's recruitment of Leibler led to a heightened focus on lobbying Australian opinion makers, Jewish leaders in Melbourne and Sydney had been concerned about Soviet anti-Semitism since the mid-1950s. Stalin's death in 1953 briefly raised hopes that his anti-Semitic policies would die with him. But by 1955 the Soviet press had begun a new anti-Semitic campaign which spread to the writers' unions, scientific bodies and the universities.

Despite Nikita Kruschev's denunciations in February 1956 of Stalin as a "brutal despot" who governed with "suspicion, fear and terror", it was clear by 1958 that the Kremlin had reaffirmed anti-Semitism as a systematic state policy.

In April 1958, the New South Wales Jewish Board of Deputies in Sydney summed up its concerns in a five-page memorandum:

> In the Soviet Union the Jews still constitute a *national group* but a group utterly unlike any other ... in the Union; it is a group deprived of any right of self expression; it has no national territory; it has seen its national languages, Yiddish and Hebrew, proscribed and the instruments of its national culture liquidated.

A month later, the Executive Council of Australian Jewry (ECAJ) at the national level, and the Boards of Deputies representing the states, outlined their views and called on the Australian government to take diplomatic action. They resolved:

> a) to ask the Government of the Commonwealth of Australia to press at UNO for the redress of the wrongs perpetrated against the members of the Jewish faith in Russia;
>
> b) to request the Conference of Jewish Organisations which is to meet again in New York on 21 May 1958 to take steps to inform world opinion of these serious crimes against Jewry in Russia; and
>
> c) to call upon the Jews in Australia to make known the serious situation …[10]

The 1958 resolution's main objectives – to persuade the Australian government to raise the issues at the United Nations and to mobilise the community's awareness – provided the framework for the Australian campaign for Soviet Jewry for the next three decades.

But it was another four years before the 1958 resolution was able to point to its first results.

CHAPTER 3

THREE LEADERS, THREE VOICES

On 9 December 1961 two Jewish community leaders, Melbourne's Sam Cohen and Sydney's Syd Einfeld, each stood for the first time for election to the Parliament of Australia. Running in second place on his party's ticket, Cohen (ALP, Victoria) became the first Jew to win a seat in the Senate. Einfeld (ALP) defeated William Aston (Liberal) to win the House of Representatives seat of Phillip, which included Bondi and the adjoining eastern beachside suburbs. But a third Jewish communal leader, Melbourne's Maurice Ashkanasy, had decided not to stand for the Senate in the 1961 elections. The Victorian ALP, dominated by the Socialist Left, had relegated him again to the virtually unwinnable fourth position as it had done in the 1958 elections.[1]

The Jewish community's political history in 1962, the critical year that followed, became the story of how Leibler drove his way, almost crashing at various points, through the obstacle course which the three leaders created by their differing responses to the Soviet Jewry issue.

Who were they?

Born in London, Maurice Ashkanasy (1901–71) came to Australia aged nine. His father, Solomon Ashkanasy, was a Talmudic scholar; his mother was the principal breadwinner, first as a hawker and then opening a clothing shop in Melbourne. Ashkanasy studied law on scholarships and was admitted to the bar in 1924, after reading with Robert Gordon Menzies – later Australia's twelfth Prime Minister – who remained his lifelong friend. After joining the Australian Imperial Force (AIF) during World War II, Ashkanasy led a daring escape with a small group in a lifeboat after the fall of Singapore. He resumed his war service in New Guinea, was mentioned in dispatches, and was discharged in 1944 as a Lieutenant-Colonel.[2] Returning to the Bar as one of the profession's youngest KCs, he acquired a reputation for "urbanity and poise".[3]

An early aspirant for parliamentary politics, Ashkanasy stood in the 1946 federal elections as the ALP candidate for the south-east Melbourne seat of Balaclava. Although he increased the Labor vote, the Liberal Party retained the seat.[4] In the 1954 federal elections, and again in 1958, he was the fourth candidate on the ALP Senate ticket, but was not elected. Writing about him in the *Australian Dictionary of Biography*, Zelman Cowen, later to be Governor-General, described him as a "firm and purposeful – if somewhat dictatorial and at times controversial" Jewish communal leader.[5]

Sydney David "Syd" Einfeld was born on 17 June 1909, three weeks after his parents, Reverend Marcus Einfeld and his wife Doris (nee Deborah Gabel), arrived in Sydney – hence the name. After leaving Fort Street Boys' High School, he wanted to attend university. But with his father's meagre salary as second reader at the Great Synagogue in Elizabeth Street, he worked to help his family. His early employment and business career, however, was somewhat chequered. Believing he was meant "to be a person serving the people" he joined the Labor Party in 1934, and became active in the Jewish Welfare Society and the NSW Jewish Board of Deputies.[6]

After some 20 years as a branch and electorate president, he won the seat of Phillip in the 1961 elections. He served in the House of Representatives, lost his seat in the 1963 elections and entered New South Wales state politics as the member for Bondi until 1971. He was then the member for Waverley for another ten years, during which time he became the NSW Minister for Consumer Affairs.[7]

"Syd" and "Ash" were the giants of Australian post-war Jewish communal history. They alternated as ECAJ president, leading the community's roof body which brought together the state Boards of Deputies in Victoria, New South Wales, Western Australia, South Australia, Queensland, the ACT and Tasmania. Under its constitution, the ECAJ's leadership rotated between Sydney and Melbourne every two years. Between 1952 and 1968, Ashkanasy had five terms in office; Einfeld had four. So strong was their dominance that critics proposed constitutional reforms to limit the term for the ECAJ presidency – but the moves failed.[8]

The two leaders shared much in common. Both came from modest immigrant families of East European origins and could relate to the new immigrants in the 1930s and 1940s. They were both active in the Labor Party at a time when the Jewish community was mostly pro-Labor. Both began their communal involvements through Jewish sport – Ashkanasy with the Judean League in Melbourne, and Einfeld with the Young Men's Hebrew Association in Sydney.[9]

Their personal styles, however, differed significantly. Ashkanasy was a brilliant intellectual with carefully managed histrionic talents and great forensic skills, which served him well at the bar. Always carefully groomed and conservatively dressed, he relished every opportunity to speak publicly. In reporting many of his speeches at the Victorian Jewish Board of Deputies (VJBD), I looked out for his slight nod in my direction when he wanted to alert me to what he regarded as a significant statement. He could be witty and charming to "the ladies" as he invariably described the women delegates to the VJBD. Yet even many of his admirers saw him as arrogant and aloof.

Einfeld was also an impressive orator, but he had a more relaxed and popular style. There was an off-the-cuff, out-on-the-stump quality to his public speaking. Ashkanasy was often confrontationist; Einfeld was more the peacemaker, seeking consensus. At times the two men clashed, most notably over the rabbis speaking for the community.[10] Ashkanasy, though nominally Orthodox, vehemently opposed any rabbinical representation. Einfeld did not see it as an issue. Despite such tensions, the two retained a mutual respect. But their biggest conflict came over the "Cohen Affair" and the surrounding dramas over Soviet Jewry which unfolded through 1962. These ructions not only threatened their personal relationship, but the organised Jewish community's unity and structure.

The third community leader who became embroiled in the Soviet Jewry campaign was Samuel Herbert (Sam) Cohen. His background was similar to Ashkanasy's and Einfeld's. Born in 1918 in Bankstown,

Sydney, to East European parents, his family moved to Melbourne in 1925. Cohen was educated at the Elwood Central School, Wesley College and then, like Ashkanasy, won a competitive scholarship to the University of Melbourne where he was the Students' Representative Council president. In 1942 he graduated in Arts/Law, and then served with Major Alfred Conlon's research section at the Directorate of Military Intelligence, Melbourne. Discharged as a sergeant in 1943, he was admitted to the bar in 1946. Specialising in industrial law, he took silk in September 1961, just three months before election to the Senate representing Victoria for the ALP.[11]

Before standing for the Senate, Cohen's main communal involvement had been as president of the left-wing Jewish Council to Combat Fascism and Anti-Semitism, "one of the most prominent and controversial organisations of post-war Australian Jewry".[12] In addition, he was also active in the United Israel Appeal, the Friends of Hebrew University, the Australian Jewish Welfare and Relief Society and the Montefiore Homes for the Aged. Although lacking Ashkanasy's authority as an orator, or Einfeld's down-to-earth style, and less experienced than either, Cohen was an effective public speaker. Through the Council, he had won a high profile within the Jewish community.

Formed in 1942, the Council initially represented a cross-section of Melbourne Jews from all political and religious backgrounds. During World War II and immediately after, the Council opposed anti-Semitism, supported the creation of Israel and cooperated closely with the VJBD.[13] After 1947, however, the Jewish writer and Communist Party member, Judah Waten, became the Council's executive secretary, followed by Ernest Platz, a German Jewish refugee and communist sympathiser. The Council's priorities and statements began to change, taking on an increasingly anti-West, Cold War tone.

In 1950 a communal conflict erupted in Melbourne between the Council and the VJBD. The issue was who should coordinate the campaign against the proposal by the Robert Menzies' government to sponsor the immigration of 100,000 displaced ethnic Germans from Eastern Europe. Just five years after World War II, the Jewish leadership feared the immigration would include former Nazi collaborators and sympathisers. The ECAJ organised protest meetings and lobbied widely. Although the ALP's strongly pro-Israel leader, Dr Herbert Evatt, supported the Jewish community and spoke at a protest rally, Arthur Calwell, who had been the Minister for Immigration in the Chifley Labor government, sided with Menzies. Given the divisions within the ALP, the strong media support for the Menzies plan and opinion polls which showed Germans were seen as "desirable immigrants", the ECAJ campaign was doomed to failure. In August 1952, Immigration Minister Harold Holt signed an agreement in Bonn with Konrad Adenauer's West German government, which led to 90,000 ethnic Germans migrating to Australia.[14]

Early in the campaign, however, Ashkanasy concluded that the Council's Communist Party links were harming Jewish interests. He singled out Waten as "an avowed Communist",[15] and proposed that the VJBD create a new public relations committee excluding the Council. Although Ashkanasy was both ECAJ and VJBD president, he could not muster sufficient support. He took the failure as a vote of no-confidence and resigned both leadership positions.[16] Cohen, at the time also the VJBD's Public Relations chairman, wrote to the New South Wales Board Public Relations chairman, William (Bill) Wolfensohn, extolling the partnership between the Council and the VJBD.[17]

The partnership, however, did not last. Within a year, Ashkanasy was back. He had managed to disband the joint VJBD/Council committee on German migration,[18] created a new PR committee – which he chaired – and had resumed the Board's presidency. Cohen resigned from the PR committee, and the Council continued its own anti-German migration campaign.

Ashkanasy's return to communal leadership with renewed support reflected the changing Cold War tensions in the Jewish world.[19] Although Stalin had turned from supporting Israel to hostility against the Jewish state, and although he had intensified the Kremlin's anti-Semitic campaign, the Council's leadership continued to support Moscow. The first reports of Stalin's turn against the Jews and Zionism began to filter through to Australian Jewry as early as July 1949. In 1951, the VJBD protested against the persecution of Jews in communist Hungary, but the Council representatives, Norman Rothfield and Sam Goldbloom, opposed the resolution.[20] They insisted that "fascist or right-wing regimes presented the sole threat to Jewish well-being and security".[21]

In 1952 the Council condemned the United States for executing the convicted "atom spies" Julius and Ethel Rosenberg. But it denied Moscow's anti-Semitic policies, vividly on display in Prague's Slansky show trials. The Council's ongoing refusal to criticise Soviet anti-Semitism led to resignations by some mainstream communal leaders, notably Walter Lippmann.[22] Others, such as the Liberal Temple Beth Israel's Rabbi Dr Herman Sanger, became increasingly concerned that the Council was "a straight-out left-wing organisation".[23] Cohen, however, continued to defend the Council, although he expressed his defence more as opposition to the Cold War, rather than as strong support for Moscow.[24]

After its expulsion from the VJBD, the Council continued under Cohen's leadership until his election to the Senate in 1961. But over the next decade it became a fringe organisation.[25] The ECAJ's 1953 call on its constituents to cut all ties with any pro-communist groups took its toll, as did the mounting evidence of Soviet anti-Semitism, especially in the years 1958–62.

The national and local Communist Party agencies closed nearly all the synagogues in the Soviet Union. In Moscow, with an estimated population of 500,000 Jews,[26] only the Great Choral Synagogue on Arkhipova Street remained open. The Soviets banned the baking of *matzot* (unleavened bread) for Passover, and made it increasingly difficult to purchase the ritual items required for Jewish religious practice. In 1960 the Communist Party newspaper *Daghestan Komunist* accused Jews of having to drink Muslim blood once a year, thereby reviving the infamous blood libel among the Soviet republic's majority Muslim population. Similar accusations led to pogroms against Jews in the Uzbek Republic in 1961 and 1962.

Most disturbing, however, were the increasing arrests for "economic crimes". Markedly disproportionate numbers of Jews faced charges of black market trading and currency speculation, and after dubious "trials" were sentenced to death.

The widespread publicity in the state-controlled media emphasised Jewish names and featured crude anti-Semitic cartoons, similar to those that had appeared a generation earlier in the Nazi press.[27]

Moscow's intensified anti-Semitism heightened the divisions between the Council's supporters and the anti-communist ALP supporters in the Jewish community. There were similar differences on the wider Victorian political scene. In the early 1950s the ALP established a New Australian Committee with Bono Wiener as its secretary. Wiener was a Holocaust survivor, a hero of the wartime Lodz ghetto and a leader of the Bund, the Jewish social democratic party formed in Eastern Europe at the end of the 19th century. Strongly anti-communist and committed to Yiddish as the Jewish national language, the Bund and its youth movement SKIF, despite relatively small numbers, was influential in the Melbourne Jewish community in the 1950s and early 1960s. This was largely due to Wiener's charismatic leadership. A tall, strongly built man who compelled attention when he rose to speak, especially in Yiddish, Wiener was a prominent VJBD executive member and a formidable participant in the VJBD's monthly open debates.

In 1955, after the ALP split over anti-communism, the party's Victorian branch moved to the left and resumed close cooperation with the Council.[28] It expelled Wiener. In 1958 long-standing Council members, Rothfield and Goldbloom, won preselection and stood unsuccessfully as ALP candidates for the Victorian parliament.[29] Cohen, however, was more successful. In October 1961, the Victorian ALP preselected him ahead of Ashkanasy for the second and safe position on the Victorian Senate ticket.

Although the Labor Party's left-wing executive argued that it had elevated Cohen, then only 41, because it was looking for "younger men", it was clear it was punishing Ashkanasy for his open defiance. As political historian Peter Medding pointed out, Ashkanasy had refused to rally support for the 1959 Australian Congress on International Peace and Disarmament, which he regarded as a communist front.

He also refused to remove Wiener, an outspoken anti-communist, from the VJBD Executive.[30]

Despite warnings that he was endangering his chances for a safe Senate seat, Ashkanasy was one of the few senior centre-right members to stand up to the party's left-wing executive during the 1960s. As Victorian ALP Senator Barney Cooney acknowledged years later in a posthumous tribute, there was a period when Ashkanasy was the only opposing voice in the party.[31]

Cohen's nomination provoked opposition from a clandestine committee of non-communist Victorian ALP members, known as the Rank and File Committee. They included some Jews, notably Oscar Rosenbess, former members of the New Australia Council, and DLP supporters,[32] who campaigned for Ashkanasy to replace Cohen. The pamphlet they circulated with the headline, "Labor yes – Sam Cohen no", claimed that "the unholy triumvirate: Ernest Platz, Sam Goldbloom and Norman Rothfield" shaped the Jewish Council's policies. It also called for Cohen to be put third on the ALP voting card, rather than second.[33] The Rank and File Committee raised funds for the ALP, but sent the money to Einfeld in New South Wales, rather than to Cohen in Victoria.[34]

The anti-Cohen campaign also attracted wider attention. The Sydney *Daily Telegraph* noted that "Jewry is getting as deeply involved in Labor-Communism as the Roman Catholic Church".[35] *The Bulletin* published an interview with Leibler by "Mugga", a pseudonym for journalist Peter Kelly, entitled "the Cohen Case". It emphasised that the VJDB regarded the Jewish Council as a "communist front" organisation.[36] The article led to a heated debate in the House of Representatives between Harold Holt, who had become the Liberal Federal Treasurer, and the Leader of the Opposition, Arthur Calwell.[37]

But Cohen was also winning supporters within the Melbourne Jewish community. Saul Same, a prominent businessman, UIA leader and strong ALP supporter, organised a meeting of 180 community representatives "to express confidence in and support for Sam Cohen".[38]

In response, Ashkanasy, as VJBD president, said that "the VJBD views with concern persistent attempts … to involve the Victorian Jewish community in the present federal election".[39] He denied Cohen's candidacy was a Jewish communal matter and emphasised that there were various shades of political opinion in the Jewish community. In the event, neither the anti nor pro-Cohen campaign made much impact. At the December 1961 federal elections Cohen, running in second place on the ALP ticket, was assured of victory.

As Australia went to the polls on December 9, the Cold War had exacerbated the partisan conflicts between the governing Liberal-Country Party (LCP) coalition and the Labor Party (ALP). After the 1955 split in the ALP, the breakaway members formed the anti-communist Democratic Labor Party (DLP). The issue divided the ALP's Socialist Left and Right factions, particularly in Victoria, as did the party's ambivalent reaction to communist influence. Although the Communist Party of Australia (CPA), had lost many of its key intellectuals after the Soviet invasion of Hungary in 1956 and some members criticised its Stalinist elements, it remained a pro-Moscow party and was still influential within the trade union movement and the ALP.

The ALP split had kept the party out of government, since the DLP's preferences mostly favoured the LCP. But in 1961, even the DLP's support was not enough to prevent a near-death electoral experience for Menzies. At the final count, the Liberal/ Country Party coalition and the ALP had equal numbers in the House of Representatives. But two of the ALP members were from the Northern Territory and the Australian Capital Territory. At the time, the territories had restricted voting rights. This gave the coalition a working majority of just two. In the Senate, however, where it needed either the DLP or independent senators for a majority, it had lost control.[40]

The coalition's shaky hold on government, the ALP's internal divisions, and the growing personal bitterness towards Menzies by some Labor MPs, set the scene for many of the spiteful and recriminatory parliamentary debates and exchanges throughout 1962. Australia's policy on Soviet Jewry would be caught up in the bitterness.

Yet the key political figure at the centre of the storm, Sir Garfield Barwick, remained above the fray throughout. In the cabinet reshuffle that followed the 1961 election, Menzies appointed Barwick as Minister for External Affairs in addition to his previous portfolio as Attorney-General. Barwick was formerly a highly successful Sydney barrister who had been in parliament for only four years. He had won the New South Wales' seat of Parramatta for the Liberals in a 1958 by-election, and then held it in the 1958 and 1961 elections. Although his eminence as a lawyer made him a natural choice for Attorney-General, Barwick had had virtually no experience in diplomacy or international affairs.

Yet it was in his new role, presiding over Australia's international relations, that he was about to become a key player in the Jewish community's lobbying campaign. As the 1962 political year began in Canberra, Barwick may not have known very much about Ashkanasy, Einfeld and Cohen. He probably had not heard about Leibler at all, and it is doubtful if he understood the passions, ideologies and internal conflicts which drove the Melbourne and Sydney Jewish communities. Nor is there any evidence that he had paid much attention to Soviet Jewry. But as the year unfolded, and as the Australian parliament and government made history, he would contribute decisively.

CHAPTER 4

WENTWORTH ASKS, BARWICK ANSWERS

On 3 April 1962, William (Billy) Charles Wentworth, the Liberal Member for Mackellar, asked the Minister for External Affairs, Sir Garfield Barwick, a Question Without Notice in the House of Representatives:

> Mr WENTWORTH. – I direct a question to the Minister of External Affairs. Is it a fact that there has recently been some recrudescence of anti-Semitism in the Union of Socialist Soviet Republics? Is this apparently inspired by the Soviet authorities or does it at least have their concurrence? What is to be the real motive behind this Soviet policy? Will the Minister have a white paper on these matters prepared for the information of honourable members, and will he provide an opportunity for discussion on it in this House?
>
> Sir GARFIELD BARWICK. – There are some indications of a recrudescence of anti-Semitism in Russia as the honourable member has said. As for the rest of his question, I think it better that I should say I will consider laying a paper on the table of the House on this matter. If and when I do, I shall speak to the Leader of the House about an opportunity to discuss it.[1]

Wentworth's question and Barwick's reply set off the chain of events that led Australia to become the first nation to raise the issue of Soviet Jewry at the United Nations. Wentworth's initial question, however, was more modest. He only sought a White Paper and a parliamentary discussion. Although many parliamentary discussions followed, Barwick never produced a White Paper.

But the results of Wentworth's question were eventually far-reaching. Rightly, therefore, he holds the distinction of being the first Australian parliamentarian to take up the Soviet Jewish cause.

Some fourteen years later it was again Wentworth's initiative and persistence which led to the landmark Parliamentary Inquiry into Human Rights in the Soviet Union. Chaired by Labor's Senator John Wheeldon, it was the first such inquiry in any Western democracy, and its documentation on Soviet Jewry was a significant contribution to international awareness about their plight.

Routinely described as "eccentric" and "maverick", Wentworth represented the Liberal Party (1949–77) in Mackellar, a seat with few Jewish constituents at the time, which stretched across the North Sydney beach suburbs from Dee Why to Palm Beach. He was a cartoonist's dream. The unruly white hair, the heavy bi-focal spectacles and the energetic body language whenever he rose in the House always attracted attention. From his political opponents, especially when he denounced communists and, as he saw it, their association with the Labor Party, there was often also derision.

When Wentworth died in 2003 aged 95, the *Sydney Morning Herald* obituary quoted his nephew Mungo MacCallum, journalist and author:

> His tragedy was that too often the extravagance of his style caused people to overlook the value of his substance. His triumph is that the substance will be recognised long after the style is forgotten and forgiven.[2]

Wentworth's question to Barwick had its origins in a letter from his private secretary to Leibler in August 1960, seeking help for an article the Liberal parliamentarian was writing on "Russia and the Jews".[3] Leibler responded and sent additional information. Wentworth thanked him and the connection was made. But Leibler did not use it for some eighteen months until 2 April 1962, when he asked Wentworth to raise the issue in parliament.[4] Enclosing the most recent VJBD resolutions protesting against the intensified persecution of Soviet Jews, and the notes of a speech he had given in Sydney on the subject, Leibler added that Wentworth's "participation in this question" would greatly help "Cohen's critics" in Victoria. It was a partisan appeal to Wentworth as the Liberals' most outspoken anti-communist.

Although he emphasised that Ashkanasy and the VJBD executive fully supported him, Leibler asked Wentworth to treat the letter, and the request for parliamentary intervention, as confidential. The request reflected the increasingly tense relationship between the Melbourne and Sydney Jewish communal leaderships and their differences on tactics and style.

Melbourne preferred an activist lobbying campaign directed towards Australian opinion makers, especially parliamentarians. Sydney emphasised "quiet diplomacy", such as the letter Einfeld wrote to the Soviet embassy in September 1962. He noted that of the 46 Russians sentenced to death for "economic crimes", 28 were Jews, thus demonstrating an "anti-Jewish bias". In reply, the embassy rejected the allegations and maintained that the accusations demonstrated an "anti-Soviet bias".[5]

Melbourne and Sydney Jewry's different ethnic and cultural backgrounds also contributed to the tensions. In the early 1960s, Melbourne's affiliated Jews were predominantly East European – Polish, Russian and Lithuanian.

The majority had arrived shortly before World War II, or as Holocaust survivors in the late 1940s and 1950s. Most spoke Yiddish, and the circulations of Melbourne's two weekly Yiddish newspapers – *Die Oistralisheh Yiddishe Nayess* and *Die Oistralisheh Yiddishe Post* – matched their two English counterparts, the *Australian Jewish News* and the *Australian Jewish Herald*.

The VJBD's monthly meetings, reflecting the more intense ideological divisions, regularly featured Yiddish speakers, often in heated rhetorical conflict. By comparison, Sydney's Board of Deputies' meetings were more sedate, apart from the attacks of Dr Hans Kimmel, Viennese pre-war refugee lawyer, who regularly disrupted NSW Board of Deputies meetings. The city's post-war Jewish emigration had been predominantly Central European – Hungarian, Czech and Austrian. Mostly they were more assimilated Jews and with less ideological baggage than the East Europeans. And Sydney's community leaders were mostly English or Australian-born Jews, few of whom spoke Yiddish.

The most divisive issue, however, especially after the Cohen Affair, arose over "channels of communication". Although all communications with federal parliamentarians from the state Boards of Deputies were supposed to go via the ECAJ as the federal body, Leibler deliberately bypassed that understanding and opened his own channel to Wentworth. It was partly because he doubted the Sydney leadership's appetite for political controversy, but mainly because he feared that Einfeld, having recently won Phillip for the ALP in the 1961 election, might refuse to pass the letter to Wentworth, a Liberal and a fervent anti-communist.

Wentworth's interest in Soviet Jewry mainly stemmed from his well-publicised anti-communism. In 1954 he made headlines when he became involved in the dramatic defection by Evdokia Petrov, the wife of Vladimir Petrov, a Soviet KGB agent who had already defected. But Wentworth also had a real concern for the underdog, for which he was much less known.

An active campaigner for indigenous Australians, he played a key role in introducing the successful 1967 constitutional referendum on Aboriginal citizenship rights. When John Gorton became Prime Minister in 1968, he appointed Wentworth as Minister for Social Services and Australia's first Minister for Aboriginal Affairs. Gorton's biographer later wrote about Wentworth:

> For all his erratic and sometimes bizarre behaviour, his flaws
> were at least those of an inventive mind.[6]

He applied that mind to the Soviet Jewry issue. Within a day of receiving Leibler's letter, Wentworth asked Barwick his question. A few days later, Wentworth wrote again to Leibler asking him to continue sending him information "which would help me in exposing Soviet anti-Semitism in the House".[7] Buoyed by Wentworth's interest and Barwick's sympathetic response, Leibler stepped up the wider political and media campaign. As he expanded his contacts outside the Jewish community, Leibler became embroiled in a growing controversy – which he helped provoke – over Cohen's official relationship to the Jewish community. Worried that Cohen did not support an activist approach on Soviet Jewry, and wary of his long involvement as a Council leader and his ties to the Socialist Left, Leibler claimed that Cohen was not entitled to speak for the Jewish community, and that on Soviet Jewry in particular the Jewish community had no confidence in the newly elected senator.

Cohen's supporters defended him, arguing that Leibler had set up a straw man to attack Cohen politically. They pointed out that Cohen had resigned as Council president, and noted that although he remained active in the Jewish community, he did not claim to speak for it. As it happened, Cohen's standing in the community rose after his election to the Senate, and many non-Council supporters agreed that Leibler and Cohen's critics were treating him unfairly. At a reception in his honour by the Victorian Friends of the Hebrew University in February 1962, one of a series of such functions, the speakers included prominent communal figures such as Judge Trevor Rapke QC and Professor Zelman Cowen, then Dean of Law at the University of Melbourne.[8]

Leibler, however, persisted in his attacks. In April 1962, after Wentworth had asked his question in Parliament, but before Cohen took his Senate seat on 1 July 1962, three Jewish leaders, including the Elwood Hebrew Congregation's Rabbi Chaim Gutnick, visited Cohen and asked him for a clear statement on Soviet Jewry. Although Cohen was prepared to criticise the prohibition of baking *matzot* (unleavened bread) for Passover, he refused to say more. Leibler intensified his criticism.[9] He claimed that unlike other Jewish parliamentarians – Baron Snider, a Liberal MLA in the Victorian parliament and Einfeld – "Cohen was not considered to have the Board's confidence."[10]

Aware that Cohen would take his seat in the Senate just three weeks later, Leibler devised eight "open questions" for Cohen, covering topics of Jewish concern, including Soviet Jewry, and circulated them as a "confidential draft" at the VJBD's June meeting. Leibler argued that if Cohen responded positively, the Board would see that he had "an affinity" with the Jewish community's interests, and he (Leibler) "… would be the first to suggest let bygones be bygones".[11] In the ensuing debate some VJBD delegates, notably Nathan Jacobson, criticised Leibler's "provocative" attitude, pointing out that Cohen was beholden to his party, not to the VJBD.[12]

After some unsuccessful attempts at mediation between communal leaders and Cohen, the VJBD dropped the questions from eight to six.

The VJBD's decision, however, did nothing to stem the controversy. An exchange of letters in the *Australian Jewish Herald* between Professor Rufus Davis, Professor of Politics at Monash University, and Dr Frank Knopfelmacher, Senior Lecturer in Psychology at the University of Melbourne, reflected the growing communal divisions.[13]

Davis, an Australian-born academic specialising in federalism, usually displayed a low-key Anglo style. But the Cohen controversy provoked a strong response. He objected to "the gratuitous ritual of submitting Senator Cohen to an unsolicited examination to determine whether he is fit to receive the patronage of the (VJBD's) political Beth Din."[14] In a pointed reference to Ashkanasy's failure to receive winnable endorsement from the Victorian ALP, Davis echoed a widespread view among Cohen's supporters that the VJBD's "unrestricted vendetta" against Cohen was due to some "deputies … using the Board to settle scores between the politically frustrated and the politically successful".[15]

Knopfelmacher was a vivid contrast to Davis. A former Czech Jew who had lost most of his family in the Holocaust, he escaped to Britain, served in the British Army's Czech unit, and completed his PhD in neuro-psychology at London University. An outspoken and often controversial anti-communist campus activist, he had attracted his first publicity in the Jewish community in 1957, some two years after arriving in Melbourne. Speaking at a lunchtime public meeting at the University of Melbourne, he had launched a withering attack on Ernest Platz, the Council's director. Platz had criticised neo-Nazism and anti-Semitism in West Germany, but had refused to acknowledge their existence in East Germany.

In one of his letters to the *Australian Jewish Herald*, Knopfelmacher argued that since Cohen had been Council president for five years, and was still on its executive, he was responsible for its failure to deviate significantly from the Soviet line and for the way its leading spokesmen continued to defend Soviet anti-Semitism.[16]

Knopfelmacher (or "Franta" as he was known on campus and to friends) was an influential academic and sharp-tongued polemicist on Melbourne's political scene throughout his three decades in the Department of Psychology. In the campaign for Soviet Jewry he wrote and spoke widely, inside and outside the Jewish community. His often scathing use of language won him opposition, especially from the Left. As an avowed anti-totalitarian – of the extreme-right and extreme-left – he became close to Leibler and his supporters during the early 1960s, and was an important intellectual figure who helped shape their ideas.

In his public statements, Ashkanasy avoided any direct references to the Cohen controversy. Although he was disillusioned that the ALP had favoured Cohen, and expressed these views privately, his public statements emphasised the larger issue of Soviet Jewry. At the VJBD's August meeting, in a statement that Wentworth later quoted in the federal Parliament, he spoke forcefully about the Jewish community's political campaign:

> We would be betraying our duty to our fellow Jews if we did not raise our voices and speak out against the destruction of our brethren in the Soviet Union. I tell you with all solemnity that if there is a risk that the position of the Jews in the Soviet Union will deteriorate as a result of our protest, then that is a risk we must take.[17]

In September 1962 Leibler organised a public meeting in Melbourne to commemorate the tenth anniversary of the 24 Soviet Jewish writers and cultural figures whose murder Stalin had ordered. The meeting attracted an audience of 350 and, as the newly installed editor of the *Australian Jewish Herald,* I reported it at length. The *Herald*'s associated Yiddish-language paper, the *Oistralisheh Yiddisheh Post,* edited by the formidable Yeshayeh Rappaport, a Yiddish journalist and writer with an international reputation, translated my report and ran it in full.

This gave me my first opportunity to talk to Rappaport about the Soviet Jewry campaign in which our two papers had become

increasingly important. We devoted many pages to local and international news coverage, as well as comment and readers' letters.
Forty years my senior, Rappaport was inspirational. Our conversations were in Yiddish. Mine was adequate; his was eloquent and
completely captivating. His knowledge of the Jewish world, his deep
understanding of the Russian Jewish experience, and his pungent
analysis of communal politics enthralled me.

In our shared view the Soviet Jewry issue was urgent, and deserved
detailed coverage. This was in marked contrast to the larger-circula-
tion Melbourne weeklies, the *Australian Jewish News* and its Yiddish
paper, the *Oistralisheh Yiddisheh Neyess*. The *News'* publisher Tony
Rubinstein and editor Hans Licht were reluctant to take strong editorial positions on communal issues, and they did not provide extra
coverage on Soviet Jewry. In the *Neyess*, editor Yitzchok Rubinstein,
Tony's brother, devoted more space to Soviet Jewry than the *News*.
But his editorial comment often criticised the VJBD and Leibler as
too militant, and generally favoured the Labor Party.

My editorial role at the *Herald*, and my subsequent involvement
with the Cohen Affair, did not come because I sought the job. The
Herald had had a long and influential history in the Melbourne
Jewish community, going back to the 19th century, and predating
the higher circulation *News*. Reuben Havin, the publisher and editor
who had owned the *Herald* and the *Post*, had sold them in December
1961 to a sixteen-man syndicate of community leaders, most of them
associated with the VJBD. But none had had any experience in publishing or journalism. The syndicate, which included Leibler, nominated him as the managing director, and appointed Monty Schaffer, a
former executive director of the Board of Deputies of British Jews, as
its first editor. Schaffer held the position for only six months. Shalom
Marantz, a travel agent, but a former editor of the Yiddish-language
Oistralisheh Yiddishe Nayess in the 1930s, replaced him.

But Marantz only lasted a month. So Leibler asked me to help out
until they could find a new editor. At the time I was 24 and had been
a television news reporter at Melbourne's Channel Nine for some
eighteen months. Leibler, himself 27, had been my youth leader in

Bnei Akiva, and we had remained friends. We shared a strong Zionist commitment, a general interest in politics, and a particular interest in Soviet Jewry. I was also close to Knopfelmacher, whose lectures in psychology and lunchtime seminars on politics and history I had attended at the University of Melbourne, and with whom I had also remained friendly. Franta's commitment to European social democracy, his passionate anti-totalitarianism, and his pungent analysis of communal and left-wing personalities, were an appealing combination.

Leibler's approach to me to edit a weekly newspaper was flattering and exciting. At first I hesitated because I thought I could not manage two full-time jobs. But as I was working the 10 am to 7 pm shift at Channel Nine, I decided I could edit the *Herald* from 8 pm to 1 or 2 am. Knowing Leibler's dominant personality and strong views, however, and aware he had a potential conflict of interest as the VJBD's Public Relations Chairman, I agreed to edit the paper on condition that while Leibler or any syndicate member could raise editorial matters, I alone would decide the *Jewish Herald's* content and editorial policy. This was part *chutzpah*, part bravado.

Leibler consulted the syndicate and, to my surprise, they agreed to my condition. And so the 13 July 1962 issue was my first as editor. I arrived at the small printing business on Brighton Road, St Kilda where the paper was published, and met our publisher Eugene Weiss, a Holocaust survivor from Hungary, and one of early founders of the Adass Yisroel, Melbourne's ultra-orthodox community. There was one staff journalist, Abe Gaffney, who later moved to Bnei Brak in Israel. He gave me a quick introduction to laying out and printing the paper.

Weiss' linotype machines were ancient and made a fearful noise as they clattered late into the night. The Yiddish-speaking linotypist, who had learned his trade in Poland before World War II, took turns with the English-speaking linotypist to melt the lead in the glowing red-hot pots, and to compose the pages in the steel frames which had to be read in reverse "on the stone". It was a skill that I thought I would never master. Yet somehow the paper appeared each week, and it became a player in the Soviet Jewry campaign.

For the next two years, I maintained my daytime job at Channel Nine, and edited the *Australian Jewish Herald* at night. David Bornstein, later a senior journalist on the Melbourne *Herald* and then the ALP member for Brunswick in the Victorian parliament, succeeded Gaffney as the production editor. Although Leibler and other syndicate members sometimes opposed my editorial decisions, publicly and privately, they never interfered directly. Throughout the Cohen Affair, I wrote all the *AJH*'s editorials, columns, and news reports that touched on the issues. Deliberately, I did not show anything in advance to Leibler, or to any of the syndicate members.

As the communal and political controversies grew, William Crawford Haworth, the Liberal member for the Melbourne seat of Isaacs (1949–69), became more interested in Soviet Jewry. Eventually he came to share Wentworth and Barwick's historical role in bringing the issue to the United Nations. Melbourne born, Haworth was a pharmaceutical chemist who had been elected to the Victorian Legislative Assembly in 1937, representing the United Australia Party. After military service in World War II, he returned to state politics in 1945 as Minister for Health. Defeated in the state elections later that year, he won Isaacs in the 1949 federal election when Menzies led the Liberal Party to victory over Ben Chifley's ALP government.

In the 1960s, before its subsequent redistribution, Isaacs included south-eastern suburbs with a large Jewish population. After Haworth contacted Leibler for information on Soviet Jewry, Leibler asked him to call on the government to raise the issue at the United Nations. Leibler chose Haworth on the critical issue rather than Wentworth because, anxious to win Einfeld's support, he believed the low-key Haworth would appeal more to the Sydney leadership than the volatile Wentworth. Additionally, the large numbers of Jewish voters in Isaacs made Haworth's intervention an understandable parliamentary response, rather than what might appear, in Wentworth's case, as a purely partisan one.

As a way of bolstering his political lobbying, Leibler actively sought press coverage in both the Jewish and mainstream press. In

September 1962, when Peter Coleman, *The Bulletin*'s associate editor, invited him to contribute on Soviet Jewry, Leibler readily agreed. Some two years earlier, Sydney newspaper proprietor, Sir Frank Packer, had acquired the Sydney-based weekly, and its first editor, Donald Horne, had transformed its often racist and anachronistic content and style. It had become an influential right-of-centre opinion journal, particularly within the Liberal Party. By September 1962, Packer, who also owned Sydney's morning tabloid paper, the *Daily Telegraph*, had sacked Horne, and had appointed Peter Hastings as editor.

As Leibler later acknowledged, Coleman's initiative to take up the Soviet Jewry issue was an important turning-point in the campaign. *The Nation*, founded in 1958 and edited by George Munster, was a smaller-circulation left-of-centre Sydney-based fortnightly, published by the *Sydney Morning Herald*'s finance editor Tom Fitzgerald. It was also influential among opinion makers, particularly in the ALP. In the months that followed, as the Soviet Jewry campaign became a major issue within the ALP, both *The Bulletin* and *The Nation* covered it extensively. But while *The Bulletin* consistently supported Leibler's campaign and the Australian government's anti-Soviet initiatives in the United Nations, *The Nation* opposed them and criticised Melbourne's Jewish leadership.

In his *Bulletin* article "The Sea of Soviet Jews – Not so different from Nazi Germany" Leibler concluded:

> The great tragedy of Soviet Jewry is that whereas the "Hell House" of Stalinism is no more, and in general most Russian citizens are considerably better off – for Jews there has been no improvement. All aspects of Jewish group survival – religion, Yiddish, or Hebrew culture, contact with Israel– are considered as subversive activities by the Government.[18]

In a long letter to the *Bulletin* the Soviet embassy's press attaché, V. Gamazeichshikov, accused Leibler of "cynicism, exaggeration and lies", and claimed that all nationalities, large and small, were equal before the law, and that there was freedom of religion in the Soviet Union.[19] The Australian communist press reiterated Gamazeichnikov's accusations, and Radio Moscow beamed three broadcasts to Australia calling Leibler a liar. The Soviet news agency, *Novosti*, ran articles denouncing Leibler by Samuel Rozin, and by Moscow's official rabbi, Yehuda Levin. The Soviet overreaction had the opposite effect intended. It added to a wider awareness about the Australian campaign and to its credibility.

Drawing on Leibler's *Bulletin* article, Haworth told the House of Representatives on 3 October 1962 that reputable international Jewish organisations believed the Soviet Union was carrying out a "determined Kremlin-directed campaign to persecute the 3 million Jews in Russia". Although he did not mention Cohen by name, Haworth claimed that the "red-lining Jewish Council … had joined with the Communist Party in attempting to rubbish these grave charges brought by official Jewry".[20] He also charged some ALP members with denying there was anti-Semitism in the Soviet Union.

In response to Haworth asking him to raise the issue at the United Nations, Barwick agreed to investigate. Although he had limited notice about Haworth's question, Einfeld supported the United Nations proposal. He emphasised that "it is a fact that for some considerable time members of the Jewish faith in Russia have suffered very serious discriminatory treatment on various levels". Wentworth also strongly supported Haworth's request saying: "We cannot ignore these things any more than we could ignore them in Nazi Germany".[21]

The Australian government's readiness to consider going to the United Nations about Soviet Jews was a first among comparable Western democracies. Australian Jewish leaders welcomed the move, and it created international interest. The London *Jewish Chronicle* reported Barwick's statement on its front page together with extracts from Haworth's speech and references to Wentworth and Einfeld.[22]

The Australian decision was especially newsworthy because President John F Kennedy's administration had backed away from any such action. Although some American congressmen and senators had asked Kennedy as early as February 1962 to raise Soviet Jewry at the United Nations, the State Department was opposed. It had argued against going public, maintaining that "private appeals to the Soviet government on humane grounds would minimise the possibility of confusing the Soviet Jewish problem with cold war issues".[23]

A week after Haworth spoke, the Sydney *Daily Telegraph* reported that some Liberal senators planned to raise the issue to see how Cohen would react. The paper noted: "If Senator Cohen comes out in defence of the Soviet Union, there will be a Jewish as well as a denominational split in Labor's ranks".[24] The prediction proved all too accurate.

CHAPTER 5

THE COHEN AFFAIR

On 18 October 1962, Senator George Conrad Hannan (Liberal, Victoria) opened the adjournment debate in the Upper House. He spoke about the "barbarous" persecution of Soviet Jews and agreed that Australia should raise the matter at the United Nations.[1] At Hannan's request, after Haworth and Einfeld had spoken on the subject a fortnight earlier in the House of Representatives, Leibler had met the senator and had provided documentation.

For Hannan, principle and politics had combined conveniently. His criticism of Soviet anti-Semitism was genuine. But he and some fellow Liberal senators also saw a chance to provoke and embarrass Cohen and the ALP. Cohen took the bait. In what historian Philip Mendes described as a "passionate, emotive and contradictory" response,[2] Cohen began by claiming that his parliamentary opponent had "delivered himself of an extraordinary series of allegations, some of which I believe have substance. But some of them are so outlandish, absurd and exaggerated that no sensible body of responsible people could pay any attention to them."[3] For Cohen, it turned out to be a serious personal and political mistake. Hannan's statement on Soviet anti-Semitism was factual, even understated.

But Cohen was angry and under pressure from the Victorian Socialist Left who had preselected him. So while he emphasised his own role in combating anti-Semitism, he tried to downplay its extent in the Soviet Union. Claiming that anti-ALP politics and a personal vendetta directed against him were the real motives behind the United Nations move, Cohen said:

> Senator Hannan has made himself the vehicle in this chamber
> for a spiteful campaign being levelled largely against me. It has
> been raised also by the honourable member for Mackellar (Mr
> Wentworth) in another place.[4]

Cohen opposed going to the United Nations and argued that the correct approach was through international dialogue with the Soviets, rather than open protest. He quoted the World Jewish Congress President Dr Nahum Goldmann to support his view. At one point, he said something even some of his supporters criticised:

> I do not find it necessary to defend the Russian system. That system apparently suits the Russian people, and the Jewish community of Russia must work out its own destiny in that system. It does no service whatever to the cause of humanity – to the cause of world Jewry – to speak in the exaggerated way that Senator Hannan spoke tonight, with little regard for balance or decency.[5]

Senator George Branson (Liberal, Western Australia) followed Cohen and began:

> As long as I have breath in my body, I will stand up in my place in this chamber and defend the rights of minorities. Where there is a minority, particularly a race of people, who have been persecuted through the ages, I reserve the right to stand up and have my say about what is happening in Russia today.[6]

Later in his speech, Branson turned to Cohen and said:

> All we have asked is for Australia to bring this matter before the United Nations. I believe that that should be done. All I ask Senator Cohen is: Does he support that? Mr Einfeld supports it.[7]

The ALP senators supported Cohen. Senator Pat Kennelly (Victoria), questioned why it had taken so long to introduce the topic into the Senate after the House of Representatives had debated it. "Was the thought behind its introduction honest, or is this only another political bang bang?"[8] Kennelly claimed that the debate was designed merely to embarrass Cohen and put him in "an invidious position".[9]

Senator Lionel Murphy (NSW) strongly supported Kennelly's accusations. He claimed that the debate was only introduced to create a division between Einfeld and Cohen, and to show that Cohen did not have the Jewish community's confidence. Murphy said he was speaking on behalf of Einfeld, who was sitting in the gallery, and claimed that Einfeld had authorised him to say:

> ... that he [Einfeld] has the utmost confidence in Senator
> Cohen, and that Senator Cohen is held in the highest regard
> by the Jewish community, that there is no division between
> Mr Einfeld and Senator Cohen, and that it is shameful that
> persons should endeavour to stir up trouble between these
> two Jewish members of our Parliament.[10]

Murphy emphasised that Cohen was an active member and patron
of a number of key organisations within the Jewish community and
that "there has been a shameful episode on the part of the Liberal
Party in endeavouring tonight to introduce anti-Semitism into the
Senate and into this country".[11]

The Minister for the Navy, Senator John Gorton, who represented
Barwick in the Senate on External Affairs, dismissed the ALP
accusations as "ridiculous". Haworth had raised the matter, he said,
at the request of some of his constituents, since he "represents an
electorate which has in it probably the largest concentration of people
of the Jewish faith in Victoria".[12] As such, he was simply carrying out
his duty to his electorate. He also noted that Einfeld had supported
Haworth's statement, so that he could not see how raising the matter
could be seen as an attack on the ALP.

Senator James Arnold (ALP, New South Wales) was the final
speaker and claimed that the "regrettable debate" had been introduced
to embarrass Cohen because "he has from time to time expressed in
Australia the view that there are some things in Russia that are not as
bad as we make them out to be".[13]

The suspension of Senator Bert Hendrickson (ALP, Victoria)
reflected the debate's emotional tone. When Hannan started to speak
about the origins of modern anti-Semitism resulting in the Nazi
murder of six million Jews, Hendrickson interjected with a comment
implying that Hannan supported Nazism. Hannan immediately
complained that the comment was offensive, and asked for it to be
withdrawn. The President of the Senate, Sir Alister McMullin, twice
asked Hendrickson to withdraw, but he refused and walked out of
the chamber. McMullin then ordered the Usher of the Black Rod to

bring Hendrickson back in the chamber. When Hendrickson again refused to withdraw his comment, McMullin suspended him from the Senate, with 26 votes to 23 supporting his decision.[14]

The Age commented that Senator's Hendrickson's suspension occurred "during the longest and one of the most heated adjournment debates in the Senate in recent years".[15] Political correspondents in *The Age,* the *Canberra Times* and the *Sydney Morning Herald* reported that officials could not recall a similar incident where the Senate President had called on the Black Rod to deal with a senator.

In a follow-up debate in the House of Representatives, Leslie Haylen, the ALP member for Parkes, a south-west Sydney electorate, attacked Ashkanasy for "betraying his faith and his party by selling this sort of stuff" to Haworth. Haylen claimed that Ashkanasy had set out to damage Cohen because he had not won safe Senate preselection and that Haworth had set out to drive a wedge between Cohen and Einfeld, "two honorable members who have an affinity both of race and comradeship which should be encouraged in this place".[16]

The Treasurer, Harold Holt, responded angrily, describing Haylen's approach as "unctuous" and denying that there was any anti-Semitic bias on the Liberal side of the House.[17] *The Bulletin* strongly supported Holt and noted that Haylen's speech was "a miserable evasion of the issue – [it introduced] a new level of cynicism, even for Mr Haylen".[18]

In the *Australian Jewish Herald's* coverage of the Senate debate, I published a front-page editorial on 26 October 1962 which attacked Cohen under the emotive heading "J'Accuse". This was a reference to Emile Zola's use of the same term in 1898 during the Dreyfus Affair in France. In a front-page editorial in the newspaper *L'Aurore,* Zola had accused the French military and government authorities of anti-Semitism and a cover-up in the false allegations of espionage brought against Captain Alfred Dreyfus, a French Jewish officer. The reference also had other overtones as the Dreyfus affair played a critical role in persuading Theodore Herzl, the founder of political Zionism in the 1890s, that the Jews needed a state of their own "to solve the Jewish problem" of national homelessness.

As the paper's editor, I chose to run the unsigned editorial down the front-page's full-length across three columns. With the word **accused** in bold type in each of six paragraphs, the editorial began:

> Senator Cohen stands **accused** of attempting to sabotage the efforts of a democratic government to raise the persecution of his fellow Jews before the conscience of the world.
>
> Senator Cohen stands **accused** of imputing insincerity to men who have soberly, intelligently and factually described the slow disintegration and destruction of a faith of the Jewish people.
>
> Senator Cohen stands **accused** of abandoning Russian Jewry. On a safe, free and ordinary Thursday night in Canberra Senator Cohen said: "I do not find it necessary to defend the Russian system. That system apparently suits the Russian people, and the Jewish community of Russia must work out its own destiny in that system".[19]

As the editorial was unsigned, and as few outside the Jewish community knew that I was the editor, it was widely assumed that Leibler had written it. In fact, I had deliberately avoided talking to Leibler during the week before the paper's publication. On Thursday, 25 October, Leibler came to the *Herald*'s office as the paper came off the press and sat cross-legged on the floor to read the editorial for the first time. After repeating expletives as he read, he told me that my editorial meant the proverbial "had hit the fan". I should prepare for "a massive backlash" against the paper from Cohen supporters.

Some 36 years later, I recalled the events in an interview with historian Phillip Mendes:

> When Sam Cohen made his speech I decided it was a big story. I was engaged and committed to the cause of Soviet Jewry. I thought Cohen had let everybody down, and this was not how a Jewish member of parliament should behave, even if there were pressures on him from the Left of the ALP. I felt [he] had to be exposed and yes, I was going [to get] Sam Cohen.[20]

Mendes wrote that the editorial "caused enormous bitterness among Cohen and his supporters". I published Cohen's claim that the paper had "grossly and viciously misrepresented" his viewpoint, and that he had been subjected to "threats, libels, and character assassination".[21] The mainstream press picked up the *Herald's* "J'Accuse" editorial and the communal controversy received wide coverage.

Some two years later, when I joined the Canberra Press Gallery as a reporter for the Channel Nine network, the Sydney *Daily Telegraph* and *The Bulletin*, I met Cohen in the Parliamentary Library. It was an awkward moment, and I was surprised when he spoke to me briefly: "So you've come to Canberra? Well, politics is a hard game, don't you think? But we all move on."

Looking back after more than 50 years, and judging the editorial in hindsight, the sensational "J'Accuse" heading on the front page, and the use of "accused" in each of six paragraphs, were unfair to Cohen. They clearly were meant to suggest, as was the case with the anti-Dreyfusards, that he was on the side of the anti-Semites. He wasn't. But in the heat of the campaign and the excitement of the controversy, I thought so at the time. It was an extreme allegation against Cohen, and he and his supporters had reason to be bitter and offended. But although the "J'Accuse" heading was unfair, the editorial itself, however hostile to Cohen, remained within the bounds of fair comment. It quoted accurately, and in context, what Cohen had said. Today, as then, I believe Cohen condemned himself out of his own mouth.

The Opposition Leader, Arthur Calwell, strongly supported Cohen, saying that he deplored and resented "the unfair criticism … concerning his recent speech in the Senate on anti-Semitism".[22] In an editorial entitled "Mr Calwell and Senator Cohen", *The Bulletin* claimed that "Mr Calwell no longer knows his right hand from his left".[23] Although Calwell had enjoyed a good relationship with the Melbourne Jewish community for many years, especially because he had supported post-war Jewish immigration to Australia, the Cohen Affair complicated that relationship.

Despite the VJBD's attempts to deny that there was any conflict with the ALP, and that the divisions over Soviet Jewry merely reflected internal communal differences, the Cohen Affair had seriously damaged the ALP's Jewish links.[24] It had shaken many in the Melbourne Jewish community, both at leadership and lay levels, who found themselves torn between their long-standing ALP sympathies and their concern for Soviet Jewry. Indeed, for some, the ALP's angry opposition to the Barwick/Menzies UN initiative became a greater and more immediate concern than whatever sympathy they may have had for Soviet Jewry. It took briefings for the Australian leaders from the visiting Yigal Allon, then Israel's Labor Minister and a former commander in its War of Independence, to reassure the community that Leibler had acted with Jerusalem's full support.

The left-wing Victorian ALP executive, led by its president Robert Holt, exacerbated the conflict by repeating the allegations that the Liberals had introduced Soviet Jewry merely to embarrass Senator Cohen. In a ten-page "secret" document leaked to the press, the party's Victorian Secretary, Cyril Wyndham, claimed that Leibler, Knopfelmacher and Wiener had orchestrated the campaign, and that Ashkanasy was known to have approved the tactics.[25] The VJBD and the *Jewish Herald* both rejected these allegations.[26]

A week after the Senate debate, on 25 October, and in response to another question from Haworth, Barwick said the item on the "Manifestation of Racial Prejudice and National and Religious Intolerance" at the Third Committee of the United Nations' General Assembly would enable Australia to speak on Soviet Jewry. He promised that Australia would raise the matter in early November.

The Jewish leadership, in both Melbourne and Sydney, warmly welcomed Barwick's pledge. Leibler was the most jubilant and excited of all. In characteristic style, and foreshadowing the prolific letter and report writer he was to become, he wrote to everybody he had contacted in the preceding months. His letter to *The Bulletin*'s Peter Coleman, commending the Sydney weekly for its crucial role, summed up his views:

> That Australia, a country geographically and ideologically far away from questions such as Soviet anti-Semitism – a country which does not have a large Jewish community acting as a pressure group – has decided to bring this matter up on a UN level is of considerable importance. I also believe that

it is the first time ... that backbenchers have raised an issue culminating in the Australian government acting on a United Nations level.[27]

The two Jewish newspapers, the *Australian Jewish News* and the *Australian Jewish Herald*, thanked the Australian government "for supporting the Jewish people". Writing to Leibler from London, Emanuel Litvinoff said:

> ... delighted to hear that the Australian government intends to raise the Soviet Jewish problem at the United Nations. If, as I believe, you are responsible for this, then you have done a great job.[28]

At the VJBD's meeting on 29 October nearly all the speakers condemned Cohen and, somewhat less emphatically, the ALP, for refusing to support Australia's plan to go to the United Nations. The meeting unanimously congratulated the Victorian Public Relations Committee under Leibler's leadership on its successful campaign, and thanked the key parliamentarians who had supported it.

Before Australia acted, however, Barwick had to persuade some of his key diplomats. Following his announcement in the House of Representatives, the Department of External Affairs cabled the Australian UN Ambassador, Sir James Plimsoll, and instructed him to ensure that the Third Committee's Australian representative, Douglas White, would raise the issue of Soviet Jewry. The cablegram emphasised that the Soviet Union should grant its Jews freedom of religion and that "the argument would follow that, should the USSR find difficulty in according to Soviet Jewry full freedom to practise their religion, it has a moral obligation under Article 13 (The Universal Declaration of Human Rights) to permit them to leave the country".[29] The cablegram also warned the delegation to be prepared for the Soviet counter-attack on Australia's Aboriginal and immigration policies.

The first part of Australia's statement, seeking freedom of religion for the Soviet Union's Jews, responded to the request from the Australian Jewish leaders. It was a welcome breakthrough and, on its own, would have been sufficient cause for celebration.

The statement's second part, however, went much further. It not only raised the emigration issue for the first time at the United Nations, but it provided a moral and legal basis for Jews to leave the Soviet Union. It thus boldly articulated what had been only implicit in the Israel-led campaign. Emigration was certainly the Lishkah's long-term strategic objective. But fully aware that Moscow would strongly resist any proposal for Jewish emigration for fear that other Soviet minorities would demand similar rights, the Israelis treated emigration as the hope that dare not speak its name. Australia was preparing to speak it.

But in New York, Ambassador Plimsoll was uneasy, and his cable to Canberra made clear his strong reservations. In 1962 Plimsoll was already the rising star in External Affairs; three years later he would become its permanent Secretary, and go on to an unrivalled career in Australian diplomacy. In 2006 Foreign Minister Alexander Downer described him as Australia's "greatest ambassador".[30]

In his 1962 cable Plimsoll argued that the timing for Australia to speak was inappropriate because President Kennedy's negotiations with Khrushchev over the Cuban missile crisis were at a delicate stage. Moreover, Australia would be isolated in its attack; it would encourage criticism of Australia from the "Afro-Asians"; and the Arabs would be hostile to such a statement. Even more telling, Plimsoll noted that Israel's representative, Michael Comay, had spoken that morning and had not referred to the treatment of Soviet Jews.[31]

Comay's avoidance of the issue, however, had not been an oversight. It reflected the divisions within the Israeli government between the "activists" and the "quiet diplomatists" unwilling to confront Moscow directly. Comay and most of the Israeli Foreign Office were in the latter camp and strongly opposed raising Soviet Jewry at the UN Third Committee. Plimsoll concluded that: "Harm can be done to Australia's interest here and Australia will gain nothing ..."[32]

Despite Plimsoll's strong reservations, the Department of External Affairs' Secretary, Sir Arthur Tange, replied that Barwick's commitment to parliament was clear and that the UN delegation would have to raise the issue. Tange acknowledged the difficulties and the unfortunate timing. He suggested that the delegation needed only to indicate the level of anti-Semitism in the Soviet Union and make a plea to permit emigration.[33]

So on 2 November, just five days after Kennedy and Nikita Khrushchev, working with the UN Secretary-General U Thant, had resolved the Cuban missile crisis, Douglas White spoke at the General Assembly's Social Committee. The Australian delegate detailed "violent and inflammatory" examples of anti-Semitism, referred to the ban on baking *matzot* (the unleavened Passover bread), noted the high proportion of Jews sentenced to death for "economic crimes", and pointed out that Jewish communities around the world had "expressed concern at the treatment of Jewish people in Russia".

As instructed, he introduced the significant additional request:

> ... should the USSR find difficulty in according to Soviet Jewry full freedom to practise their religion, it should, we believe, permit them to leave the country. Indeed, it had a moral obligation to do so under article 13, paragraph 2, of the UN Declaration of Human Rights, which said: "Everyone has the right to leave a country, including his own, and to return to his country."[34]

The Soviet delegate, Mrs T N Nikolaeva, responded immediately, claiming that such "slanderous and false calumnies" had been introduced "solely to embarrass the Soviet Union".[35] A second Soviet delegate, Y A (Jacub) Ostrovski strongly defended his country's record on Jews, claiming that there was racial discrimination in the United States in clubs and other organisations.[36] There was also an adverse Arab reaction. But other countries, including the United Kingdom and the United States, supported Australia.

More significant than the immediate reactions to Australia's initiative was its longer-term impact on American and Western diplomacy on Soviet Jewry. Most important, although unpublicised at the time, was how the Australian intervention tipped the balance inside Israel's cabinet. Israeli historian Yaakov Roi notes that Israel had previously feared that raising Soviet Jewry "in an arena where the Arabs and some African states took every opportunity to attack

Israel and Zionism – its very intervention on behalf of Soviet Jewry would arouse irrelevant antagonism that would bring more harm than good to the cause."[37]

Australia's move, however, united the previously divided Israeli government behind pursuing the issue openly at an international level. The prevailing Israeli government view now was that "if Australia was prepared to raise the issue, then the Jewish state could not afford to stand on the sidelines".[38] Israel warmly – and repeatedly – thanked Australia "for its active" leadership at the United Nations.[39]

That leadership was no less significant because Barwick's contribution to a turning point in 20th century Jewish history was unwitting, and some Australian diplomats were unwilling.

In devising a way to use an item on the UN Third Committee's agenda as procedural cover for raising Soviet Jewry, Barwick's creative legal mind, or someone else's in External Affairs, opened a previously closed window. The Australian diplomats may have drawn on similar language which some United States Congressmen had proposed. But it was language which the State Department had rejected.

For its part, Australia had framed Soviet anti-Semitism as a human rights issue, and had publicised it for the first time in an international human rights context. Canberra may not have immediately grasped what it had done. But Moscow did. Together with the other repercussions, short-term and long-term, the Soviets' fervent denunciations justified the descriptions "unprecedented" and "historic" for the Australian initiative.[40]

What, then, might explain Barwick's role? Why did he respond to the requests from Liberal backbenchers? And why, despite the advice he received from senior Australian diplomats to the contrary, did he insist that Australia should speak up at the United Nations?

The simplest explanation is that it was hardly surprising, at the height of the Cold War, that Australia would criticise the Soviet Union. It reflected both Menzies' and Barwick's world views. Barwick's own strong opposition to communism, in Australia as a political movement, and internationally, as reflected in his opposition to the Soviet and Chinese varieties, predated his position on Soviet

Jewry. As External Affairs Minister, Barwick's concerns about communism influenced his decision to support South Vietnam and the commitment of Australian military advisers to Saigon. In July 1962 he attacked the Soviet's role at the United Nations, which he said Moscow and its satellites used as "a platform for propaganda".[41]

In 1954, still as a barrister, he had represented the Australian Security Intelligence Organisation (ASIO) during the Petrov Royal Commission into Soviet espionage in Australia. His experience during the Commission is said to have influenced his decision as Attorney-General in 1960 to introduce controversial amendments to the Crimes Act, which specifically targeted the Communist Party. Against the background of his long-standing inclination to exploit anti-communism as a political weapon against the ALP, Menzies certainly, and Barwick also, would have welcomed the divisions and tensions within Labor and the Left which the Soviet Jewry issue provoked.

But Barwick was also a strong supporter of individual human rights. At the start of his political career, he explained his "credo":

> I stand for people. I stand for individuals and for their freedom
> to live their own lives.[42]

Given this view, his opposition to communism internationally and domestically, his desire to support the Liberal backbenchers who had raised the issue, the perceived political benefits of creating conflict within the ALP, and his reputation for being his own man who did not always accept External Affairs' advice, Barwick's initiative accords with both political ideology and temperament.

Yet whatever Barwick's motives may have been, there is no record of any self-reflection on this issue. He does not mention Soviet Jewry in his memoirs *A Radical Tory – Garfield Barwick's Reflections and Recollections*,[43] and David Marr's comprehensive biography *Barwick* does not refer to it either.

In retrospect, however, it is clear that Barwick's initiative left a legacy. At the height of the Cold War, he acted against the prevailing balance of diplomacy in the Australia–United States alliance. Usually Washington led and Canberra followed. This time Canberra had not consulted Washington and had even gone against the State Department line. It had taken the lead unilaterally, and it had attracted notice for it – from its allies, and even more from the Soviet Union. In a letter to Leibler, Moshe Decter summed up the view from New York:

> Australia's succinct and marvellous United Nations intervention was of great value and significance. It was unprecedented in that this was the first time that the problem of Soviet Jewry was discussed at the UN on an official governmental level. It was valued on two counts:
>
> a) it helped to make the Soviets more aware than ever before of the concern felt in the West about Soviet Jews;
>
> b) it impressed other UN delegates with the seriousness of the question … so that the door has been opened for further and more systematic efforts by the UN.[44]

With considerable prescience, Decter argued that the Australian initiative mattered greatly because a) "the Soviets are known to be morally vulnerable on this problem, so that the UN was the most appropriate forum; and b) any discussion or action on this problem at the UN serves as a morale booster to isolated and disadvantaged Soviet Jewry".[45] Decter would be proven right on both counts.

CHAPTER 6

CHANNELS OF COMMUNICATION

First came the gratitude and euphoria. Then the communal recriminations. Australia's historic moves in the United Nations, welcomed throughout the Jewish world, had created new divisions at home, exacerbated old ones, and fuelled heated personal and organisational differences. For Leibler it was a sweet-bitter time. In a speech to the VJBD he described Australia's initiative as "the most significant step by an Australian government since the announcement of support for a Jewish State".[1]

But he also spoke of the aggravation, personal attacks and communal divisions. Yet it had all been worthwhile because "to know that one has been involved in a campaign which may, perhaps, be instrumental in helping to alleviate the suffering of three million Jews … is the ultimate reward that anyone in communal life can receive".[2]

In his private letters to Litvinoff, however, Leibler was more ambivalent. He was remorseful about the rifts he had created, especially the harm he had done to the Jewish relationship with the ALP. He could have been more effective if he had briefed the ALP earlier, so that "much of our present heartbreak might have been avoided".[3] As if to underline the point, the ALP's Senator Pat Kennelly told Leibler that had he been briefed he would have spoken differently about the Cohen affair.[4]

Leibler also confided to Litvinoff that the campaign had led to "probably the [community's] most vicious and unfortunate domestic upheaval". He feared that the ECAJ's upcoming annual conference would be "explosive".[5] The fears were well founded. The Sydney based ECAJ councillors insisted that Victoria had not only acted unilaterally, but by ignoring the "channels of communication", they had undermined the roof body's unity principle.

On 20 November 1962 the veteran Sydney Jewish leader, Horace Bonham Newman, moved successfully at the New South Wales Jewish Board of Deputies to censure the Victorians.[6] Again, Einfeld was caught between his ECAJ and ALP roles. Although he had strongly supported the Menzies government's plan to go to the United Nations, he had not briefed the ALP senators on the Jewish leadership's unanimity. As a result, the ALP senators all supported Cohen and, unusually for the ALP, opposed taking a human rights issue to the United Nations.

A few days after the Newman resolution, the conference met in Sydney at the Great Synagogue in Elizabeth Street. In a charged atmosphere, the ensuing debate almost led to the ECAJ's disintegration. Some of the NSW delegates threatened to keep the ECAJ executive in Sydney until March 1963 if the meeting did not censure the Victorians. In response, Ashkanasy threatened that if the ECAJ did not move to Melbourne as the constitution required, the VJBD would withdraw from the ECAJ.

Faced with a potential split in Australian Jewry, the meeting accepted a compromise resolution which emphasised the need to maintain the "channels of communication", but removed any censure of the Victorians. Some of the NSW delegates criticised the compromise. But Newman argued it had been necessary "in order to preserve the ECAJ".[7] Einfeld agreed. The conference ended with the ECAJ executive moving to Melbourne for the next two years. Ashkanasy was the incoming ECAJ president, Leibler the secretary.

The Cohen Affair and the fault lines it highlighted among Australian Jews marked a turning point in Melbourne's communal politics. In the ongoing conflict between the Jewish Left, as represented by the Council, and the mainstream communal leadership, the Left had become increasingly marginalised. Cohen's claim that the Liberal Party had raised the issue of Soviet Jewry only to embarrass him and the ALP, his minimisation of Soviet anti-Semitism, and his refusal to support the United Nations' move, had damaged his standing. Even otherwise sympathetic commentators, such as the *Australian Jewish*

News columnist Pamela Ruskin, were critical. Ruskin wrote:

> Senator Cohen convinced himself that the matter was raised
> to embarrass him rather than from any genuine concern for
> the Jews of Russia. This is very probably true, but one must ask
> Senator Cohen *why the issue should embarrass him* [emphasis
> Ruskin's].[8]

Even more than the damage to Cohen's personal standing, from
which he partly recovered before his death in 1969, the Cohen Affair
significantly weakened the Council and the remnants of its left-
wing support in the Jewish community. The Soviet Jewry campaign
had benefited from the Menzies/Barwick government's Cold War
stance and its anti-Soviet policies. And the opportunities for the
government to exploit the differences within the ALP, certainly for
its more strident anti-communist senators and backbenchers, also
helped. But the decisive drive which defeated the once influential
Jewish Left came from a coalition of new-generation activists led by
Leibler and their more seasoned mentors: Ashkanasy, Wiener and
Knopfelmacher.

Which is why the campaign proved to be so important long after
and well beyond the Soviet Jewry issue. It heralded a new stage in the
Australian Jewish community's willingness and capacity to pursue
its domestic and international interests, even if it meant entering the
"political thicket". As Philip Mendes has noted:

> From this time onwards, Jewish leaders began to speak out
> increasingly publicly and loudly in defence of Jewish interests,
> including support for Zionism and the state of Israel.[9]

Australian Jews had mobilised and lobbied on other major issues
before Soviet Jewry. In 1947–48 a small group of Sydney Jewish
leaders had helped to persuade Labor's External Affairs Minister
Herbert Evatt to support the partition of Palestine and the emergence
of Israel. In 1950 a broader coalition of Melbourne and Sydney
leaders could not prevent the Menzies government, supported by
Labor, from allowing 100,000 German settlers to come to Australia.

But the successful 1962 campaign to bring Soviet Jewry to the
United Nations reflected a greater militancy, especially in Melbourne,

a new sophistication in engaging and informing sympathetic parliamentarians, and a new readiness to involve the mainstream media.

The Cohen Affair, however, has remained the subject of some historical controversy. In 1999, Rodney Gouttman, a lecturer at the University of South Australia, concluded that the Affair "had all the hall-marks of a conspiracy". After obtaining access to contemporary ASIO files, he argued that a handful of opponents had plotted secretly to ruin Cohen's political career and, in the process, to inflict damage upon the ... [ALP].[10]

Gouttman was both right and wrong. Although a small group of Cohen's opponents did conduct a mostly clandestine campaign against him and bitterly opposed the dominant Socialist Left faction in the Victorian ALP, they were marginal players. They certainly did not shape the Affair's main events.

As someone directly involved, both as a journalist and activist, I believe the evidence supports my recollection: the decisive events were far more public, the main participants were far more open, the issues were far more basic. The key drivers were not the handful of Gouttmann's "conspirators", but the VJBD led by Ashkanasy and Leibler, the students and activists who demonstrated and lobbied their parliamentarians, and the community's "silent majority" who knew that Soviet anti-Semitism was real. For Leibler and his Melbourne supporters, helping Soviet Jewry was the driving motivation, rather than undermining Cohen or attacking the ALP. Yet given the Left's dominance of the ALP's Cold War policy agendas in the 1960s, Leibler's sense of urgency, and his temperamental impatience, it was inevitable that he would chose to enlist the Liberal Party. To that extent Leibler undoubtedly exploited the Liberal Party's readiness to use anti-communism as a stick with which to beat Labor.

But as the campaign developed, Leibler hoped that Einfeld's influence in the ALP would lead to a bipartisan commitment which would strengthen the Australian case in the United Nations. It was not to be. And despite his attacks on Cohen, Leibler insisted that he was non-partisan in defending Jewish interests. He was prepared to criticise any Australian politician, Liberal or Labor, who associated with anti-Semitic governments or organisations. He cited his strong opposition to James Killen, the Queensland Liberal MHR who, earlier in 1962, had agreed to a lecture tour by the racist and anti-Semitic League of Rights.

Yet it is also clear that he was especially vitriolic about Cohen, and that he also worked very closely with Wiener and Knopfelmacher, whom the communist Left and many in the ALP regarded with suspicion and hostility. But although Leibler shared many of Knopfelmacher's anti-Soviet views, he did not agree with him on Israel or on other Jewish issues. Indeed, the two men were to fall out bitterly and spectacularly some eighteen years later over their different attitudes to boycotting the Moscow Olympic Games. But in 1962, and as Leibler has maintained since, he always regarded the political alliances he formed, and any exploitation of Liberal and ALP differences over anti-communism, as means to an end, not ends in themselves.

At the beginning of November 1962, at the height of the key parliamentary debates, Leibler made this case to Alan Reid, the veteran Canberra correspondent for the Sydney *Daily Telegraph*, who was known for his critical reporting of the ALP's Left.

> This whole business from our point of view was not a stunt to get Cohen. Our concern was for Soviet Jewry. Unfortunately Calwell's statement, and Einfeld's apparent tacit support are forcing the Jewish community to choose between Cohen and Soviet Jewry – a ridiculous state of affairs.[11]

In the months that followed the "explosive" ECAJ conference, some of the personal tensions and bitterness between Sydney and Melbourne subsided, or were papered over. In November 1963, just twelve months after his controversial Senate speech, Cohen joined Einfeld to hand a protest letter to the Soviet Ambassador in Canberra about the persecution of Soviet Jews. Leibler wrote to Cohen congratulating him. By joining Einfeld to protest, Leibler said Cohen had "closed the book" on the past, and on the divisive issues in the Jewish community.[12]

The cooling of tensions during 1963 meant that the Melbourne-based ECAJ could now follow up the Soviet Jewry campaign, free of provoking any partisan divisions. The less turbulent political environment also meant that Leibler had time to take stock. His reappraisal, in close consultation with the Lishkah in Israel and his international counterparts, led to two new directions. First, he set out to establish contact with the Communist Party and the Left, the "enemy" which had so vehemently opposed his campaign throughout 1962. Second, and largely arising from his dialogue with the CPA, he decided to confront Dr Nahum Goldmann, the World Jewish Congress president and the champion of "quiet diplomacy".[13]

Both these initiatives lay ahead of him. Throughout 1963 he worked on consolidating Australia's "breakthrough" at the United Nations. On 22 October 1963 Ashkanasy wrote to Menzies, saying he hoped that Australia would not drop the issue.[14] On 30 October 1963, just twelve months after he had first raised Soviet Jewry, William Haworth spoke again in the House of Representatives quoting the United States Secretary for Political Affairs, Averell Harriman, about the suppression of Jewish religious rights in the Soviet Union. In response, Barwick asked Australia's Ambassador to the United Nations, David Hay, to confer with the United States Ambassador, Adlai Stevenson, and instructed him to raise the issue again regardless of any formal agenda difficulties.

When Hay met with Stevenson, however, he learned that the United Nations Committee was so far behind in its agenda that it was unlikely that Religious Intolerance would come up in that session. Stevenson noted that in 1964 the UN was planning to draft a convention on Religious Intolerance, and that Australia could raise the matter at that stage.[15]

Barwick issued a press statement about the delay[16] and External Affairs assured Ashkanasy that the the Department had instructed Hay "to take advantage of any opportunity which presents itself, publicly or privately, to help promote some effective action".[17] An impatient Leibler wanted to press for Australia to raise it as an emergency item. But Decter explained that the pro-Soviet Jewry network had failed to persuade any government to raise the issue, and so it would have to wait until 1964.[18]

On 30 November 1963, Menzies went to the electorate early and won government with an increased majority. In the swing against the ALP, however, Einfeld lost the seat of Phillip to the Liberal William Aston, whom he had beaten in 1961. With Haworth, Aston continued to raise Soviet Jewry in the House of Representatives. During 1964, however, Australia became less active on the issue at the United Nations.

In April 1964, speaking in the House of Representatives, Aston condemned *Judaism Without Embellishment* by Trofim Kichko, a crude anti-Semitic publication by the Ukrainian Academy of Sciences which had gained international notoriety. On one of the rare occasions where he spoke publicly on the issue, Menzies joined Aston in his condemnation. He promised a "forceful" statement confirming Australia's opposition to racial and religious intolerance at the United Nations General Assembly's 19th session. Said Menzies: "We will speak up, and, I hope, be heard with some effect".[19] But Menzies did not fully keep his pledge. At the General Assembly's 20th session in late 1965, Australia made a general statement criticising anti-Semitism, but did not refer specifically to the Soviet Union.

In large measure, Australia's less active role on behalf of Soviet Jewry was due to Barwick's retirement from politics. In July 1964 the Menzies government appointed him as the High Court's Chief Justice.[20] Leibler and his supporters were especially disappointed at Barwick's departure. The Minister for External Affairs had left his mark on the campaign, and on Jewish history.

CHAPTER 7

FROM RIGHT TO LEFT

From their earliest meetings in 1959, the Lishkah's Avigur and Levanon repeated a key message to Leibler and his international associates: Find "independent" communist leaders, not beholden to Moscow, to endorse the Soviet Jewry cause as a human rights issue for the international Left. Prominent left-wing intellectuals, such as Bertrand Russell and Martin Luther King, had begun to criticise Soviet anti-Jewish policies in the late 1950s. The Socialist International had also passed a resolution calling on the Soviet Union to end its discrimination against the Jews. So the "next challenge for Soviet Jewish advocates was to involve Western communists in the Soviet Jewry debate".[1]

Leibler's first Melbourne meeting with senior CPA leaders was held in February 1964 in the Melbourne city office where he ran the family's diamond business. It was with Bernard (Bernie) Taft and Rex Mortimer, close friends and members of the CPA's Victorian Central Committee. Taft, who was Jewish, was the party's executive director. Mortimer was the editor of *The Guardian*, the CPA's Melbourne weekly, and co-editor of the Marxist quarterly *Arena*. A former barrister planning to study for his doctorate in Indonesian politics at Monash University, Mortimer had acquired a reputation on the Left for his more independent line.[2] The communist leaders had asked for the meeting after Leibler had sent Trofim Kichko's *Judaism Without Embellishment*, a crude Soviet anti-Semitic tract, to Alec Robertson, the editor of *The Tribune,* the party's Sydney weekly.

Kichko's extremism had jolted the CPA. Just months before, the party had republished a pamphlet by the American Jewish communist, Herbert Aptheker, which rejected any criticisms of Soviet anti-Semitism. Aptheker's pamphlet even included a foreword by Melbourne communist, Harry Stein, also Jewish, arguing that the Soviet Jewry campaign was just another Cold War attack on communism.[3]

In his autobiography, *Crossing the Party Line*, Taft, who had known Leibler as a child (their fathers had been friends) described the first meeting:

> I went to Leibler's office with some trepidation. It was an extraordinary meeting. Leibler gave me the feeling that he expected Communists to have horns. He measured every word ... treating us with great suspicion. I suppose we were not exactly sure whom we were dealing with either.[4]

From the outset, Leibler insisted that he was strongly anti-communist, but that in dealing with the CPA his only interest was Soviet Jewry. Mortimer was impressed. In a conversation with Waten, he described Leibler as "very suave and no fool either ... he was a smooth operator".[5] Waten agreed that the CPA had "never taken him lightly", but called him a "bastard".[6]

Taft regarded the Kichko book as "scandalous".[7] But he complained about the pressure from Leibler for a public statement, claiming that "(Leibler) thinks I am only living for him".[8] The contacts with Leibler nevertheless continued. Some of the exchanges had the CPA's official endorsement. But in others, Taft and Mortimer saw an opportunity to collude against the hard-line CPA leadership in Sydney.[9]

One result of Leibler's contacts with the CPA was that the Australian Security Intelligence Organisation (ASIO) opened a file on "Isi Joseph Leibler", and followed his activities.[10] Although ASIO did not tap his phone, they tapped the CPA members' phones and transcribed every conversation they had with – or about – Leibler. The CPA leaders and Leibler usually assumed ASIO was recording their dialogue; indeed they often joked about it.

For their part, however, the ASIO officers reported every conversation with deadpan routine. They also included in the files every newspaper article in the Jewish and mainstream press about Leibler. Which is why Leibler's ASIO files provide a detailed – and intriguing – record of an important chapter in the history of the

Australian Left and the Jewish community's political development.

In March 1964, Leibler arranged to print 20,000 copies of the Kichko book, complete with its confronting anti-Semitic images, and distributed it to opinion makers around Australia. It was a risky move and created controversy in the Jewish community. Temple Beth Israel's Rabbi Dr Herman Sanger argued that the idea may have been well intentioned, but it had been a serious mistake. He was not alone. But the book's wide distribution helped to raised awareness, especially in the media, about Soviet anti-Semitism.

In response to world-wide criticism, the Communist Party of the Soviet Union (CPSU)'s Ideological Commission reviewed the Kichko book, and concluded that there were many "errors". When Moscow withdrew the book in April 1964, Mortimer welcomed the Soviet decision and called on Moscow to prosecute Kichko.[11] Despite Moscow's action, the Moldavian State Publishing House published F S Mayatsky's *Contemporary Judaism and Zionism*, another extreme anti-Semitic book, just five months later. In a letter to the Soviet embassy, the ECAJ protested that the book "revives canards of medieval and modern anti-Semitism".[12]

As part of his dialogue with the CPA, Leibler had also sought a rapprochement with Cohen and the Council. In June 1964 he offered to help the Council reaffiliate with the VJBD. But he told Cohen he had reservations about Platz, who denied there was anti-Semitism in the Soviet Union, and Waten, whom he described as an unrepentant Stalinist.[13] But Cohen defended Platz who, he claimed, was highly regarded within the ALP.

Nothing came of Leibler's proposal. Waten and Solomon Factor, another veteran Jewish communist, opposed Leibler's overtures. Waten claimed that talking to Leibler was "a waste of time" because "he had his views on everything and everything else was just manoeuvres".[14] And in a conversation between Waten and Platz, which ASIO recorded, they agreed they would only try to rejoin the VJBD if they were sure that they had the numbers.[15]

In the event, the VJBD did not readmit the Council. Waten continued to criticise Leibler, describing him, Knopfelmacher, and

Ken Gott (a former CPA member and now strongly anti-communist) as a "dangerous group".[16] The ASIO telephone transcripts show that other CPA members also continued to suspect Leibler's motives.[17]

In July 1964, the moderate socialist journal, *Dissent*, devoted a whole issue to Soviet Jewry. In the introduction the editors, Leon Glezer, Peter Samuel and James Jupp, noted that the Kichko book had highlighted the problem of Soviet anti-Semitism. They criticised Waten for claiming "only eighteen months ago" that Soviet anti-Semitic publications were Western "forgeries", and emphasised the need to defend human rights "wherever they are being attacked".[18] Leibler welcomed the *Dissent* special issue as an important development on the moderate Left. He wrote to Litvinoff:

> Soviet anti-Semitism is assuming a very important role in Australian politics. Weird though it may seem, the question, "What is your attitude on Soviet anti-Semitism"? ... is ... a gauge to assess political postures.[19]

Litvinoff urged Leibler not to lose the Left's moral support. "In the long run, we think their influence on the situation may be far reaching".[20] Leibler took Litvnoff's injunction seriously, and persevered in his dialogue.

By November 1964, however, he was growing impatient because the CPA had still not made a formal statement. So to force the issue, he told the *Australian Jewish Herald* that Taft and Mortimer had commented on CPA attitudes to Soviet Jewry. The paper reported that Taft had criticised the Kichko book. But it also reported that Mortimer had welcomed Bertrand Russell's praise for the CPA as one of the few communist parties prepared to condemn Soviet anti-Semitic propaganda. Mortimer had also said that he wished the CPA would be more active on the issue, but that he was not authorised to make a formal statement.[21]

After the *Jewish Herald* article appeared, Mortimer confided to Leibler that the CPA's Victorian State Committee had "carpeted" him and criticised him strongly. But for Leibler the comments from Taft and Mortimer were a breakthrough, and justified the months of "rather painful negotiations and discussions".[22] *The Bulletin* described the Taft and Mortimer comments as "a new struggle for power and influence among the communist leadership … the beginnings of a new division between Moscow and Rome".[23] When Leibler told Mortimer the *Bulletin* article would create "bedlam" on the Left, the ASIO transcript notes that "they both laughed".[24]

The Bulletin was referring to an emerging group within the CPA that had aligned itself with the Italian Communist Party. Under Palmiro Togliatti's leadership, the Italian communists had become more critical of Moscow and followed a more independent line. To add to the dynamics of change within the CPA during 1964, a pro-Maoist group led by Melbourne barrister Ted Hill had split away and formed the Communist Party of Australia (Marxist-Leninist).

In Israel, the Lishkah closely followed the Australian Left's divisions and Leibler's dialogue. At their request, Leibler travelled to Britain, France and New York to meet leading Jewish communists, including Morris U Schappes, editor of *Jewish Currents*, and Paul Novick, editor of *Morgen Freiheit*. Their discussions focused on the dilemmas the Jewish Left faced in dealing with Soviet anti-Semitism.[25] From his international meetings, and from his association with Mortimer and Taft, Leibler's own view of the Left, and especially of the Jewish Left, had become more nuanced.[26]

But Leibler's dialogue with the CPA, and his apparent transition from militant "Cold War warrior" to a moderate negotiator with the communists, was too much for some Jewish community leaders. They criticised him as an "irresponsible young upstart" who had sold out.

Leibler's dialogue also reflected yet another difference between the Melbourne and Sydney political cultures, Jewish and non-Jewish, which had surfaced during the Cohen Affair. Although those tensions had eased by mid-1964, the publication of *The Bridge*, a new Sydney Jewish quarterly, revived them.[27]

The new journal's editor, Haim Brezniak, was a successful pro-Soviet businessman. Born in Poland in 1914, he arrived in Australia in 1939 and had married Paula Taft, Bernie Taft's sister. He joined the Jewish Unity Association (JUA), the Sydney equivalent of

Melbourne's Left-leaning Jewish Council, and in 1948 became editor of *Unity*, a literary journal for the wider Sydney Jewish community. In the same year, the Commonwealth Investigation Service (CIS) – ASIO's precursor – began its surveillance of the JUA. The CIS claimed that although the organisation's primary aim was to combat anti-Semitism, it also acted "as a cover to disseminate communist propaganda".[28]

Unity had ceased publication in 1951. In mid-1964 a consortium of Jewish academics and Sydney community leaders led by Dr Alan Crown, then a lecturer in Semitic Studies at the University of Sydney, launched *The Bridge* under Brezniak's editorship. Leibler regarded Brezniak, who was not a CPA member, as a "fellow traveller", and worried that he and the new journal could undermine his delicate negotiations with Mortimer and Taft in Melbourne. Brezniak's failure to mention Soviet Jewry in *The Bridge*'s first issue, confirmed his fears. When Leibler published a critical review in the *Australian Jewish Herald*, republished in Sydney's *Australian Jewish Times*, it sparked another acrimonious debate.

Dr Joachim Schneeweiss, a prominent Sydney Zionist leader on *The Bridge*'s editorial board, described Leibler as "that knight errant ... that stormy petrel of many a battle, both real and imagined". He accused Leibler of "character assassination" and described his review as "a tendentious and incompetent piece of bigotry, irrelevance, and downright rudeness".[29] The September 1964 meeting of the NSW Jewish Board of Deputies debated the controversy and reignited some of the Cohen Affair tensions.

In response to the controversy, *The Bridge* published a supplement on Soviet Jewry in its third edition. It featured an introduction by Professor Julius Stone, Challis Professor of International Law at the University of Sydney, and a leading pro-Israel advocate. There were also articles by prominent American Jewish writers Abraham I Katsh and Ben-Zion Goldberg, both with pro-Moscow leanings, and a reprinted speech by Dr Nahum Goldmann. Overall, the supplement's tone and content, especially Goldmann's warning against "over-zealous activity" – a clear reference to Leibler-style activism – combined to minimise Soviet anti-Semitism.

When Einfeld, now again ECAJ president, said the ECAJ would reprint 1000 copies of *The Bridge*'s supplement, Leibler asked Ashkanasy to intervene. The supplement was due to appear in 1965 just before Leibler's own booklet *Soviet Jewry and Human Rights*. Following pressure from Ashkanasy, Einfeld only reprinted 200 copies. After Leibler published his booklet in March 1965, Brezniak acknowledged that Mortimer's endorsement was significant. Arising from Leibler's dialogue with the CPA, Mortimer had expressed an unprecedented condemnation of Moscow's anti-Semitism which shook the Australian Left (see Chapter 8: Italian Liners and the Party). Brezniak had little choice but to acknowledge Mortimer's important declaration. But he could not quite bring himself to welcome Leibler's booklet. Eventually, Brezniak criticised Moscow in *The Bridge* in September 1965, referring to "the dark years of 1948–52" when Stalin ordered the murder of Jewish writers and cultural leaders.

In his clash with Brezniak during *The Bridge* controversy, in his dialogue with the CPA, and in his battles with the Jewish Left, one recurring theme increasingly frustrated Leibler – "the Goldmann alternative". Since 1948 Goldmann had led the WJC, an international roof body which he had helped to establish in 1936. By the early 1960s it loosely represented Jewish communities in some 65 countries. The WJC, however, was essentially a one-man show, a vehicle for Goldmann's international diplomacy.

Born in 1895 in Visnieva, now in Belarus, Goldmann was one of the most influential Jewish and Zionist statesmen of the 20th century. According to his biographers: "Goldmann was a profoundly idiosyncratic and iconoclastic character ... a master of political theatre." He could be both "the charming diplomat, a bon vivant [who] enjoyed the pleasures of life" and also "a political loner ... acerbic, sharp, and unpredictable". A self-described womaniser, Goldmann could joke about his relaxed lifestyle: "Every fourteen days Goldmann takes two weeks of vacations."[30]

But Goldmann, a brilliant networker, had also built an international reputation among liberal-minded Jewish and non-Jewish opinion makers. He argued it was wrong to claim there was Soviet anti-Semitism, because under the Soviet constitution all citizens had equal rights, and Moscow officially recognised its Jews as a national minority. When he did criticise the Soviet Union, Goldmann argued only that Moscow did not support the Jewish national minority as much as it did others. He expressed his views in a widely quoted 1963 article:

> But, to sum up, it would be false and unjust to accuse the Soviet policy of an openly anti-Semitic policy, and to think that the physical and even economic existence of Jews in the USSR is seriously threatened. The real problem of Soviet Jewry concerns their life as a distinct community, their right to maintain their identity and survival as a distinct Jewish entity.[31]

At international forums, Goldmann emphasised his preference for "quiet diplomacy" in contrast to Leibler's support for public protests and political action.[32] Since the Cohen Affair, when Cohen had cited Goldmann in the 1962 Senate debate, communists and many on the Left had done the same. Even many Jewish leaders, especially in Sydney, who accepted the evidence for Soviet anti-Semitism, were nevertheless uneasy at Leibler's combative style and the political entanglements he attracted. To them, Goldmann's emphasis on "quiet diplomacy" seemed the safer bet.

With Ashkanasy's strong support, however, and confident that he reflected Israel's view on active protest, Leibler decided to confront the pre-eminent world Jewish leader. Privately he dubbed him the "King of the Jews".[33] But he had no illusions that he was up against a formidable opponent. He had his first chance to confront Goldmann publicly at the WJC executive meeting in Geneva in June 1965. The London *Jewish Chronicle* reported the clash:

> Leibler, whose published survey – Soviet Jewry and Human Rights – has attracted world attention, thrustfully advocated a harder line in Jewish approaches to the Soviet Union in order to enlist support of non-conforming leftist circles. Dr Goldmann, in turn, with a formidable display of forensic fireworks, insisted that his quiet diplomacy was the better

course. In general, the consensus was that Dr Goldmann won on points, but Mr Leibler's perspicuity and tenacity was admirably commented upon.[34]

Leibler continued to insist that "the only means whereby the plight of Soviet Jewry could be alleviated would be by an intensification of the protest movement within the Free World".[35]

In 1965 the American Jewish leadership mobilised on Soviet Jewry for the first time. They began their protest campaign with two major events – a rally at Madison Square Garden on 3 June, followed by a vigil in Washington on 4 June. On 10 June, Goldmann responded on the *New York Times* front page. He claimed:

> Accusations are being made against Russia which are not justified, and which can only delay the solution of the problem, and even harm Soviet Jewry.[36]

Goldmann's views attracted wide international press coverage and created unease among Jewish leaders. The Israeli cabinet was also concerned and Prime Minister Levi Eshkol cabled Goldmann seeking an explanation.

Litvinoff, concerned that Goldmann was now a serious threat to the international campaign, urged Leibler to take up "an outspoken position". The next opportunity to debate Goldmann would be a month later at the Strasbourg conference, a special WJC meeting on Soviet Jewry for only 25 invited participants, including Leibler. He told Litvinoff:

> I am at a complete loss as to what to do in Strasbourg. This meeting is Goldmann territory, but I will play it by ear.[37]

At the time Leibler was 30. Goldmann had celebrated his 70th birthday just a few days before the Strasbourg meeting. Leibler had won some limited standing in the international Soviet Jewry movement, but he was still seen as a young newcomer at the WJC. Trying not to overplay his hand against the doyen leader, Leibler said that in disagreeing with him, he was not behaving out of *chutzpah*. But he claimed that Goldmann's statements "cut the feet from those raising the questions in Left quarters", and provided ammunition for Russian Jewish apologists for the Soviet regime such as the Yiddish writer, Aron Vergelis, the editor of *Sovietish Haimland* (Soviet Homeland), a Yiddish monthly.[38]

Leibler also criticised Goldmann's opposition to public protests.

> ... *Shtadlonus* [intercession] and private diplomacy used since 1956 have been abysmal failures ... The only approach ... is a militant campaign to mobilise public opinion ... And let's not hear any talk about restraint. Principled, factual, well documented approaches, yes! But based on militant public campaigns, not on *shtadlonus* or silent diplomacy.[39]

To his surprise and relief, the WJC's governing board gave Leibler a standing ovation. In an hour-long reply, Goldmann accused Leibler and his critics of "extreme naivety and even stupidity", emphasised his right to decide on tactics, and accused the activists of undermining any chance he had of reaching an understanding with Soviet authorities.[40]

Commenting on the debate, the London *Jewish Chronicle* noted:

> Dr Nahum Goldmann might well believe that he was on the verge of an understanding with the Soviet authorities on the Jewish question, and that an understanding was torpedoed by open denunciation of Soviet practice. One is bound to approach such a view with an open mind and also with some scepticism. Such hopes have been harboured before.[41]

For Leibler the debate was not just about policy and tactics. It had become personal. In devoting so much of his response to attacking Leibler and mocking his youth and lack of experience, Goldmann's condescension had backfired. The veteran leader significantly boosted the Australian's status, and the Strasbourg conference proved to be a turning point for Leibler's international recognition.

On his return to Melbourne, Leibler wrote that so long as "WJC meetings are democratic gatherings I will speak my mind and if the price will be to be showered with personal abuse, too bad".[42]

Addressing the VJBD, he described Goldmann:

> The President is completely omnipotent, not responsible to anyone for his public statements ... Everyone is terrified of antagonising Dr Goldmann. He is, undoubtedly, World Jewry's most outstanding spokesman ... head and shoulders

above all … He has a very sharp tongue and contempt for public opinion – so there is … a cult of personality.[43]

At the WJC Plenary Session in Brussels in August 1966, Leibler renewed his attack on Goldmann, focusing on the debate over tactics.[44]

The London *Jewish Chronicle* reported:

> Dr Goldmann said that while others liked to beat the drum, he himself preferred to play the flute. One of his most persistent critics … the Australian Mr Isi Leibler, complained that the Congress President's role was not to play one instrument but to conduct the whole orchestra. To which Dr Goldmann retorted: How can I be the conductor when I have no assurance that my baton would be followed?[45]

In addition to disagreeing over tactics, Goldmann also differed with Leibler and the Israelis over the campaign's main goals. Goldmann was reluctant to press Moscow on the right to emigrate to Israel. He feared that the emigration issue might detract from the religious and cultural campaign within the Soviet Union. Taking the lead from his Israeli colleagues, however, Leibler highlighted the right to emigrate: "It is our sacred responsibility to continue exerting pressure to bring this about."[46]

The tensions between the Melbourne Jewish leadership and Goldmann reached a peak after November 1966, when Ashkanasy resumed the ECAJ presidency. At Leibler's urging, Ashkanasy wrote to Goldmann outlining the Australian success in establishing dialogue with the communists and proposed that the WJC should do likewise.

Goldmann responded that the WJC was active in the area, but that they had to "do it very discreetly without any publicity – otherwise the Communists would refuse to do anything".[47] Ashkanasy replied that he was not aware of anything the WJC had done with Communist parties, and that Soviet representatives often quoted Goldmann to defend their policies.[48] Goldmann's reply was short: "You know we differ on this matter, and it is no use continuing the polemics in correspondence." Ashkanasy replied: "We shall not desist: with those who think as we do, we shall go forward."[49]

On 14 February 1967, the Melbourne-based ECAJ executive circulated a six-page letter, which Leibler had drafted, to all the WJC's members and constituents. The letter claimed that Goldmann was out of step with the leading Soviet Jewry organisations, that his reliance on quiet diplomacy was harming the cause, and that overt pressure on Moscow was essential.[50]

Some WJC members rejected Leibler's claims, even calling for the ECAJ's disaffiliation from the WJC.[51] Dr Gerhardt Riegner, the veteran WJC Executive Director, deplored the letter and defended Goldmann's record.[52] Dr Joachim Prinz, chairman of the WJC's Governing Council, claimed that Leibler had so distorted Goldmann's views as to falsify them.[53] The Canadian Jewish Congress chairman, Michael Garber, also supported Goldmann, as did the CJC's executive director, Saul Hayes, who dubbed the controversy "L'Affaire Russe".[54] But Avraham Abba Cohen, the president of MAOZ, the Israeli organisation for Soviet Jewry, strongly supported Leibler.[55]

The Leibler-Goldmann debate continued at the WJC Governing Council in Jerusalem in July 1967, as did the correspondence. Neither man conceded. In 1969 Goldmann and Riegner visited Australia for the WJC. While in Melbourne, community leader Walter Lippmann quietly arranged a meeting with Taft and other CPA members without informing Leibler. The WJC leaders maintained the contact with Taft after their Australian visit.[56]

But by the early 1970s, Goldmann and the WJC were relegated to the sidelines. The Jewish movement's very public protests and bold demonstrations inside the Soviet Union had overtaken the Goldmann-Leibler debate. In risking arrest, loss of jobs and KGB harassment, the Russian activists had ensured that the international movement, with the great advantage of free expression in the democracies, would now follow their militant example. The time for "quiet diplomacy" as the international campaign's main vehicle was over.

Although Goldmann continued as WJC president until 1977 (he died in 1982) he was no longer a key player in international Jewish affairs.

CHAPTER 8

ITALIAN LINERS AND THE PARTY

Writing of the memorial gathering at Monash University for Rex Alfred Mortimer (1926–79), historian Terence H Irving noted that his friends recalled his "cosmic pessimism and day to day good cheer".[1] As the most significant communist intellectual he met during the four years of dialogue with the CPA, Leibler remembers him with respect and affection. By any measure, in the history of the Australian Left, Mortimer was a game-changer.

Leibler's booklet *Soviet Jewry and Human Rights*, the Australian campaign's most influential publication, owed its origins to Mortimer's invitation in November 1964 to write about Soviet Jewry for *Arena*. Leibler submitted 30,000 words rather than the 5000 he had been allotted. Although Leibler offered to pay for printing the essay as a supplement, Mortimer faced heavy pressure from the CPA not to publish anything. He feared expulsion, even a split in the party, if he did. So Leibler published a print-run of 10,000 independently, and the essay appeared in March 1965. Mortimer endorsed it and wrote:

> The question of Soviet Jewry is one that concerns me seriously. As a Communist I cannot but react to any manifestations of discrimination and prejudice wherever they may occur.
>
> I do not share your political views. I am also aware that people of notoriously inhumane views have involved themselves in campaigns about Soviet Jewry for the sole purpose of discrediting the USSR … However … I am convinced that the massive documentation you have assembled poses a substantial and disturbing problem for Marxists and people of the left everywhere … [2]

More than 50 years on, when the Soviet empire and Marxist-Leninism seem as remote to a new generation as the Middle Ages, it is difficult to convey the significance of Mortimer's guarded statement. It was unprecedented for an Australian communist, and among the very first of its kind in any communist party. Internationally, it added to the growing awareness about Soviet anti-Semitism. In Australia it exacerbated the growing rifts within the CPA and the wider Left towards Moscow and international communism.

Writing in *Labor News*, the leading left-wing historian, Brian Fitzpatrick said: "We were wrong. It's not fun to admit this; but the evidence is irresistible."[3] Leibler saw Fitzpatrick's admission as a "complete capitulation".[4] He had been one of Cohen's strongest supporters in 1962 and had opposed going to the United Nations. In *Outlook*, another left-wing journal, Helen Palmer wrote: "Leibler documents the whole development of Soviet anti-Semitism with credible objectivity."[5] And in *Arena* Marxist academic Lloyd Churchward, a senior lecturer in Political Science at the University of Melbourne, criticised Leibler's methodology, but agreed that the evidence of Soviet anti-Semitism could not be ignored.[6]

The publicity surrounding *Soviet Jewry and Human Rights*, its favourable reception within the Left, and even in some sections of the CPA, presented a dilemma for Moscow's supporters in Australia. During a conversation which ASIO recorded between Margaret Hearn and Professor Courtney Oppenheim at the Australia-Soviet Friendship Society, they agreed that the book was "no flash in the pan" and had to be "taken seriously".[7] But they were not sure how to react.

A similar dilemma faced the CPA leadership. Early in 1965, after Lance Sharkey had stepped down due to ill health, Laurie Aarons succeeded him as general secretary. His brother Eric Aarons had become vice-president. Within the CPA, Sharkey was known for his "notorious prejudice" against Jews, and the rise to party leadership by the Aarons brothers who, like Taft, were Jewish, stirred some of the internal anti-Jewish undercurrents.[8]

As Laurie Aarons' son Mark has noted, this had its own ironies as Leibler's relationship with Mortimer developed. During late 1964, in the leadership transition period from Sharkey, Laurie Aarons had visited Moscow and had clashed with two senior Kremlin officials: Mikhail Suslov and Yuri Andropov. As the Soviet Ambassador in Budapest in 1956, Andropov had been involved in Moscow's suppression of the Hungarian revolution, and later as KGB head he would help to crush the Czech uprising in August 1968. In 1982 he succeeded Leonid Brezhnev.

When Laurie Aarons met him in 1964, Andropov, together with Suslov, was a member of the CPSU Secretariat, the Kremlin's most senior leadership group. Aarons' clash with them was a foretaste of the CPA's eventual complete break with Moscow after the "Prague Spring" in 1968. Quoting from the ASIO files, which reported a conversation between Mortimer and Laurie Aarons after Aarons had taken up "cultural (and) Soviet Jewish matters ... on the highest levels" in Moscow, Mark Aarons comments:

> In light of the subterranean anti-Semitic campaign inside the CPA, it was ironic that one of Laurie's first clashes with Moscow concerned the systematic oppression of Soviet Jews ... Laurie's and Eric's ASIO files for this period contain dozens of reports on this subject, culminating in a mild, but nonetheless accurate, public criticism of Soviet policies.[9]

In early 1965, however, although Mortimer had emerged as the spokesman for the Euro-communists or "Italian liners", he and his supporters were still in a minority. Whatever their private doubts and leanings, the party's Sydney-based leadership and most members still followed the broad Moscow line. This meant that Mortimer's endorsement of Leibler's book attracted a CPA commission of four leading members: Eric Aarons, Malcolm Robertson, the *Tribune's* editor, Paul Mortier, a CPA journalist, and Mortimer. They rejected Mortimer's endorsement and asked him to withdraw it. Mortimer "decided that he was mistaken".[10]

The commission published a booklet entitled *Soviet Jewry – A reply to Mr I. Leibler.* It claimed that communists opposed all forms of racism, condemned anti-Semitism wherever it occurred, and challenged many of Leibler's citations. But it conceded the Kichko book's authenticity and acknowledged some expressions of Soviet anti-Semitism.[11]

Writing from London to the *Australian Jewish News*, Leibler pointed out that the CPA's publication at least conceded that there was a Jewish problem in the Soviet Union. This was very different from just a year earlier, when Waten had claimed that the issue was simply a Cold War provocation, based on fabricated evidence. Leibler argued that the CPA's publication tried to paper over the differences between diehard Stalinists, as represented by Waten, and those supporting the more liberal approach of the Italian communists, as represented by Mortimer.[12] In his autobiography Taft agreed that, at the time, the party had "tried to have a bob each way".[13]

On his return to Australia in September 1965, Leibler met Eric Aarons, Robertson, and Taft in Sydney. The CPA leaders began by questioning Leibler's motives. In his meeting report Leibler wrote:

> ... I asked them why their motives weren't suspect and why I shouldn't assume that the CPA was still acting merely as the local Soviet post office. They took this quite well and assured me that they now realised that I was genuinely concerned with Soviet Jews, rather than fanning anti-Soviet propaganda.[14]

As Eric Aarons was due to visit the Soviet Union, he undertook to raise Soviet Jewry in Moscow. Leibler followed up the Sydney meeting in November 1965 by inviting Laurie Aarons to his Melbourne home in Caulfield. Over dinner he pressed for a CPA statement on Soviet Jewry. Laurie assured him that the CPA would review the issue when brother Eric returned from Moscow, and that if he confirmed the claims of anti-Semitism "the CPA would take militant action, even if this meant openly criticising the Soviet Union".[15]

When Eric returned, his first meeting with Leibler began with an abusive exchange. Just as the meeting was ending, however, Eric "became very sociable, dropped his formal manner and agreed to a draft statement". Leibler wrote afterwards: "Eric is a very tough nut".[16] The Aarons' statement was due to appear in *The Tribune*. But during a conversation with Mortimer, Leibler discovered that Eric had altered the statement. Leibler was furious, describing him as "that rotten bastard ..."[17]

Eventually the two men agreed on a statement in which Eric claimed the Soviet Union treated all its citizens equally, and that

Jewish religious life was declining due to assimilation. He also claimed that Jews were allowed to emigrate if they wished to join relatives in other countries. But he conceded there was some anti-Semitism which deserved condemnation.

Despite its limitations, Leibler welcomed the statement as a potential "breakthrough". He claimed Eric and the CPA had gone further than any other Western Communist Party in condemning Soviet anti-Semitism.[18] Privately, Leibler believed Eric had agreed to the statement because the Kremlin officials had given him "the run-around" and had treated him arrogantly.[19]

Leibler's next publication, in May 1966, was a booklet entitled *Soviet Jewry and the Australian Communist Party – Documents*. It included newspaper reports, reviews of *Soviet Jewry and Human Rights* and all the correspondence with the CPA, including exchanges with Laurie and Eric Aarons.

At the time, I was *The Bulletin*'s News and Foreign Editor and living in Sydney. But I had maintained close contact with Leibler and had continued to write about Soviet Jewry. In the booklet's introduction which Leibler had asked me to write, I noted that the documents showed how painful it had been for Australian communists, after years of stubborn and vehement denials, to even admit to some Soviet anti-Semitism. I argued the Soviet Jewry issue had become a litmus test. It not only distinguished the new modernisers from the CPA's old-time Stalin dogmatists, but threatened to split the modernisers themselves between the revisionist intellectuals – led by Mortimer in Melbourne – and the still suspicious party bureaucrats – led by the Aarons' brothers in Sydney. I saw them as interdependent "bicycle riders".

> For the time being both these groups are riding tandem – with all the looking over the shoulder and watching the man in front that is implied in the metaphor.[20]

Ashkanasy welcomed the new booklet and praised Leibler's role:

> Leibler has been among the leaders. He not only makes history, but he writes and records it and in writing and recording it he makes more history.[21]

Einfeld, now again ECAJ president, also commended the booklet, as did Melbourne academic Newman Rosenthal, and Professor Zelman Cowen, then Dean of Law at the University of Melbourne.[22] *The Bulletin*, the *Catholic Worker* and Santamaria's *News Weekly* featured favourable reviews.[23] Encouraged by the booklet's reception, Leibler said he hoped Soviet Jewry campaigners would similarly confront other communist parties in other Western countries.[24]

Although he had welcomed the Aarons' statement, Leibler also saw it as equivocal, and continued to press Taft and Mortimer for something stronger. Taft refused to cooperate and advised Mortimer to do the same. He claimed that Leibler was only "doing it for Zionist purposes".[25] Mortimer, however, had developed strong views, and expressed them as "a personal statement" in the *Australian Jewish Herald*.[26] It was a true landmark moment in the Soviet Jewry campaign, as it was to become for the CPA and the Australian Left.

Mortimer declared:

> A Socialist Government has a bounden duty to campaign actively against any racialist manifestations ... Where racialism and anti-Semitism find organised and even official expression, then the Soviet leaders cannot disavow responsibility ...[27]

Importantly for the Left, at the height of the civil rights campaign in the United States, Mortimer compared the status of Soviet Jews to that of the American Negroes. He also claimed Moscow was not doing enough to encourage peaceful negotiation in the Arab-Israel conflict. And he pointed out that although the Soviets had assured the CPA delegation led by Eric Aarons that they would allow Jews to emigrate to join family members, this had not happened, and that Jews who applied for emigration permits still faced obstacles. Mortimer concluded:

> As a Communist and one who recognises the great contribution of the Soviet Union to social programs, I am convinced that all progressives must continue to express their point of view on the question until the injustices have been remedied.[28]

Leibler told VJBD members that Mortimer's statement was "... a remarkable document ... from a leading Communist ... [which]

indirectly refutes all the lies and evasions peddled by Communists in recent years ..."[29] On a personal level, Leibler described Mortimer as a "brave man who was taking a courageous stand ..."[30]

Mortimer's decision to speak out was not a sudden one. His growing disenchantment with the CPA's "old guard" and the Soviet Union had begun years earlier. He was especially disillusioned with the show trial of dissident authors Andrei Sinyavsky and Yuli Daniel between September 1965 and February 1966, when the Moscow Supreme Court sentenced them to seven and five years of hard labour. Their "crime" had been to publish their satirical novels overseas under pseudonyms, Abram Terz (Sinyavsky) and Nikolay Arzhak (Daniel). Daniel was Jewish, and the Moscow trial was accompanied by an anti-Jewish propaganda campaign in the official Soviet media.

Historians see the Sinyavsky-Daniel trial as a turning point which ended the limited period of intellectual "thaw" under Khrushchev, and marked the beginning of Brezhnev's period of intellectual "stagnation". But it was also "the birth of the Soviet dissident movement ... Little did they (Sinyavsky and Daniel) realise at the time that they were starting a movement that would help end Communist rule."[31]

By the time Sinyavsky and Daniel were sentenced, Mortimer had resigned as *The Guardian*'s editor and was working on his doctorate. Leibler believed that it was only a matter of time before the CPA would expel him.[32] But although the CPA censured Mortimer, he remained in the party. After his statement's publication, Mortimer told Leibler that Eric Aarons was "having fits and coldly informed me that my aims are now naked, viz the splitting of the CPA".[33]

Leibler called Taft and Eric Aarons to try to prevent them from repudiating Mortimer's statement. In the ensuing angry telephone conversation, Eric accused Leibler of trying to split the CPA. He followed up with a statement to all CPA members on 18 November 1966, challenging Leibler to show his concern for human rights and speak out against the Vietnam War. Eric also quoted Goldmann to show that the Soviet Jewry issue had nothing to do with anti-Semitism. He claimed that Moscow's opposition to Israel was based on its government's "aggressive" policies. As for Mortimer, Eric told party members that he had expressed a personal view which the CPA had not authorised.[34]

But Mortimer remained unrepentant. Despite pressure from Laurie Aarons and other senior party colleagues, he refused to retract. Recounting a speech to Jewish progressives in early December, Mortimer told CPA member John Sendy that "the discussion was quite amicable – there were many strains of opinion represented" and that it had been "quite pleasant and informative".[35] After this meeting, however, leading Jewish communist Sol Factor was angry with Mortimer, and told Sendy: "He won't get away with it". But he said he did not want Mortimer to resign because he believed that "resignation is worse than expulsion".[36]

As Leibler wrote to Litvinoff, however, the CPA was in a quandary: they were reluctant to expel Mortimer because they wanted to maintain their more liberal image. But the party leadership thought his dissent had gone too far.[37] On 11 December 1966, the Victorian CPA State Committee, with fifteen members present, met in Melbourne to consider the Mortimer statement. Mortimer told the Committee that "time would prove whether he was right or wrong" and that "anti-intellectualism still existed in the Party, even at the highest level". He added that "there were inadequate moves in Communist countries to give full freedom to the people".[38]

After Mortimer's presentation, every speaker endorsed the CPA statement repudiating his views. Some were harsh. Andy Wallace accused him of "misleading the Party" and said that "Leibler is an unprincipled scoundrel". Geoff Sayn noted that Mortimer's action was "deplorable and indicative of the indiscipline of the intelligentsia". Even Taft did not support his friend, commenting that "ideologically the Communist Party had stood still" but that Mortimer's action was "inexcusable". He claimed that "there was no anti-Semitism in the Soviet Union".[39]

After the State Committee meeting, some members assumed that Mortimer would suffer the same fate as Ian Turner, a dissenting writer and academic whom the CPA had expelled in 1958.[40] But Mortimer survived, and continued to support a more independent CPA as part of a broader "Coalition of the Left" within Australian politics.

Although Leibler's four-year "dialogue" with the CPA had led to some criticism of Soviet anti-Semitism, the tensions with the CPA continued. After the June 1967 Six-Day War between Israel and its Arab neighbours, Waten continued his hard line support for Moscow. He repeated a Soviet propaganda claim at the CPA's 21st Congress that "[Israel's] destruction of Syrian and Egyptian air bases [in the Six-Day War] was definitely carried out by British and American bombers".[41] When Leibler claimed that CPA members had confirmed that Waten had made the allegations about Israel, Waten wrote:

> Knowing something about Mr Leibler's pathological anti-Communism and his uncritical acceptance of dubious reports and documents which confirm what he wants to believe, I can only conclude that once again he has been taken in by a fabrication.[42]

At first Leibler engaged Arnold Bloch & Associates to demand an apology from Waten, or face a writ for defamation. But Waten refused to apologise and, after legal advice, Leibler dropped the proceedings.

In September 1967, the Communist Party of the Soviet Union (CPSU) wrote confidentially to the CPA referring to the "worldwide Zionist campaign to discredit to the Soviet Union" and appealed to the CPA "to fully align itself with the CPSU on the Middle East question". The CPSU said that the CPA had to take very strong steps to ensure that it "spoke in one voice".[43] The Aarons brothers wanted to maintain party unity, and under pressure from the "hardliners", led by Richard Dixon and Waten, they replied and promised full solidarity with the Soviet Union. Under pressure, Taft also agreed.

But Moscow's request for solidarity came as Leibler stepped up his protests to the CPA about the increasingly anti-Semitic language from Soviet leaders and their UN diplomats after Israel had defeated Moscow's Arab allies in the 1967 Six-Day War. Leibler singled out the labelling of Zionists as Nazis by the Soviet UN Ambassador Nikolai Fedorenko. Speaking in the UN General Assembly Federenko said:

> The Israelis take their arguments from the same garbage heap of history and from the arsenal of the most famous

criminals in history. They follow the bloody footsteps of Hitler's executioners who always accused the victims of their aggression.[44]

Leibler pointed out that Egypt's President Gamal Abdel Nasser openly admitted Nazis after 1945 and had used Nazi scientists. He also criticised Poland's Premier Władysław Gomułka and his government's anti-Semitism. The CPA's Richard Dixon replied, and an acrimonious correspondence ensued. Leibler distributed copies to the VJBD arguing that once Israel and Soviet Jewry had became major international issues, the CPA had reverted to its traditional pro-Soviet line.

In November 1967, the tensions flared again when Ashkanasy, as ECAJ president, published an advertisement in *The Australian* headed: "Open Letter to the leaders of the Soviet Union on the Occasion of the Fiftieth Anniversary of the Bolshevik Revolution." Ashkanasy criticised the Soviet Union for its persecution of Jews, stating: "For today, the evidence is overwhelming that you are the main single enemy of the Jewish people."[45]

While speaking to Hyrall Waten, Judah's wife, ASIO recorded the Jewish Council's president Lou Jedwab, who was also a CPA member, describe Ashkanasy's attack on the Soviet Union as "a vicious, ghastly thing".[46] In a later statement, Mischa Frydman, secretary of Melbourne's Jewish Progressive Centre, a pro-Moscow group with links to the CPA, rejected Ashkanasy's claim that the Soviet Union was the main enemy of the Jewish people. He cited neo-Nazism in Germany and "[Eric] Butler's group" in Australia as more dangerous.[47]

The Ashkanasy advertisement led to further debate at the ECAJ annual conference a few weeks later. Einfeld, representing the NSW delegates, complained that Ashkanasy had not consulted him, and that the advertisement's wording was too extreme.[48]

Whatever impact the Soviet Jewry campaign had made on the CPA's internal divisions, the Soviet invasion of Czechoslovakia in August 1968 overshadowed it. Even more than the Soviet invasion of Hungary in 1956, this threw Australian communists and the Left into disarray.[49] Mortimer had been travelling in Europe when the

Soviet troops marched into Prague to suppress Alexander Dubček's attempts to develop "Communism with a human face". In May 1969, he resigned from the CPA because, he argued, the changes in the party had not gone far enough, and that it was "caught between the past and the present".[50]

Commenting to Litvinoff about Mortimer's resignation, Leibler wrote:

> I would love to induce him to make Soviet anti-Semitism one of the public issues over which he broke out. But he has just come back from Eastern Europe and Czechoslovakia and this is the only thing he is interested in at present.[51]

Litvinoff replied that Mortimer's decision "will probably be the making of him as a human being".[52]

Taft's road to disillusionment with communism took longer. He defended the 1968 Soviet invasion of Czechoslovakia, and only left the CPA in 1984. Leibler maintained contact with Taft, whom he described in 1971 as a "skilful and adroit intriguer".[53] Taft later claimed that in the 1970s he operated as a link between the CPA and Bob Hawke. But by then, the CPA was no longer a player in the Soviet Jewry campaign.

CHAPTER 9

EXODUS VIA *SAMIZDAT*

Mark Azbel was a young Jewish physicist at Moscow's prestigious Physical-Technical Institute in June 1967 when Israel won its lightning victory in the Six-Day War. In his memoir *Refusenik*, Azbel recalls the widespread Jewish reaction:

> The incredulity, the joy, felt by all of us is something I could never describe. Of course we couldn't express it publicly: any celebration had to be quiet and behind closed doors … It would be hard to convey the internal transformation that took place among Soviet Jews. They acquired a totally new outlook, a new soul …[1]

A feature of this "internal transformation" was the 1958 bestselling novel *Exodus* by the American writer Leon Uris. Although many critics panned Uris' potboiler about the founding of Israel, the story of its hero Ari Ben-Canaan stayed on the American bestseller lists for a year. In 1960 *Exodus* was also a widely successful pro-Israel movie.

In the Soviet Union during the 1960s, however, and especially after the Six-Day War, the book's impact on Soviet Jews was even more profound. For them, *Exodus* became "a moral touchstone and rallying point":

> It circulated underground in *samizdat* form [secretly written and distributed literature], where its sheaves of onion-skin encouraged an entire generation of young Soviet Jews to reclaim their Jewish identity. That Soviet authorities were quick to imprison those who possessed a copy of *Exodus* underscored its symbolic resonance.[2]

As Azbel explained, Soviet Jews were proud of belonging to a people who could fight:

> What a different world it became when the most notable event

in one's national consciousness was not the familiar tale of
persecution and defeat, but a triumph ...[3]

Israel's victory not only dramatically changed the way Soviet Jews
saw themselves; it changed the way the Soviet leadership viewed
the Jews and Israel. For Moscow, the Arab debacle was a political,
economic and diplomatic defeat. One measure was the $2 billion
loss in military equipment, which it had supplied to its Arab allies.
But the Kremlin was also uneasy that Israel had become a symbol of
resistance to Soviet power which might resonate throughout its East
European Communist satellites.

In response, Moscow launched a propaganda campaign against
Zionism as a "world threat". Reverting to the Stalinist era, the Kremlin
equated Israel, Soviet Jews and world Jewry with an "international
force" conspiring against communism. Historian Howard M Sachar
notes that "the term 'Zionist' once again became interchangeable
with 'Zionist Jew', or with the 'rich Jewish bourgeoisie' and the new
propaganda campaign soon assumed Nazi-era characteristics."[4]

In October 1967, the Soviet media rehabilitated Trofim Kichko and
published extracts from his crude and discredited *Judaism Without
Embellishment*. In January 1969 *Sovetskaya Rossiya* compared
Zionism with Fascism, implying that Jews were Nazis, and that ...
"Zionism is the ideology that justifies war, killing and oppression".[5]
Pravda referred to "the Israeli barbarians", "a reactionary Zionist
doctrine" and the "fraudulent call" that "All Jews are Brothers!"[6]
During 1969 the anti-Zionist campaign escalated with the nation-
wide distribution of Yuri Ivanov's *Beware Zionism*, a communist
version of the infamous anti-Semitic forgery, *The Protocols of the
Elders of Zion*, first published by the Tsarist secret police.[7]

In concert with the propaganda campaign, Moscow increased its
active discrimination against Jewish religious and cultural life. But the
increased restrictions, coupled with the refusal to allow emigration
to Israel, spurred the growing Jewish nationalist movement. Israel's
victory in the Six-Day War had encouraged the Zionist underground
into the open. Now it began to spread beyond the main centres of
Moscow and Leningrad. When the restrictions failed, Moscow

tried to introduce some concessions, such as the limited printing of Hebrew prayer books and, in 1968 and 1969, the production of *matza* (unleavened Passover bread). But the Zionist movement continued to grow.[8]

In October 1969, John Bowan, a junior diplomat in the Australian embassy, and later to become Prime Minister Bob Hawke's senior adviser on International Affairs, reported on the celebrations at the main Moscow synagogue on Arkhipova Street during the Jewish festival of Simchat Torah:

> It was a rather inspiring experience. Arkhipova Street was already blocked by the crowd … Some groups danced horas, while others sang [Israeli] songs … The majority of the 5–10,000 crowd was young and [came] to demonstrate nationalist solidarity rather than religious fervour …[9]

By 1970 it was estimated that at least 80,000 Soviet Jews – and possibly as many as 240,000 – had applied to leave for Israel. An application to emigrate was a courageous act. It could result in job and housing discrimination, the expulsion of children from school, refusal of university entrance, and the risk of being branded as traitors. Leibler described those applying as "true heroes … They are the finest Jews in the world and the only genuine Zionists outside Israel".[10]

But applying to leave also struck at some of the Soviet Union's core ideological tenets and strategic interests. The Kremlin presented the Communist state as the ideal society where everyone enjoyed full equality. Moreover, if Jews were allowed to leave, the Kremlin feared it could destabilise many other minority ethnic groups. And as the Arabs' superpower patron, the Soviets were reluctant to help boost Israel's population.[11]

The Soviet refusal to grant exit visas, however, led to a growing wave of internal protest and opposition. Groups of Jews began appealing to Soviet and international organisations, demanding the right to emigrate as outlined in the Universal Declaration of Human Rights.

The first such group to attract significant international attention were eighteen Georgian Jews who petitioned the United Nations on

6 August 1969. Another letter, to UN Secretary-General U Thant, and signed by 531 Georgian Jews, ended with the cry: "Israel or death." In March 1970, 39 Moscow Jews wrote supporting this petition,[12] and in an appeal to Soviet leaders, 37 Leningrad Jews wrote:

> Our motives are not social or political; our motives are deeply national and spiritual. We want to live in the re-born State of our ancient people … We want to live in our historic motherland, in our own country.[13]

It was the Georgian Jews' petition, however, which changed the Israeli government's response to the new and burgeoning movement in the Soviet Union which had taken them by surprise. Writing to the UN Human Rights Commission, the Georgians said:

> We believe that our prayers have reached God. We know that our appeals will reach people because we are not asking a great deal. Let us go to the land of our forefathers.[14]

The Georgians sent an accompanying letter to the "Friends of Anne Frank" at the Netherlands embassy in Moscow which had represented Israel's interests since the Soviet Union broke diplomatic relations with Jerusalem in June 1967. The letter asked the Dutch to send the second letter to Israel's Prime Minister Golda Meir. It called on her to submit the petition to the United Nations, to publish it in the Israeli press and broadcast it on Israeli radio. The third letter, to Yosef Tekoah, Israel's Ambassador to the United Nations, asked him to distribute the petition to all UN members and release it to the international press.

As Leonard Schroeter recounts in *The Last Exodus,* the letter had "dramatic repercussions" for the Israeli government. The eighteen families, not having heard for 100 days from the United Nations, the Netherlands embassy, Prime Minister Meir, Israel radio or Ambassador Tekoah, wrote again to each of them.

But as the Georgian Jews discovered, the problem was not that the Israel government had failed to receive the petition.[15] The problem was that the Israel government, advised by Avigur and the Lishkah, still believed that the primary method for enabling Soviet Jews to emigrate would ultimately be through secret negotiation. This was the method which had worked for Romanian, Bulgarian and Polish Jews during the 1950s and 1960s. Although the Lishkah encouraged active protests on Soviet Jewry from outside Israel, hence Leibler's confidence to battle against Dr Goldmann's "quiet diplomacy", it was far more cautious about the Israeli government directly endorsing such activism by Soviet Jews themselves.[16]

The growing publicity, however, and the concerns repeatedly expressed by some Knesset members, had led Meir, even before she had received the Georgians' petition, to meet a delegation of 20 new Soviet immigrants. They told her that Israel's reluctance to offer outspoken support to the new wave of Zionist fervour in Russia was "a betrayal of Soviet Jewry". The new immigrants' blunt talk shook the Israeli leader. She became visibly emotional as they spoke. Together with the prospect that the Georgians' petition would soon become public, the meeting forced her hand.

Meir had good reason to be emotionally involved with Soviet Jews. When she came to Moscow in 1948, as the new State of Israel's first Ambassador, the widespread excitement among so many Jews aroused Josef Stalin's paranoia. On her first Rosh Hashanah, the Jewish New Year, Meir arrived at Moscow's Great Synagogue to a tumultuous welcome from an emotional crowd. Some 50,000 Jews lining the surrounding streets chanted her name and shouted "*Am Yisroel Chai*", "The Jewish people live!"

A few weeks later on 7 November, the Soviet Foreign Minister Vyacheslev Molotov held a diplomatic reception for Meir, and his wife Polina Molotova welcomed her in Yiddish. When Meir asked her how she knew Yiddish, Molotova replied: "*Ich bin doch a yiddishe tochter*" – "But I'm a daughter of the Jewish people after all". When they parted tearfully, Molotova said: "If things go well for you, then things will be good for Jews all over the world."[17]

Things did not go well, however, for Molotova. Just weeks after she met Meir, Stalin ordered her arrest for treason and she spent five years in the Gulag. Nor did things go well for Soviet Jews. Historian Simon Sebag Montiefore dates Stalin's persecution of the Jews from the encounters with Meir:

The synagogue "demonstration" and Polina's Yiddish shtick outraged (Stalin) ... confirming that Soviet Jews were becoming an American Fifth Column ... On 20 November 1948, the Politburo dismantled the Jewish Committee and unleashed an anti-Semitic terror ...[18]

On 19 November 1969, almost 21 years to the day after that visit, and 106 days after the Georgians' first appeal, the Israeli Prime Minister read it to the Knesset as requested. She said:

We sincerely believe the day will come when we shall witness a large wave of immigration from the Soviet Union of old and young alike ... We cannot abandon our legitimate interest in the fate of Soviet Jewry for the sake of some doubtful friendship with the Soviet Union, a country which, by its actions in this region, has put a question mark on our very existence.[19]

Just five months later, in March 1971, Meir welcomed a group of 102 Soviet immigrants on arrival at Tel Aviv Airport. As she spoke in Yiddish to them, she had tears in her eyes, telling them she didn't believe they would ever come. She expressed the hope that all Jews who wanted to come from Russian would be able to come.

Among these new arrivals were some who, just two weeks earlier, had staged a hunger strike in Moscow to press their appeal for exit visas. In response to international protests, the Soviets had begun to ease emigration restrictions. But in 1970, they had granted exit visas to only 1000 Jews. By April 1971, however, the Australian embassy in Moscow reported that they had issued over 2000 in four months.

Between February 1968 and October 1970, following a new strategy which the Zionist leadership in the Soviet Union promoted to "internationalise the protest", Soviet Jews sent 220 individual and collective petitions to the United Nations, Israel, prominent Western leaders, and to senior Soviet officials.[20] As the appeals calling for the right to emigrate increased, so did the Israeli Knesset's calls on Western democracies "to exert the full measure of their influence so that the Jews of the Soviet Union who so wish may be enabled to migrate to Israel".[21]

The Knesset's Speaker, Reuven Barkat, appealed to other Parliamentary Speakers, including the House of Representatives speaker, Sir William Aston. External Affairs advised him to reaffirm Australia's support for Soviet Jewry, and to mention that Australia had regularly raised the issue in the UN Third Committee.[22]

The Soviet Union's increasing anti-Semitism after 1967, and the growing internal Zionist movement in response, helped bring a new generation of Jewish communal leaders in Australia to the fore. As ambitious in Sydney as Leibler had been in Melbourne, Marcus Einfeld was 32 when, in May 1970, he chaired the first meeting of a new national body for Soviet Jewry. It would operate under the ECAJ's auspices. With the support of veteran Sydney leader Gerald Falk, now ECAJ president, and the NSW Board of Deputies, the new body moved the campaign's public face to Sydney from Melbourne, where Leibler and Ashkanasy had set its direction and tone for its first decade.

Born in 1938 in Sydney, Marcus Einfeld was the only son of Billie and Sydney Einfeld. Educated at Sydney Boys' High and the University of Sydney, Marcus graduated with BA and LLB degrees in 1960. After a decade at the Sydney bar, and working for the World Jewish Congress in London in the early 1970s, he returned to Sydney to resume his career as a barrister. He later became president of the Human Rights and Equal Opportunity Commission, and then a Federal Court judge.

During the 1980s and 1990s Marcus won an international reputation for championing a wide variety of humanitarian and social justice causes. In 2009, however, he became the first Australian superior court judge to be convicted for perjury and attempting to pervert the course of justice. He received three years imprisonment.

In 1970, just a month after Marcus assumed the Australian campaign's leadership, a failed attempt by Soviet Jewish activists on June 15 to hijack a light plane at Leningrad Airport dramatised the plight of Soviet Jewry internationally, and galvanised the Australian Jewish community.

During 1969 Moscow had granted some 3000 exit permits for Jews who had received invitations from Israel. But with an estimated backlog of over 200,000 requests, and desperate at the slow pace of the Soviet response, some activists had proposed the hijack plan to publicise their demands. The Leningrad Zionist Committee, after consulting the Israeli government, rejected the plan as unrealistic and a threat to the movement. But an ex-political prisoner, Edward Kuznetsov, and a former military pilot, Mark Dymshits, decided to proceed. The KGB arrested them at Leningrad's Smolny Airport before they could implement the plan, and rounded up a further 32 alleged conspirators who went on trial in Leningrad, Riga, Kishinev and other cities over the ensuing eighteen months.

In July 1970, as the Campaign's new public voice, Einfeld circulated a booklet entitled "Soviet Jewry – What is the Tragic Truth?" and produced "Let My People Go" badges, posters and stamps. Working with Doron Ur, the Victorian Board of Deputies' Director, Einfeld also called on Australian Jews to send Rosh Hashanah cards (for the Jewish New Year) to Soviet Jews who had applied to emigrate.[23]

In August 1970, as the protests grew against the Leningrad hijacking arrests, the Australian Campaign asked Christian clergy to join Jews in a week of prayer for Soviet Jewry. Marcus drafted a petition addressed to the UN Secretary-General, U Thant, and sought signatures from leading Australians. Wentworth, now the Minister for Social Services, said that as a minister he could not sign but expressed his ongoing support.

The public rally for Soviet Jewry on 30 August at the Sydney Town Hall drew a capacity crowd of nearly 3000. Tall and imposing, looking very much the fast bowler he had been for Sydney's Maccabi Cricket team, Einfeld spoke on a stage ringed by banners proclaiming "Let My People Go". Also on stage were Gordon Samuels QC, later to be a NSW Governor, and the Reverend Graham Hardy, a leading Presbyterian clergyman. Having honed his oratorical talents at the bar and at many public meetings, Marcus impressed the overflow crowd with his call for protest:

> The Jews in the Soviet Union suffer from a form of oppression far more subtle than that practised by the Nazis … The major threat to Soviet Jewry is not the destruction of life, but the obliteration of the Jews as a people.[24]

The rally called on the Australian government, by acclamation, to step up its protests against Moscow. Just two days later, on September 1, an ECAJ delegation, which included Leibler and Walter Lippmann from Melbourne, met Prime Minister John Gorton, the Leader of the Opposition, Gough Whitlam, and MPs in Canberra. Marcus coordinated the meetings with Labor's Jewish MPs, Joe Berinson, Barry Cohen and Dr Moss Cass.[25] Einfeld also asked to meet the Soviet Ambassador, Nicolai Nikolayevich Mesyatsev, but Mesyatsev refused.[26]

The delegation was in the House of Representatives when David J Hamer, a Victorian Liberal MP, asked McMahon about the government's response to the Sydney rally's call. The External Affairs Minister's reply was non-committal:

> We do not believe in discrimination of any kind practised in any way because of a person's religious beliefs or because of his race.[27]

Although Marcus Einfeld had won the ECAJ's Sydney-based leadership's full confidence, Leibler and many Melbourne leaders remained sceptical. The ideological and personal differences between the Melbourne and Sydney communities which had so dogged the campaign in the early 1960s had eased. But they had not disappeared.

After the Canberra meeting, Einfeld asked Gorton to sign the petition to the UN. Arguing against the request, External Affairs described it as "an emotive and propagandist document" which exaggerated Soviet Jewry's problems, and used immoderate language, such as "inhuman discrimination" and "spiritual genocide".[28]

As it had done for a decade, External Affairs also maintained that the petition would probably provoke Soviet criticism of Australia's treatment of its Aborigines, its administration of Papua New Guinea, and its immigration policies. It would also risk encouraging Arab requests for similar expressions of concern about the plight of Arabs in Israeli occupied territories. Finally, following Trade Minister John McEwen's recent visit to Moscow, criticism of the Soviet Union's "domestic policies" might "adversely affect" trade and commercial prospects.[29]

Einfeld's petition appeared in *The Australian* on 24 October 1970. Many leading Australians had signed it; Gorton had not.[30] But while External Affairs had advised Gorton not to sign, it had suggested that Australia should express sympathy for Soviet Jewry in the United Nations Third Committee, as Australia had done previously. Gorton approved a statement, scheduled to be introduced under item 53 which called for "the elimination of all forms of racial discrimination". It requested the Soviet Union:

> ... to desist from policies or practices of discrimination against citizens of Jewish origin, and to give permission to those who so wish, to emigrate. Not to do so is clearly incompatible with the letter and spirit of the Charter, the Universal Declaration of Human Rights and the International Covenant on Civil and Political Rights.[31]

At the same time, however, an Australian Aboriginal delegation was planning to present a petition to the Third Committee, also under item 53, seeking their "rights to the land which we have traditionally occupied".[32] Australia's UN Ambassador, Sir Laurence McIntyre, pointed out that raising Soviet Jewry issues under the same item would invite a strong reaction from the Soviets, and would persuade other delegations from Africa and Arab countries to embarrass Australia.

Instead he proposed to raise it under item 12, in the "Report of the Economic and Soviet Council", noting that the United States also planned to raise the issue under that heading.[33] Australia's delegate did so on 11 December 1970, following a similar statement by the United States.

As on previous occasions harking back to November 1962, Australia had again raised Soviet Jewry at the United Nations. It remained one of the few countries which had done so consistently. At the same time, however, the issue presented Australia's diplomats, as they saw it, with a juggling act. On the one hand, directions from Prime Ministers or foreign ministers had required them to protest at the UN against Soviet anti-Semitism, and to call for free emigration. But until late 1970 the government's directions to External Affairs had always followed a direct request from the Jewish leadership, or had come via a parliamentarian's request, usually after approaches from the same Jewish leadership, or from constituents.

There is no evidence that in the eight years which followed Barwick's initiative in 1962 to bring the issue to the UN, External Affairs, acting on its own, ever recommended raising the issue. As the diplomats saw it, they believed they had to protect Canberra's wider bilateral relationship with Moscow, however fragile it became at various points during the Cold War, and Australia's interests in the world body. For the most part, and here the Australian embassy diplomats in Moscow were usually much more empathetic than their Canberra colleagues, Soviet Jewry did not fit easily into that assessment.

During Gorton's time as Prime Minister, therefore, much depended on the degree to which Soviet Jewry issues came directly to his attention, or were left to McMahon, whose default position was to accept his department's advice. Thus when the first Leningrad hijack trial was pending in December 1970, the ECAJ asked McMahon to inquire whether Moscow would persuade the Soviet court not to imprison the would-be hijackers.

In his reply on 23 December, McMahon claimed a direct approach to the Soviet authorities would be "counter-productive". Instead, he suggested the ECAJ should approach the UN Commission on Human Rights through the UN Secretary-General. McMahon's reluctance to take the matter up bilaterally reflected the department's advice that:

> ... We need to be careful that we do not intrude too far on the principle of non-interference in domestic affairs – a principle which we, generally, strongly support.[34]

But after the first trial on December 24 in camera, Gorton rejected the diplomatic advice. Kuznetsov and Dymshits were condemned as traitors and sentenced to death by firing squad. The rest received prison sentences from ten to fifteen years of "corrective labour".

The draconian sentences provoked widespread international protests. Commenting 40 years later in the *New York Times*, author Gal Beckerman wrote:

Italian longshoremen in Genoa refused to unload Soviet ships. Students in Stockholm marched with torches through the streets. Even Salvador Allende, Chile's Marxist president, called for clemency. In Israel, air-raid sirens blasted through the cities and 100,000 people gathered in front of the Western Wall. In Washington, Richard Nixon held an emergency meeting with Leaders of Jewish groups.[35]

In the Knesset, Prime Minister Meir appealed to parliaments, governments, religious and intellectual leaders, to call for an annulment of the sentences.[36] Meir wrote to Gorton, asking him to do whatever he deemed appropriate. As on most previous occasions, Foreign Affairs (the Department had changed its name from External Affairs in November 1970) advised against any action. In a handwritten memo the unidentified writer said:

> These people are Soviet citizens, dealt with presumably in accordance with Soviet 'law'. We invite retaliatory complaints with either (i) the aborigines (ii) PNG (Papua and New Guinea).[37]

But the writer added an opinion which Foreign Affairs had not previously expressed:

> We have always failed to see what special interest Israel as State has in relation to people, citizens of other States, who happen to be Jewish. Do we, for instance, concede to Israel some rights in connection with Australian citizens of the Jewish race?[38]

Not for the first time, the advice from Foreign Affairs on Soviet Jewry was narrowly conceived and out of step with the growing international protests. Despite his diplomatic advice, Gorton wrote to UN Secretary-General U Thant, noting that the trial had been held in camera, that had Jews been permitted to emigrate freely the incident would not have happened, and that the sentences were very severe. He asked that "such severe punishment of what appears to have been an attempt at escape will not proceed".[39] The Israeli media welcomed Gorton's statement[40] and Leibler described it as "extraordinarily good". Most Australian newspapers also supported it.[41] The *Sydney Morning Herald* described the death sentences as a "barbaric penalty" and compared the Leningrad trial with the concurrent Burgos trials in Spain, where a military tribunal had sentenced six Basque nationalists to death.[42] And the *Canberra Times* editorialised:

> Those of us lucky enough to live in a society which permits disgruntled citizens to leave if they want to, will retain a great deal of sympathy for those less fortunately placed.[43]

Other public figures also spoke up. Opposition leader Gough Whitlam said he had telephoned the Soviet Chargé d'Affaires in Canberra to express his concern at the death sentences. Australian religious leaders, including the apostolic delegate, Gina Paro, also protested to President Nikolai Podgorny, as did the Communist Party, the Aboriginal Advancement Council in Perth, Robert J. (Bob) Hawke, president of the Australian Trade Union Council (ACTU) and the Federated Clerks Union federal secretary, Joe Riordan.[44]

Einfeld and the students' Hillel Director in Melbourne, Henry Shaw, coordinated an all-night vigil by students and Zionist youth movements outside the Soviet embassy in Canberra. Shaw led prayers, student leader David Mittelberg spoke, and the demonstrators tied a protest letter to the embassy gates.[45] The Perth Jewish community also held a protest rally.[46]

As the international protests against the Leningrad death sentences grew, left-wing activists and communist parties – Italy's and Australia's included – joined Western governments in their appeals to Moscow. The distinguished Soviet nuclear scientist Andrei Sakharov wrote to President Podgorny, describing the proposed executions as "unjust brutality" and said that "the reason for the action of the accused was restriction by the authorities of the legal right of tens of thousands of Jews who wish to leave the country".[47]

In response, the Soviets commuted the death sentences to fifteen years hard labour. A Foreign Affairs memo suggested that this was partly due to the world outcry, but also because the Soviets did not "want to appear more brutal than the 'Franco Fascists'".[48] The Spanish authorities had commuted the death sentences of the six Basque separatists to life imprisonment.

In 1979 the Soviets freed Dymshits, Kuznetsov and three other dissidents, in exchange for two Soviet spies arrested in the United

States. When the would-be hijackers and their families arrived in Israel, large crowds welcomed them as heroes. A third member of the group which had planned the hijack, Yosef Mendelevich, was freed in 1981.

CHAPTER 10

PRISONERS OF ZION

For all the growing awareness in the Jewish world and Israel about Soviet Jewry, it was not until the Leningrad hijacking trials, first in December 1970, and then in May 1971, that the issue became front page news and captured international attention. And it was not until June 1971 that 27 national Jewish organisations in the United States – secular and religious – created one organisation with Soviet Jewry as its sole mandate. For the next sixteen years, culminating in Freedom Sunday on 6 December 1987, when 250,000 participants marched in Washington proclaiming "Let My People Go", the National Conference on Soviet Jewry (NCSJ) spearheaded the American movement.

Between the first and second hijacking trials, in February 1971, the international movement also gathered momentum when the WJC convened the First World Conference on Soviet Jewry in Brussels. The Second Conference (Brussels 1976) and the Third Conference (Jerusalem 1983) which followed, were also known as the Brussels Presidiums.

The first conference exceeded its organisers' hopes. It attracted 790 representatives from 42 countries, more than twice the numbers expected. Former Israel Prime Minister, David Ben-Gurion, former United States Ambassador to the United Nations, Arthur Goldberg, and four Soviet Jews who had recently arrived in Israel, were among the speakers. Veteran campaigners, Litvinoff and Decter, prepared the conference's briefing papers.[1] Leibler, Marcus Einfeld and VJBD Youth Chairman, Gary Gepner, represented Australia. Recognising Australia's role and Leibler's growing reputation, the conference nominated him as one of two consultants on the Political Commission; Einfeld was appointed to the Judicial Commission.

At its conclusion, the Conference's declaration, entitled "Let My People Go!" commended Soviet Jewry's historic struggle for "their national identity and for their natural and inalienable right to return to their historic homeland of Israel".[2] At Israel's request, the Presidium circulated the declaration to all United Nations members. The Soviet Union denounced it.

The diary Leibler kept during the conference reflects his excitement at an "extraordinary demonstration of international Jewish public opinion" and what he saw as an historic turning point for the Soviet Jewry movement. In a clear reference to a repudiation of Goldmann's approach, he wrote:

> No longer do we hear people understating the plight of Soviet Jewry. Anti-Semitism is no longer a taboo expression. No more are we warned against over-zealousness. No longer do we gloss over the primary objective: freedom of emigration for Soviet Jewry.[3]

Leibler believed a Jewish renaissance was underway in the Soviet Union. Five years earlier, he wrote, the analysts were predicting that within a generation, Jewish life would disappear from the Soviet Union. But now the "Jews of silence were no longer silent … they are unbelievable heroes signing open protests knowing that there would be government reprisals against them". For Leibler, this was "an unfolding miracle".[4] Marcus Einfeld was also moved, and described the Brussels Presidium as "a unique historical occasion".[5]

But there had been tension between the two Australians. ECAJ President Nathan Jacobson had nominated Leibler to lead the delegation. But when Leibler arrived in Brussels he was incensed to find that Einfeld had claimed to be Australia's main delegate. The Melbourne leader told Einfeld, just three years his junior, that he was "a newcomer" to the cause, that he might have done some good work on Soviet Jewry, but that he should know his place.[6] Einfeld refused to step down. It took a telegram from Jacobson to the Jewish Agency's chairman, Aryeh Louis Pincus, who was also chairing the Presidium, to confirm Leibler's role, and for Einfeld to concede.[7]

Following the widespread publicity, much of it anti-Soviet, which the Brussels conference received internationally, Australia's diplomats discussed it with Soviet diplomats in Canberra. During a private dinner at the Soviet embassy in late February, a senior Foreign Affairs official, F B Cooper, attended a dinner hosted by V N Smirnov, the Soviet Counsellor. Reporting on the conversation, Cooper said he had asked Smirnov:

> Why not let them go? The Soviet Union [is] surely not so short of people that it needs to place a virtual ban on Jewish emigration.[8]

Smirnov responded that the Soviet Union was short of skilled labour and Jews were highly skilled. Moscow was not prepared to let them go to Israel "if this meant assisting the Israeli war effort". Cooper said he could understand that about young people, but why not let the elderly go? Smirnov offered the standard reply that Jews had their own autonomous region. But Cooper cut him short.

> ... I pointed out that the so-called Jewish autonomous region was in a remote area, that only about 20 per cent of the population living there was Jewish, and that the majority of Soviet Jews lived elsewhere. Smirnov did not pursue the subject.[9]

Although the second hijack trial was also held in camera, the Soviet news media reported it extensively, and intensified their anti-Jewish propaganda. All the defendants received prison sentences, ranging from one to ten years. Together with those jailed after the first Leningrad trial, they became known as the "Prisoners of Zion".

The sentences sparked a renewed series of international protests. Jewish communities in every Australian state held rallies, and the ECAJ called on Canberra to condemn the trials. Marcus Einfeld, hoping to attend the trial as a lawyer, tried unsuccessfully to obtain a Soviet visa. The *Sydney Morning Herald* published a protest letter from leading rabbis, Sydney's Dr Israel Porush and Melbourne's Dr Isaac Rapaport.[10] In Sydney, 40 Zionist youth movement leaders wearing prison clothes chained themselves together on the Town Hall's steps.[11]

In July 1971, a group of Jewish women, led by Sydney's Fitzi

Fishman, Bertha Porush and Phyllis Glasser, and Melbourne's Mina Fink, tried to present a petition with 5000 signatures to the Soviet embassy in Canberra. If the Soviets would not allow a refusenik family they had adopted to emigrate to Israel, the petition asked for the children to be allowed to travel alone. At first, the embassy refused them entry. But when a Melbourne woman, Yetta Coopersmith, telephoned and said she was "a perfectly harmless middle-aged grandmother", embassy staff allowed her and Bertha Porush to speak to a Soviet official. But he refused to accept the petition.[12]

The Australian government's response was more muted than after the "first" Leningrad trials in December 1970. In March 1971 McMahon had replaced Gorton as Prime Minister. Unlike his predecessor, however, who did not always follow the diplomats' advice, McMahon was more cautious, and more readily accepted Foreign Affairs' guidance. In response to Jacobson's telegram of 11 May 1971 asking him to condemn the Leningrad trial, McMahon's answer was vague.[13]

When Jacobson persisted, Foreign Affairs repeated its concerns: no other foreign governments had reacted to date; hijacking was a serious crime; this was a domestic matter; and Australia was negotiating bilateral proposals with the Soviet Union.[14] The memo noted, however, that "we accept that the Government is already under some domestic Jewish pressure, and this is likely to increase". The diplomats suggested either a suitable public statement or calling in the Soviet embassy's Counsellor for "an informal discussion".[15] After meeting Smirnov, Cooper reported:

> The atmosphere was relaxed and friendly and no bones were broken, but Smirnov made it quite clear that, so far as he was concerned, we should mind our own business.[16]

In October 1971 Foreign Affairs again discussed whether to raise Soviet Jewry in the UN Third Committee. Opposing any action, Cooper wrote:

> The Israeli case is demonstrably thin this year and I believe that, if necessary, we should tell them so. In any case, we have our own interests to consider.[17]

As a handwritten note on the memo testifies, the Australian officials had become increasingly impatient with the Israel Ambassador Shlomo Erell's representations:

> It's about time the Israelis realised that we have our own problems with the USSR without taking on theirs![18]

After other governments had spoken on Soviet Jewry, however, Australia referred briefly to the problem of racial discrimination, and the need to allow emigration if governments could not eliminate prejudice, as for example with Jewish minorities. But the presentation avoided any specific reference to the Soviet Union.

In April 1971, the Israel Foreign Ministry's Director, Gideon Rafael, visited Australia, hoping to create improved understanding with Indonesia. He met Indonesia's Foreign Minister, Adam Malik, in Canberra, and while there he thanked the Foreign Affairs Secretary, Sir Keith Waller, for Australia's support on Soviet Jewry, Rafael told Waller that Moscow was allowing some Jews to emigrate but the numbers were "nothing compared with the requirements". Although Soviet anti-Semitism was a deep-rooted problem, Raphael emphasised that Moscow had shown that it was "amenable to public pressure".[19]

Waller had reason to be well informed about Soviet Jewry. After Moscow severed diplomatic relations with Jerusalem in 1967, the Netherlands acted as Israel's consular representative. As the Australian and Dutch embassies in Moscow had developed a close relationship, the Dutch often shared confidential information about Jewish emigration. But it was a sensitive connection which the Australian Ambassador, Fred Blakeney, was guarded about. Reporting to Canberra in May 1971, Blakeney explained that Ambassador Tammenoms Bakker had said "he felt able to speak freely only because our conversation took place in his embassy's 'safe room'". He concluded his report with a strong appeal to "protect Bakker and the Netherlands embassy here, and restrict circulation of the memorandum accordingly".[20]

As the Australian embassy in Moscow reported, the Soviets hoped that by allowing Jewish activists to emigrate they would undermine the movement. The reverse happened. As the year progressed, the Jewish demonstrations and sit-ins increased. Periods of restriction followed periods of greater flexibility. In December 1971 Moscow allowed 5000 Jews to leave, and proposed a target of 20,000 for 1972. By early 1972 the Netherlands embassy in Moscow was processing Israeli visas at the rate of 3000 a month.

From Washington DC, the Australian embassy's counsellor, David Sadlier, reported that the Soviets were allowing more Jews to emigrate "primarily due to the hard-headed tactics of Jews within the Soviet Union as well as the concern expressed by foreign communist parties (including the CPA) over the Soviets' treatment of its Jewish population".[21] After the United States Congress agreed to provide Israel with a grant of US$85 million to help resettle Soviet Jewish emigrants, the International Committee for Soviet Jewry also asked Australia for financial aid. Canberra, however, rejected the request.[22]

As the clamour for exit visas grew, and as many of those applying were scientists, engineers, doctors, academics and highly skilled technicians, Moscow introduced a new deterrent. On 3 August 1972 the Presidium of the Supreme Soviet enacted a decree which, after the Council of Ministers ratified it on August 14, became known, notoriously, as the "diploma tax" or the "ransom tax".

Those applying for visas would first have "to compensate" the Soviet Union for their education, but on an exorbitant scale. In theory the "diploma tax" was not discriminatory since it applied equally to Jews and non-Jews. In reality, however, the tax only affected Jews.[23] It was clear to the emigration movement that the new decree was a major effort to "discourage and halt the exodus".

As the Leningrad trials had done, the new Soviet law attracted immediate international protests. On 23 August 1972 the Knesset condemned "this shameful decree" and called for its repeal.[24] ECAJ president Jacobson flew to London for an emergency protest meeting of international Jewish organisations and cabled Prime Minister McMahon to ask him to press Moscow "to withdraw this barbaric decree".[25]

More far-reaching than the protests it provoked, and like the

Leningrad trials, the diploma tax galvanised the international Soviet Jewry campaign. More than most, the Australian Jewish community was prepared. In many ways it had been ahead of its counterparts in other Jewish communities, first under Leibler's leadership in Melbourne in the 1960s and then (1970–71) under Marcus Einfeld's in Sydney. After Einfeld moved to London in 1972, Robert Goot, at the age of 25, and representing a new generation of communal leadership, succeeded him as chairman of the Australian Campaign for the Rescue of Soviet Jewry (ACRSJ).

An official at the Federated Clerks Union, Goot found himself thrust quickly into the communal and political arena. Born in New Zealand in 1947, Goot came to Australia at twelve with his two older brothers and his mother, Etla, a single parent. From 1972 to 1976 he represented Australia regularly at international conferences and immersed himself in the Soviet Jewry campaign. At 31, while the NSW Jewish Board of Deputies' youngest president, Goot resumed his legal studies and in 1980 became a barrister. In the following three decades Goot served as a Moriah College president, a Sydney Jewish Museum president, ECAJ president (2007–10, re-elected 2013) and as a World Jewish Congress vice-president. Looking back, however, the Soviet Jewry campaign, as it became for many, was his definitive "training ground" in political activism and communal leadership.[26]

As the campaign against the diploma tax gathered momentum, three federal MPs – David J Hamer (Liberal), Phillip E Lucock (Country Party) and Joe Berinson (ALP) – organised an all-party petition signed by 62 MPs, addressed to the Soviet Union's President Nikolai Podgorny calling for the tax's repeal.[27] Another protest petition, organised by Professor Julius Stone and signed by 276 leading Australians, appeared in the *Sydney Morning Herald*.[28] The ECAJ welcomed the Stone petition, and sent another – with 1000 signatures – to the Soviet embassy.

In Adelaide, Professor Leon Mann, a professor of social psychology at Flinders University, coordinated a petition from academics protesting against the dismissal of Professor Benjamin Levich from Moscow University. After applying to leave for Israel, Levich had become a symbolic figure in the protests. He had not only lost his position; he was expelled from all scientific councils and education boards, and prevented from lecturing, publishing and attending conferences.[29]

In addition to its petitions and letters, the Australian campaign, which had developed its media skills and connections, stepped up its public protests. On 3 September 1972 some 200 demonstrators, bussed in to Canberra from Sydney, placed 50 bags, each containing $200 in 50 cent pieces, outside the Soviet embassy's gates. The $10,000 represented the tax payable by a Jewish university graduate who wanted to leave the Soviet Union.[30]

In September 1972 the ECAJ invited a former Soviet refusenik, Professor Dori Parolla, to visit Australia. After the Soviets had refused him an exit visa for ten years, Parolla had divorced his wife so that she, and his son and daughter, could emigrate to Israel. His case attracted international attention when his eight-year-old daughter wrote a widely publicised "Dear Comrade Kosygin" letter, asking the Soviet leader to "please permit our father to come to us". After fifteen months the Soviets had let him leave.

Now reunited with his family and teaching at the Hebrew University, Parolla said in Sydney that Australia's role as the first country to raise the issue in the United Nations had been important, and that ongoing Western protest was vital for Soviet Jewry. It had been a key factor in his own release.[31] Although the Soviets thought that they could silence the Jewish dissident movement by letting its leaders leave the Soviet Union, Parolla said that Soviet Jews were more active than ever, and that "no other minority in the Soviet Union has shown anywhere near the courage, the determination, the willingness to go through fire, that our fellow Jews are demonstrating daily".[32]

As the community campaign grew, the McMahon government responded cautiously.[33] In reply to a parliamentary question, McMahon said Australia was a nation that "received immigrants" and so had "a definite interest in promoting the free movement of peoples in accordance with the Universal Declaration of Human

Rights. The Government will take such opportunities as are open to it, both in the UN and elsewhere, to press for the observance by all countries of the provisions of the Declaration".[34]

In addition to McMahon's direct inquiry to Soviet Ambassador Dimitri Musin, the Foreign Affairs Minister, Nigel Bowen, raised the issue in New York with the Soviet Foreign Minister, Andrei Gromyko. Bowen later reported:

> Mr Gromyko immediately made it clear that he was not prepared to discuss the question. He asked that (we) should move to more important matters … and avoid 'artificial issues'. We should concentrate on our growing economic exchange and other useful contacts … Whenever subjects that verged on propaganda were broached he said he detected "the smell of moth-balls".[35]

Gromyko and the Soviet leadership soon found that the increasing protests were about more than "artificial issues". In the first wave, the growing outcry came from some governments and from the international scientific and academic community. On 1 October, 21 Nobel Laureates expressed their "dismay" at the "massive violation of human rights". On 31 October, in a two-page advertisement in the *New York Times*, 6000 professors from 200 American and Canadian universities urged Moscow to rescind "this benighted decree and remove all arbitrary bars to the free movement of people".[36]

Even more potent, however, was the political response in Washington, as reflected in the US Senate's amendment to the East-West Trade Relations Act. Introduced on 4 October 1972, and authored by Senator Henry "Scoop" Jackson, a pro-Israel and anti-Soviet Democrat from the state of Washington, the amendment won the support of three-quarters of the US Senate (76 senators). Charles Vanik (Democrat, Ohio) and Wilbur Mills (Democrat, Arkansas) later co-sponsored the amendment in the House of Representatives where it also won majority approval.

The amendment foreshadowed Congressional readiness to reject Most Favoured Nation (MFN) commercial status for the Soviet Union unless it rescinded the diploma tax. At first Moscow responded quickly to the Congressional signals from Washington by exempting 190 Jews and their families from the tax. At the same time, the Soviet Deputy Interior Minister Boris Shumilin emphasised that their policy had "not changed and will not change".[37]

In practice, however, the international protests, the pressure from the Jackson-Vanik amendment, and the emerging détente between the Nixon-Kissinger administration and Moscow, meant that the Soviets did not enforce the new regulations. The years 1972 and 1973 became the peak years of Soviet Jewish emigration: 31,500 left in 1972 and 35,000 in 1973.

As the Australian embassy cabled Canberra in December 1972:

> Legal loopholes plus international protest had largely negated the effect of the tax … The Soviet authorities had apparently hoped, by generously granting more exit visas in 1972, to lessen the backlog of applications. Instead, the backlog has built up.[38]

The report came from the embassy's Second Secretary, John C Powys, who worked closely with a Dutch diplomat, Hans Heinemann. Powys' cables provide a vivid account of the Jewish emigration story. They also attest to an important diplomatic relationship between Australia and the Netherlands at a sensitive time in the Cold War. As the Netherlands embassy represented Israel's diplomatic interests in Moscow, it came under close KGB scrutiny. Powys asked Canberra to consider Heinemann's frankness and to ensure he was fully protected as a source.[39]

Describing the obstacles facing visa applicants, Powys explained that this included the requirement that the fees had to come from liquid assets, because the authorities had confiscated their other property. The Soviets also often cancelled one family member's exit visa, forcing the family to choose between emigrating and leaving someone behind. Powys reported:

> The [Jewish emigrants] were only allowed to take 100 roubles [about $25] out of the USSR. There are very torrid scenes at airports when people try to smuggle out jewellery etc. … Elderly Jewish women emigrants, highly distraught, and surrounded by tearful relatives, have had every single item in their baggage minutely examined, and frequently damaged.[40]

Heinemann invited Powys to the Netherlands embassy to observe the process. On the day he visited there were around 50 prospective emigrants inside, and some waiting in the street outside:

> They all seemed to already have exit and travel documents; some looked relieved to be at the end of a long bureaucratic trail; most looked anxious and harried, as if they expected things could still go wrong.[41]

Powys wrote that the Jewish question had become most sensitive for the Soviet authorities who were unsure how to handle it. This led to inconsistencies. As they were susceptible to Western pressure and Jewish protests, they had hoped that increasing emigration would defuse the agitation. But this had not happened. Since the Soviets feared similar demands from other nationalities, the Australian diplomat concluded, the growing international coverage of the Jewish question, "one of the sorriest blots on the Soviet record", was seriously disturbing Moscow.[42]

It would soon disturb Moscow even more.

CHAPTER 11

HENRY J AND HENRY K

The *Washington Post* is on 15 St NW in the United States capital, and the Soviet embassy is on 16 St NW. Beginning in 1972, small groups of Jewish students, often joined by older demonstrators, would hold lunchtime vigils across the street from the embassy to protest about Soviet anti-Semitism. Sometimes they carried placards, sometimes they sang, but mostly they just stood quietly. As the Washington correspondent for *The Australian* (1969–73) I had an office in the Post's building, and would often stop to talk to the demonstrators during my lunch break.

In the spring of 1973 Mark Yampolsky began a hunger strike opposite the Soviet embassy. Yampolsky was a former Russian jazz drummer and mathematics student who had emigrated from the Soviet Union to Israel in November 1972. But the Soviet authorities had refused to grant exit visas to his in-laws, Dr and Mrs Isaac Poltinnikov, and his sister-in-law Victoria. So Yampolsky began a hunger strike in Washington in protest, while his wife Eleanora did the same outside the Soviet embassy in London.

Yampolsky's hunger strike received some limited media coverage in its first few days. But he made international news when he wrote a letter on the seventh day of his fast to Deputy Secretary of State Kenneth P Rush, and challenged his prediction that Soviet anti-Semitism would increase if Congress did not grant it MFN trade benefits and credits. The *Jewish Telegraphic Agency* reported that Yampolsky gave his return address on the letter as "opposite the USSR embassy, 16 St NW Washington DC". Senator Henry Jackson, the principal author of the MFN amendment that was blocking the trade befits, supported Yampolsky and circulated his letter.

Soviet representatives had "been all over Washington", Jackson said, threatening that his amendment would lead to anti-Semitism. But anti-Semitism was so rampant in Russia that it was hard to imagine how it could get worse. It was a rebuke to Rush, and another shot in the battle between Jackson and the Nixon-Kissinger administration. On the eighth day of Yampolsky's fast, Jackson visited him in the evening and urged him to end his fast. He assured him that he had achieved his objective, and would continue to support him. An exhausted Yampolsky accepted Jackson's advice.

Jackson is deservedly one of the great heroes of the Soviet Jewry story. But he is also one of the great American statesmen of the Cold War, not widely known or understood outside the United States. He was a moderate liberal Democrat on domestic issues, but hawkish on defence and security. Of Norwegian ancestry and a believing Lutheran, strongly pro-Israel and anti-Soviet long before détente began under Nixon, "Scoop" Jackson was widely respected as "a stubborn yet thoughtful warrior … a close friend and supporter of John Kennedy, yet … offered the job of Defence Secretary by Richard Nixon."[1]

Jackson's key adviser was Richard Perle, an international relations specialist who had studied under Hedley Bull, an Australian professor at the London School of Economics, and later at the Australian National University. Perle was Jewish and an "intense, razor-sharp scourge of the Soviets who despite his cherubic smile, later earned the sobriquet Prince of Darkness [when he became Assistant Secretary of Defence in the Reagan administration] … Among the kinder things Kissinger called him at the time [during the MFN arguments were 'ruthless', 'a little bastard' and 'a son of Mensheviks who thinks all Bolsheviks are evil'."[2]

Viewed from the Kremlin, the Jackson amendment directly negated the Nixon-Kissinger drive towards détente. It also aroused suspicions that the United States Congress would not support Nixon on major East-West agreements such as the Strategic Arms Limitation Talks (SALT). Viewed from the White House, Nixon and Kissinger worried that Jackson's tough stand on MFN could endanger the long-planned Nixon-Brezhnev summit in Moscow scheduled for June 1973.

Kissinger was especially irate. First, because in uniting Jews, human rights activists, trade unions, neo-conservatives and paleo-conservatives, Jackson was building a significant political coalition against détente. And second, because Jackson and Perle presented a serious intellectual alternative to his policies for dealing with Moscow. For Kissinger, who prided himself as a heavyweight in the battle of ideas, the philosophical case against Moscow which Jackson and Perle were building around the MFN amendment stung his pride.

In addition to reporting for *The Australian*, I was also the Washington correspondent for the *Jerusalem Post* (1970–73). So I had a special interest in Soviet Jewry issues and the Washington senator. Being the *Post*'s correspondent, whose English-language reports were translated for the Hebrew-language daily, *Al Hamishmar*, the left-wing Mapam party's daily, I also joined the Israeli press corps teams whenever Prime Minister Meir visited Washington.

Golda's four visits to the Nixon White House were always big news in the United States, but even more so in Israel. They were great assignments for reporters, because they made news. The agendas always included vital military and economic aid, critical political and diplomatic support, and indispensable intelligence exchange. Golda and the Israel Ambassador in Washington, Yitzhak Rabin, briefed the Israeli press corps at length after each meeting. At the embassy residence, Rabin's wife Leah served Earl Grey tea to Golda, her traveling entourage, and Israeli journalists. Between cigarettes and cups of tea, Golda herself could usually be persuaded to tell stories about her past travels.

On this evening, she told us how she had arrived at the Vatican just a few weeks earlier to meet Pope Paul VI, but without a hat. Golda never wore hats. When told that as a matter of protocol she needed to wear a head covering, her long-serving secretary Lou Kaddar arranged for the El Al flight that had brought the Israeli leader to Rome to fly back to Tel Aviv and return with a Persian lamb hat. As the photos show, the hat arrived just in time for the historic meeting, the first time an Israeli Prime Minister had been received in the Vatican. Golda said that the only comparably emotional official encounter was her arrival in Moscow in 1948 as Israel's first Ambassador.

But riveting as her stories were, Golda did not tell us that evening that the Jackson amendment had now also become an issue in the Washington-Jerusalem relationship. Although some of Meir's and Rabin's biographers later wrote in passing that the subject came up during the fourth visit to Nixon, its significance did not become clear until December 2010. That was when the Nixon Presidential Library released a new batch of transcripts of conversations taped in the Oval Office.

On one of the recordings, dated 1 March 1973, Nixon and Kissinger talked about Soviet Jews. Kissinger said:

> The emigration of Jews from the Soviet Union is not an objective of American foreign policy. And if they put Jews into gas chambers in the Soviet Union it is not an American concern. Maybe a humanitarian concern.

Nixon responded:

> I know. We can't blow up the whole world because of it.[3]

Meir and Rabin did not live to learn about the deeply disturbing views Kissinger and Nixon expressed about Soviet Jewry just after they had left the White House. But they did learn something during their meeting about how seriously the Jackson amendment bothered the two men.

Earlier in the day Meir and Rabin had met Kissinger. The main topic on their agenda, as it had been on Meir's three previous visits to Washington, was how to bring Israel and Egypt to the negotiating table, and how to respond to Israel's requests for American economic and military assistance. Jerusalem was concerned at the increasing flow of advanced Soviet weaponry into Egypt and Syria.

But having withstood the 1970–71 War of Attrition against Egypt on the Suez Canal, the Meir government had accepted Moshe Dayan's strategic "concept", i.e. that the Arabs would not attack Israel, and if they did, Israel would defeat them within days. Thus, while Meir came to Washington confident about Israel's deterrent strength – tragically misplaced as the Yom Kippur War later that year demonstrated – she was less certain whether she could cope with the White House's diplomatic pressure.

In fact, her first meeting with Kissinger which preceded the combined session with Nixon, went badly. She and Rabin had feared that Nixon, having won a second term in a landslide against Senator George McGovern in the November 1972 elections, and having celebrated a triumphant inauguration just weeks earlier, would demand major concessions from Israel about returning the Sinai, conquered in the 1967 Six-Day War, to Egyptian sovereignty. The Kissinger meeting seemed to confirm their fears.

When Meir returned to Blair House, the VIP residence for visiting heads of government across the road from the White House, Rabin's biographer Dan Kurzman reports her as telling her Ambassador:

> If what the President has in store resembles what I got from [his] people [Kissinger] I'm better off packing my things and returning home before my meeting with him.[4]

But Kissinger, ever the negotiator, then phoned Blair House, spoke to Rabin, and dangled a carrot. If Israel conceded most of the Sinai it had occupied in the 1967 Six-Day War, just keeping a few patches, the United States would provide generous aid as a reward. Meir agreed.

The meeting with Nixon began on a bright note when he greeted Rabin with a cheery "Happy Birthday" and a box of souvenirs. The Ambassador had forgotten it was his 55th birthday, but he had reason to celebrate. In a generous and supportive mood, Nixon went on to pledge a significant upgrade of long-term American military and economic aid for Israel.

But Nixon and Kissinger wanted something in return from Meir. When the Israeli leader pleaded with them to put pressure on Moscow to release Soviet Jews, Nixon and Kissinger asked her to persuade American Jews to drop their support for the Jackson amendment. Meir was in a difficult position. Israel, more than ever, was now heavily dependent on American political, economic and military support. But she stood her ground and said: "You must understand my situation. I cannot tell the Jews in the United States not to concern themselves with their brethren in the Soviet Union."

The taped conversation – Kissinger's own "smoking gun"– must now be understood in the light of Meir's rebuff. Despite unprecedented generosity and support for Israel, Kissinger's attempt at "linkage" had failed. He had tried to use American Jewry's affection and respect for Meir as leverage for United States foreign policy. But he had found there was a line Meir would not cross.

After Meir and the Israelis had left the White House, and unaware that Nixon was secretly recording everything, Kissinger is heard on the tape as he bangs the table angrily in exasperation and declares that if the Soviet Union "put Jews into gas chambers" it would not be "an American concern". To compound his callous remarks about Soviet Jews, Kissinger adds the charge of treason against American Jews:

> I think that the Jewish community in this country on that issue (Soviet Jewry) is behaving unconscionably. It's behaving traitorously.

The Kissinger remarks were front-page news in December 2010, as were additional disclosures from the tapes which confirmed that Nixon regularly indulged in crude anti–Semitic and racist slurs. At first, Kissinger refused to apologise. But after some two weeks of outraged reaction from Jewish and non-Jewish quarters, Kissinger issued an apology of sorts, but said his statements had been taken out of context. Much of the comment and analysis that followed the Kissinger revelations understandably revolved around the spectacle of Kissinger, the court-Jew who had himself escaped the Nazi gas chambers, toadying to Nixon.

As Jonathan S Tobin wrote in *Commentary*:

> It is one thing to see human rights as irrelevant to American policy, but quite another to express indifference to the possibility of genocide.[5]

More than four decades after Jackson introduced the amendment, the Kissinger-Nixon exchange, however grotesque, raises a fundamental question at the heart of the Soviet Jewry campaign. Who was right about the Jackson amendment? In his defence, and clearly taken aback by the backlash against the tape's release, Kissinger argued that he had been right; that his quiet diplomacy with Moscow had enabled more Jews to leave than the Jackson amendment; and that in fact the Soviets reduced the emigration rates in response to Jackson's pressure.

Viewed in the short term, Kissinger was right. Jewish emigration from the Soviet Union reached 35,000 in 1973, and then, despite the Jackson amendment, declined to 14,000 in 1975 and 1976. But despite their denunciations and their attempts to slow down the emigration rate, the Soviets had to face the pressures arising from Jackson's ongoing support in the Congress. In the years 1978–79, as Moscow worked to win over Congressional opinion on the SALT II agreements, as well as for important trade agreements, the Soviets allowed 28,000 Jews to leave in 1978 and an unprecedented 51,000 in 1979. The Soviets had taken notice of the trade agreement which the United States had reached with Hungary in 1978 after Budapest had promised to allow free emigration.

In the longer term, however, Kissinger was wrong. Nobel Laureate and Soviet dissident scientist Andrei Sakaharov described the Jackson amendment as a "policy of principle", and the Twentieth Century Fund judged it as "the single most effective step" the United States took to respond to Moscow's "new serfdom". Their judgments were more right than Kissinger's. As was Perle's in 2010 when he told a Kennan Institute conference at the Woodrow Wilson Centre that it was "the single most important piece of human rights legislation of the last century" and may never be surpassed.

Perle was hardly a disinterested observer; indeed he was deeply, sometimes dogmatically, involved. To some, therefore, his view seems too sweeping. But on closer examination, and given the amendment's ongoing impact on Moscow, Perle's assessment holds up. In favour of it we have Leonid Brezhnev's own testimony.

After the collapse of the Soviet Union, the Russian authorities released a vast number of highly classified documents. Among them are the minutes of Politburo meetings which show just how disconcerting the Jackson amendment was for Brezhnev and the Kremlin. We now know that Brezhnev himself wanted to lift the diploma tax to comply with Jackson-Vanik. But much "to his noticeable agitation" the Soviet bureaucracy did not follow his orders until it was too late.[6]

Some 40 years later, it seems odd to point out that Brezhnev understood better than Nixon and Kissinger why the Jackson amendment was as powerful a weapon as it became. It certainly contributed far more to the Soviet empire's downfall, and so ultimately to the historic emigration of a million Jews to Israel, than Kissinger's diplomacy. And in hastening the Soviet collapse, Jackson and Kissinger's "traitorous Jews" also did more for the cause of freedom, let alone the United States' realpolitik interests, than all of Kissinger's grand designs for détente.

CHAPTER 12

"YOU PEOPLE ARE HARD TO PLEASE"

It was the time of the duumvirate. For fourteen days in December 1972, after Gough Whitlam had led the Labor Party to its first victory in 23 years, the new Prime Minister and his deputy Lance Barnard shared 27 ministries between them. Whitlam was Foreign Minister, a portfolio he retained for most of the government's first year. During that time, Whitlam took Australian foreign policy in new and often controversial directions. He formally recognised communist China; ended all Australian involvement in the Vietnam War; sought a greater role in the United Nations and in relations with the Third World; emphasised "even-handedness" in the Arab-Israeli conflict, and became the first Australian Prime Minister to visit the Soviet Union.[1]

In keeping with these changes in foreign policy, particularly on the United Nations and the Middle East, he distanced himself from the Australian Jewish community and from the Soviet Jewry campaign. Senator Don Willesee, who became Foreign Affairs Minister in 1973, followed Whitlam's lead, relying heavily on advice from Foreign Affairs. Dating back to the Menzies-Barwick period, Foreign Affairs had been consistently less willing than the Coalition governments to condemn the Soviet Union on Jewish issues. Under Whitlam, they became more influential. For the Jewish communal leadership, concerned by Whitlam's increasingly pro-Arab policies, Canberra's indifference on Soviet Jewry was an added frustration.

Tensions between the Jewish leadership and Whitlam over Soviet Jewry had first surfaced when he was Opposition Leader. In September 1970, when an ECAJ delegation went to Canberra to meet Prime Minister Gorton, they also met Whitlam. At first Whitlam claimed that he had not heard about Soviet Jewry's problems, and said he was astonished that they were so serious. After Leibler and Marcus Einfeld had outlined the issues, Whitlam said that the "hawks" in the (Liberal) government were "busting themselves to curry favour" and that appeasing the heavily Jewish electorate of Phillip was the primary consideration". The (Liberal) government, Whitlam insisted, was only using Soviet Jewry to "gain favour with the Jewish community".[2]

After Whitlam's querulous response, Leibler asked Barry Cohen, a Jewish Labor MP who also attended the meeting, to pursue the issue within the Labor Party. Cohen had a relative in the Soviet Union who had signed a petition calling for the right to emigrate to Israel.[3] Eventually, Whitlam said he would raise the issue with the Socialist International, the umbrella body for Labour and Social Democrat parliamentary parties, and also with the Soviet embassy.

Jewish leaders were not alone in asking the Whitlam government to intervene on Soviet Jewry. The Australian Council of Churches called for condemnation of the diploma tax, and the National Council of Women in Australia also sought action.[4] Whitlam responded:

> I understand ... from recent press reports that the Soviet authorities have now announced significant revisions to the education tax regulations, which will have the effect of mitigating their impact. In these circumstances I do not think that this would be an appropriate time for the Australian Government to take up this matter with the Soviet Government.[5]

The Whitlam government was slow to find "an appropriate time". In September 1973 when Whitlam spoke about human rights in the Soviet Union, he referred only to the dissident movement, but not to Soviet Jewry.[6] In October 1973 on United Nations Day, and again in December, Whitlam delivered major addresses on human rights. Although he decried the Liberal Party's record as "one of negligence and inaction", and listed his government's achievements in signing United Nations Human Rights Covenants on civil, political, economic, social and cultural rights, he did not mention the abuse of human rights in the Soviet Union.[7]

The Whitlam government's failures on Soviet Jewry were not due to ignorance or lack of advice. Canberra was aware that international protest and criticism could influence Moscow's policies towards Jews, and that Australia could play a role in the campaign. Indeed, the reports of Australian diplomats in Moscow consistently underlined the point.

At one stage, the Netherlands embassy in Moscow told Australian officials that the Soviets granted exit visas inconsistently and that the timing varied from a few days to many months. The Dutch said that this was an area where the West might persuade the Soviets to be more flexible.[8] In March 1973, after the Soviets had granted exit visas to nearly 40,000 Jews, the Australian Ambassador to Israel, Rawdon Dalrymple, reported that Israel's Minister for Immigration, Natan Peled, had said that Israel did not want to appear to be totally dependent on the United States, hence representations to Moscow from other countries, including Australia, were very important.[9]

In Canberra, Israel's Ambassador Moshe Erell twice asked the government to raise Soviet Jewry during the impending visit to Australia by the Soviet Minister for Foreign Trade, Nikolai Patolichev. Erell argued that Patolichev should not return to Moscow and report that Australia had changed its policy under Whitlam. The Soviet visitor, Errel said, would know that the McMahon government had raised Soviet Jewry with Foreign Minister Gromyko, and with the Soviet embassy in Canberra.

The Foreign Affairs memo on Errel's request suggested that the Prime Minister or other ministers could mention the issue "unabrasively" either to Patolichev himself, or to one of this accompanying officials.[10] A hand-written note later commented that Willesee did not raise the issue with Patolichev. Whitlam nevertheless instructed Foreign Affairs to say: "It is understood that this matter was raised with the Soviet Minister for Foreign Trade during the latter's visit to Australia".[11] But there is no evidence to support Whitlam's instruction.

As Foreign Affairs Minister, Senator Willesee mirrored Whitlam's stance. When the DLP's Senator Jack Kane asked about Soviet Jewry, Willesee referred to previous statements at the UN Third Committee meetings in 1970 and 1971 under the Gorton government. But he could not point to any similar statements by the Whitlam government.

In reply to a letter from Opposition Leader Billy Snedden in January 1974, Willesee said Australia had refrained from protesting directly to Moscow, because the Soviets would see it as "interference in a domestic matter". It would just be an irritant in Australia's relations with Moscow and the only approach was to continue to raise the issue at the UN in appropriate forums.[12]

Willesee was again non-committal after Senator Kane asked about the leading Soviet ballet dancer Valery Panov, whose case had attracted international attention. After Panov and his wife Galina, another leading dancer, had applied for exit visas, the Soviet authorities had imprisoned Panov and then expelled them both from Leningrad's Kirov ballet company.[13] When the Kirov Company toured Australia in 1973, Jewish communities staged large public protest rallies in Sydney, Melbourne, Adelaide and Perth. The Panovs were eventually allowed to leave in 1974. In 1976 they toured Australia, performing to standing ovations.

Internationally, 1973 was marked by the Yom Kippur War when Egypt and Syria surprised Israel on 6 October in a combined attack. The war was an historic turning point in the Middle East. But it also had an impact on Soviet Jewish emigration.

The emigration rate did not change during the war, and for the three months after the war the arrivals from the Soviet Union actually increased. But as the newly powerful Arab oil producers increased their pressure on Austria, Chancellor Bruno Kreisky's government closed its transit facilities for Soviet Jews en route to Israel. Previously, Austria had allowed Israel's Jewish Agency to house Soviet immigrants in Vienna's Schoenau Castle for up to a week. Now emigrants would only be permitted to remain for 12–14 hours on Austrian territory, before Israel's El Al airline had to fly them to Israel. Schoenau's closure prompted Jewish demonstrations in Australia, requests for Canberra to intervene, and protests to the Austrian government.[14]

In May 1974 Whitlam called an early election. ALP leaders,

especially in Melbourne, were concerned about maintaining Jewish donations and support which had been significant in Whitlam's earlier campaigns, especially in 1972. In Melbourne, Labor's Jewish fundraisers estimated that as much as 60 per cent of the party's private donations had come from the Jewish business community. But since winning government, Whitlam had alienated many Jews with his "even-handed" policies and pronouncements on the Israeli-Arab conflict, which were reflected in Australia's support for one-sided UN resolutions criticising Israel.

Whitlam's standing had eroded even further during the 1973 Yom Kippur War. As I was serving both as the VJBD's Community Director and the ECAJ's National Director, I experienced Whitlam's "even-handed" policy first-hand in Canberra on Tuesday, 9 October. It was the fourth day of the Yom Kippur War. A seven-man delegation of Sydney and Melbourne Jewish leaders, called together by ECAJ President Lou Klein, had flown to Canberra to meet Whitlam. We were alarmed and despondent, as was the Jewish community. We were still in shock from the surprise attack on Israel by Egypt and Syria three days earlier on Yom Kippur, the Day of Atonement, the holiest day in the Jewish calendar.

The war was going badly for Israel on both the northern and southern fronts. There had been heavy Israeli casualties on the Suez Canal and in Sinai, and the northern front with Syria appeared near collapse. The fortunes of war eventually changed in Israel's favour, but on 9 October Israel was desperately calling for a ceasefire. We had come to Canberra to ask Whitlam to support it. His deafening silence to that point, especially his refusal to condemn a clear breach of international law, was disturbing and disappointing.

The Prime Minister had agreed to see only two leaders, so it fell to Lou Klein as ECAJ president, to choose who would accompany him. When he chose me, as the ECAJ's professional adviser, this set off a heated argument with Leibler, by then VJBD president. Standing toe-to-toe with Klein in a corridor in the old Parliament House, Leibler insisted that as the senior ECAJ vice-president, and as an elected leader, he should accompany him. But Klein told Leibler he was too aggressive and would provoke Whitlam, thus ruining any chance of eliciting a statement. For his part, Leibler made it clear he thought Klein and I would not be aggressive enough.

In the event, after the shouting died down, Leibler accepted Klein's ruling. I joined Klein in the Prime Minister's office with Whitlam and his foreign policy adviser, Gordon Bilney, who later served as a Labor MP from South Australia. We presented our case for Australia to condemn the attack on Israel and to call for a ceasefire. But Whitlam, courteously adamant for an hour, made it clear Australia would not be commenting.

Whitlam blamed Israel for the war because, in his view, it had been too intransigent in its negotiations with Egypt and had held on to the Sinai for too long. But he said he wasn't worried about Israel because it would eventually win. "I know who started this war and I know who'll finish it," he said. His main argument for silence was that Australia's UN Ambassador Sir Laurence McIntyre was serving as President of the UN Security Council during October. As such, he said, Australia could not take sides. It was a specious argument, and we tried to explain why. But he did not budge. Klein and I left his office with nothing. The word spread quickly through the main Jewish communities of Melbourne and Sydney that although Israel faced severe danger, Australia would not condemn the Arab aggressors, or even support a ceasefire. Whitlam compounded his loss of support among Jewish voters when Australia continued to support the one-sided UN resolutions criticising Israel for retaliatory raids into Lebanon after Palestinian terror attacks.

Not surprisingly, therefore, when Whitlam called an early election in May 1974, Labor leaders were worried that Jewish donors and supporters would abandon the ALP. Labor asked United Israel Appeal leaders and ALP donors, Isador Magid and Saul Same, to organise a meeting for Whitlam. Under pressure from Leibler, then VJBD president, Magid and Same agreed to invite community leaders and Whitlam critics to a breakfast at the Chevron Hotel in St Kilda Road.

In the four decades since, "the Chevron breakfast" has assumed almost legendary proportions in the Jewish community. As the

VJBD's Community Director at the time, I was one of the breakfast's organisers who coordinated the event with Jewish lawyer and Victorian ALP President, Peter Redlich.

The breakfast proved to be a disaster for Whitlam's standing in the Jewish community. It started badly over the scrambled eggs and bagels. Almost as soon as Whitlam began to speak, he angered most of the audience by equating Israeli retaliatory attacks on PLO bases in Lebanon with Palestinian terrorist attacks on Israeli schools:

> There have been actions of a terrorist nature by Israel. Israel also has killed innocent people, women and children, maybe not so many. But there have also been crimes by the protagonists of Israel. I will condemn them too. The bullying of Lebanon by Israel gets no public support. Israeli civilian women and children, Lebanese women and children, are all sacred alike. I condemn the terrorist attacks which have brought shame on both.[15]

But it was Whitlam's hectoring that did the most damage. He warned the Jewish community that there were now as many voters of Arab background in Australia and that they could not expect political leaders to support only Israel. Then, answering a question, and visibly showing his annoyance at having to defend his policies, Whitlam rocked forward on his toes, his face reddening as he said: "You people are hard to please."[16] The condescending use of "You people ..." infuriated his audience. Prefacing a question, the veteran Zionist Federation president, Robert Zablud, said he hoped that Whitlam did not mean "You people ..." to be derogatory. Whitlam did not respond. He had burned his political bridges with the Jews.

After the meeting Leibler described Whitlam's approach as "disappointing and unacceptable".[17] Whitlam told Labor supporters he had felt ambushed, and accused the Jewish leadership of trying to blackmail him into supporting Israel. His attitude affected not only the government's relationship with the Jewish community on Israel, but on a range of issues, including Soviet Jewry.

In November 1974, before Whitlam's planned visit to the Soviet Union in January 1975, he met a senior Soviet Foreign Ministry official, V P Suslov, who was visiting Australia. During the meeting

Whitlam outlined his government's efforts to overcome "the phobia" against the Soviet Union, which he said the previous government had "manufactured". He noted that one of his first foreign policy initiatives was to extend de jure recognition to the Soviet's incorporation of the Baltic States of Estonia, Lithuania and Latvia. Whitlam claimed that the previous "artificial situation" was due to the Baltic immigrants in Australia, a number of whom were "professional anti-Communists".[18]

Regarding Soviet Jewry, the Foreign Affairs record showed Whitlam's antagonism towards the Jewish community had continued:

> The Prime Minister went on to say that there had always been a good deal of agitation in Australia against the Soviet Union from Jewish circles, although the gradual increase in the size of the Arab population in Australia meant that this pressure was being balanced. Nevertheless the Jewish community was still well organised. Thus questions were now being asked whether the Prime Minister intended to raise the issue of Jewish migration when in Moscow.
>
> Mr Suslov replied that emigration to Israel from the Soviet Union was now greater than at any time in the past. He said only a very limited number of persons were not permitted to leave and these were prevented for security reasons (e.g. persons connected with defence or missile production) or because they were criminals).
>
> Mr Suslov made it clear that there was no reason which would prevent the Prime Minister from raising this issue in Moscow, on the understanding that no statement should be made about any such discussion until after the Prime Minister's departure from Moscow.[19]

But Whitlam's public position was less dismissive. When Snedden again asked in parliament about Soviet Jewry, Whitlam replied that the Soviet government was aware of Australia's strong feelings on issues of human rights. While very few Soviet Jews had applied to immigrate to Australia, Whitlam said that if they did, they would do so through the normal channels of family sponsorship. He said he would consider raising this issue during his Moscow visit.[20] When questioned on the topic during a television interview, Whitlam said: "You can certainly rely on it that I will use what influence we have, and we do have some, to mitigate the illiberal features of Soviet rule."[21]

While in Moscow, Whitlam did raise Jewish emigration with Leonid Brezhnev and Alexei Kosygin. Although he conceded it was "an internal matter" for Moscow, he said the criticism of Soviet policies affected Australian-Soviet relations. Whitlam also said that "further progress in this direction would assist the growth in the future of friendly and cooperative relations which exist between Australia and the Soviet Union".[22]

As agreed, Whitlam did not publicise his Moscow discussions until his return to Australia. When some elements became known, however, ECAJ president Jacobson thanked him for raising the issue.[23] In February 1975, reporting to the ALP National Conference in Terrigal, New South Wales, Whitlam said that Kosygin had claimed applications for exit visas were decreasing. As for applications for family reunions by Soviet Jews wanting to emigrate to Australia, each would be considered on its merits. Also at the conference, and in one of his more outspoken criticisms of the Soviets, Whitlam strongly criticised Moscow's expulsion of the dissident writer, Alexander Solzhenitsyn. The expulsion had made international headlines and had aroused widespread condemnation.[24]

Whitlam's mixed record in dealing with Moscow made little impact on the Australian Soviet Jewry movement. But there were other factors which had slowed it down. After the 1973 Yom Kippur War, the rise of Arab petro-dollar power led to an intensified international anti-Israel campaign, especially at the United Nations. It was quickly reflected within the ALP's Left, sections of the trade union movement, and on university campuses. At first, taken aback by the extent of the anti-Israel assault, the Jewish community regrouped and reorganised its pro-Israel activities. But the new focus weakened the Soviet Jewry campaign. As did the internal debate within the international Soviet Jewry movement over the *noshrim* – "the drop-outs". *Noshrim* was the name given to the increasing numbers of Soviet Jews who were not going on to Israel after receiving their exit visas, but breaking their journey at the Vienna transit point and then emigrating to the United States, Canada and Australia.

Aligning themselves with the Israeli government's position, Leibler and the majority of Australian Jewish leaders insisted that Soviet Jews had to go directly to Israel. They argued that if they were left free to choose their destination after obtaining a visa to go to Israel, that would undermine the movement's campaign. For them the slogan "Let My People Go" meant "Let My People Go to Israel". Although only a minority of Australian Jewish leaders demurred from the Zionist insistence, American and other international campaigners were almost evenly divided. In the United States especially, the awareness that so many of the American Jews were descended from forebears who had fled persecution in Tsarist Russia led to a more vehement, and at times, bitter debate.

But despite a slow-down, the Jewish community's grassroots protests against the Soviets continued through the mid-70s. In March 1975 a "Russian Spectacular" entertainment group toured Australia and university students, led by Danny Epstein and Danny Katz, staged an all-night vigil outside the group's motel in Kings Cross. Sydney's Rabbi David Freilich conducted a Passover Seder service in the street to highlight the restrictions preventing Soviet Jews from celebrating Passover. A month later at Passover time, after Soviet police had closed the Moscow Synagogue, 400 demonstrators protested outside the Soviet embassy in Canberra.

In November 1975, after the Governor-General, Sir John Kerr, dismissed the Whitlam government, Malcolm Fraser won the December 13 election with the largest majority in Australian political history. Much closer to the United States in his view of Australia's foreign policy than Whitlam, Fraser came to office in Canberra with a reputation for a strong anti-Soviet outlook and as a Cold War warrior. He contrasted his approach to international relations with Whitlam's in his first major foreign policy speech as Prime Minister on 1 June 1976 when he told Parliament: "We must be prepared to face the world as it is, and not as we would like it to be."[25]

But Fraser also had a long-standing opposition to apartheid, and a commitment to human rights generally. During his eight years as Prime Minister the Soviet Jewry campaign would find him a sympathetic and engaged supporter.

CHAPTER 13

FREEDOM RIDE TO CANBERRA

On the Tuesday after the first Monday in November, 2 November 1976, Americans went to the polls and chose Jimmy Carter over Gerald Ford as the 39th President of the United States. In Australia it was the 115th Melbourne Cup Day, a public holiday to mark a thoroughbred horse-race. Although only Melbourne observes the holiday, Australians everywhere follow "the race that stops a nation".

In Canberra it was another parliamentary sitting day. Which was why Rabbi Ellis "Adi" Sultanik and some 60 supporters from the North East Jewish Community Centre in Doncaster, an outer Melbourne suburb, had chosen it for a "Freedom Ride" protest to the national capital. Sultanik was a young American rabbi, the suburban Community Centre's first, and had only taken up the post a year earlier. An ordained graduate of Yeshivah University, New York, Sultanik had come to Orthodox Judaism as a teenager. He had visited the Soviet Union in 1973, and had run Soviet Jewry protests in New York. Slightly built, but passionate, militant and media savvy, Sultanik was impatient. He thought the campaign was flagging and needed new directions.

Having made the ten-hour trip from Melbourne through the night, Sultanik and his congregants gathered outside the Soviet embassy wearing prayer shawls and tefillin, the small leather boxes and straps for morning services. To dramatise the contrast with Jewish boys in the Soviet Union who were forbidden to study Hebrew, fourteen-year-old Michael Becher led Hebrew prayers.

Sultanik blew the shofar, the ritual ram's horn. Although he said after the protest, "We marched around the Soviet embassy seven times blowing the shofar, but the walls did not come tumbling down," the "Freedom Ride" did yield important results for the Soviet Jewry movement.[1]

In planning the Canberra journey, Sultanik had drawn on his American experience of voters visiting their Congressmen in Washington. He arranged for briefings in advance to the Doncaster Centre's local member, Neil Brown (Liberal), Victorian Senator Alan Missen (Liberal), a noted civil libertarian, and West Australian Senator John Wheeldon (Labor). While in Parliament House the demonstrators visited 40 parliamentarians in both the House of Representatives and the Senate to make presentations and leave information packs.

The Freedom Ride's main objective was to highlight a petition with 20,000 signatures – representing some 80 per cent of Melbourne's adult Jewish population – which called on the Soviet Union to respect the freedom of religion and the right to emigrate clauses in the Helsinki Accords. The Soviet Union, together with 34 other states from both the communist and Western blocs, had signed the Accords in 1975.

The Accords had been the culmination of the Conference on Security and Cooperation in Europe which United States President Gerald Ford and Soviet President Leonid Brezhnev had convened to improve Cold War relations. Brezhnev had welcomed the Accords as a diplomatic victory because he had focused on the sections which effectively sanctioned Moscow's territorial conquests in Europe after World War II.

But in the fourteen years that followed, until the collapse of the Berlin Wall in 1989, it was the human rights sections which proved to be far more potent, indeed historic. Inside the Soviet Union they emboldened the Jewish movement and other dissidents. Internationally, they gave the Soviet Jewry movement an increasingly powerful basis for their lobbying. As Sultanik readily understood.

When the Soviet Ambassador refused to receive the Freedom Ride's petition, as expected, he asked Bill Wentworth, now again a backbencher, to submit it to the House of Representatives. Wentworth did so the same day. The petition asked the Soviet Union to respect the Helsinki Accords they had signed, allow emigration to Israel, free the Prisoners of Zion, end anti-Semitism, and permit the practice of Judaism.[2]

But Wentworth, inventive as ever, did more than present the petition. He proposed that the Joint Committee on Foreign Affairs and Defence (JCFAD) should seek the Soviet Ambassador's "advice" on Moscow's policies, and that the Committee should also examine the situation facing Soviet Jews.[3] Kim Edward Beazley, the Labor Member for Perth and Education Minister in the Whitlam government, was the JCFAD's deputy chairman. In his memoirs, *Father of the House*, Beazley acknowledged Wentworth's role:

> Most petitions are forgotten as soon as they have been presented, but Wentworth worked skilfully.[4]

The House of Representatives unanimously endorsed the proposal, as did Senator Sir Magnus Cormack, a Victorian Liberal who chaired the JCFAD. When the Soviet embassy said that if Australia inquired about Soviet Jews, Moscow would consider an inquiry about Australia's Aborigines, Beazley said he would welcome it. In his view the Helsinki Accords meant "everyone put the searchlight on everyone else's backyard".[5]

Although the proposed inquiry had won bipartisan support, it took another ten months before the JCFAD formally considered it. The delay, in part, was due to Foreign Affairs resistance to demands from Cormack and Wentworth for documentation. In February 1977 Wentworth threatened to take the delay to the party room. But Foreign Affairs continued to insist that his requests were unreasonable and would reduce "our ability to perform other, more important tasks".[6]

While Sultanik waited for the JCFAD to begin its hearings, he formed a separate group, The Australian Committee for the Rescue of Soviet Jews, and began his own lobbying campaign. It was largely independent of the ECAJ, Leibler and Goot, the mainstream movement's leaders. In early 1977, after the Soviets again restricted the supply of *matza* for Passover, Sultanik left packets of *matza* on the Parliament House steps addressed to every federal MP and senator. He asked Peacock to deliver the *matza* to Moscow via the diplomatic mail. In reply, Foreign Affairs explained that the delivery would breach international conventions, and that the Soviets would resist such pressure.[7]

Three Liberal parliamentarians, Roger Shipton (Victoria), Jack Birney (NSW) and Senator Peter Baume (NSW) took *matza* to the Soviet embassy and asked officials to send it in the diplomatic bag to the Moscow Synagogue. Embassy officials refused and suggested Australia Post.[8] A few months later Birney and Shipton visited the Soviet embassy again and presented a petition signed by 38 MPs protesting against the imprisonment of psychiatrist, Dr Semyon Glazman, and dissident physicist, Dr Yuri Orlov.[9]

By mid-1977, the Australian Soviet Jewry movement, in its mainstream groups, or in breakaway networks such as Sultanik's, was organising protest meetings, demonstrations, petitions and letters on a weekly basis. In July, Goot led 1000 participants at a candlelight vigil outside Sydney's Soviet consulate.[10] Later that week Peacock met a rabbinical delegation of Rabbis Sultanik, Michael Alony, Uri Themal, Richard Lampert, Brian Fox, Chaim Gutnick and Simon Silas.[11] It was the first time that Orthodox and Liberal rabbis, rarely seen in public together, had jointly met a Federal Minister, or cooperated so openly on Soviet Jewry.

Peacock's briefing memo for the meeting pointed out that Soviet–Australian trade was very much in Australia's favour, so that any boycott would disadvantage Australia more than the Soviet Union. But the memo also noted that Australia should tell Moscow that full détente was not possible if it maintained its current policies on human rights which "undercut the basis for the development of mutually beneficial relations".[12]

The rabbis asked Peacock to support another site instead of Moscow for the 1980 Olympic Games, to make Australia's agreements with Moscow conditional on improvements in human rights, and to facilitate the visit of a rabbinical delegation to the Soviet Union. Peacock was friendly and said he would consider their requests. But his letter rejected almost all their proposals.[13]

Trade sanctions would not be effective, he wrote. The government did not welcome a rabbinical visit to the Soviet Union, and Moscow would see it as interference in internal affairs. Australia would not lead an international Olympic Games boycott. While Canberra shared the rabbis' sense of outrage and concern on human rights, and would continue to speak out when the Soviet Union breached its international obligations, any Australian response beyond that "must be carefully measured":

> In the key issues of détente – the Strategic Arms Limitation Talks, a comprehensive nuclear test ban, mutual and balanced force reductions – the whole international community has an intense and growing stake. It would not be in Australia's interests, or in the interests to the world at large, to return to a course of confrontation with the Soviet Union.[14]

Peacock's reply highlighted the dilemmas and dissonances which lay at the core of the Soviet Jewry movement during the 1970s era of détente. For all their insistence that their campaign was not meant to be anti-Soviet, but merely pro-Jewish and pro-human rights, the movement became a key player in the superpower relationship between Washington and Moscow. By extension, that affected relations between all Western capitals and Moscow. Canberra was no exception.

One of the American movement's leading professionals, Myrna Shinbaum, summed it up retrospectively:

> It was always our belief – and our strategy – that the road to Moscow was through Washington; that the Soviet Jewry issue could only be resolved by government to government intervention. History has shown that strategy was correct.[15]

From the 1960s, when Leibler successfully pursued Australian intervention for Soviet Jewry in the United Nations, the Australian movement had followed the same strategy. On a much smaller scale that meant "the road to Moscow was through Canberra". Allowing for the basic differences between the two political systems, another parallel developed as the movements grew in each country. The strategy of pursuing "government to government intervention" came to include both the executive and the legislature. In Washington that meant lobbying the White House and the Congress. In Canberra it was the Cabinet and the Parliament.

The rabbinical approach to Peacock, which Sultanik had organised independently, provoked protests from the ECAJ leadership. Sultanik defended his actions, arguing that the rabbis were the community's spiritual leaders. There had been many calls for the rabbinate to become more active on Soviet Jewry, he said. Yet when they did so they were condemned. The ECAJ rejected Sultanik's views, but he was undeterred.[16] A month later he led a prayer service outside the Palais Theatre in St Kilda where the Russian Berioska Dance Company was performing.[17] And some six months later, despite Foreign Affairs' objections, Sultanik and Sydney rabbinical colleague Michael Alony visited the Soviet Union.

Australia's Ambassador to Moscow, Murray Bourchier, was an experienced senior diplomat. He quickly concluded that "Alony was an excitable naïve sort of person, but also and most reassuringly, that Rabbi Sultanik was very sensible [and] had [him] under firm control". On 10 February 1979 Rabbi Alony visited the Moscow Synagogue and Bouchier accompanied the rabbis "out of respect for the Australian Jewish community".[18]

On their return, Sultanik and Alony were among the final few contributors to give evidence to the JCFAD subcommittee's public hearings on Human Rights in the Soviet Union, the direct result of Wentworth's presentation to Parliament of the Freedom Ride's petition on Melbourne Cup Day, 2 November 1976. It had taken the JCFAD another eleven months to establish the subcommittee and hold its first hearings, and Sultanik was appearing before it more than two years later.[19] But for the young American rabbi, it was a moment of personal satisfaction and vindication.

The JCFAD had finally discussed Wentworth's petition in late August 1977. There was heated debate on whether to widen the inquiry to consider human rights infringements in other countries. But the Committee decided to restrict it to the Soviet Union, and on 6 September appointed a subcommittee to conduct the hearings and prepare a report.

Foreign Affairs officials did not welcome the inquiry. Their main concern was that the Soviets would see it as "unwarranted interference". On 20 September 1977, Peacock met the Soviet

Ambassador, Alexander Basov, to explain. After outlining the "positives" in Australian–Soviet relations – joint cooperation in agriculture, shipping agreements, and consular arrangements – Peacock emphasised that the inquiry was a parliamentary initiative. As the record of meeting reports, he told Basov:

> It was not our intention to interfere in the internal affairs of the Soviet Union. We were, of course, obliged to bring some dissident cases to the attention of the Embassy because these cases had been brought to our attention by the public and we could not be indifferent to such public concern. Because the JCFAD enquiry was a parliamentary action and not a Government one it would have to take its course. Both Lib-Country and Labor Party parliamentarians were involved. The Government hoped that the enquiry would not interfere in the internal affairs of the USSR. The Minister added that the enquiry was not starting with a set of preconceived notions but would seek to be as objective as possible.[20]

Basov reacted angrily, insisting that the inquiry would not help Australian–Soviet relations, and that it was unthinkable that the Soviet parliament would ever behave that way.

The Inquiry's first chairman was Kim Edward Beazley, who had held the seat of Fremantle since 1945, and had been Minister for Education in the Whitlam government. The Inquiry's first hearing began on 7 October 1977, with statements from two Foreign Affairs officials in camera, and then with its first public session later that day.[21] Whatever concerns Peacock may have had about the inquiry, he instructed his senior officials to give evidence to it, and appeared himself on October 19 to underline his department's readiness to cooperate fully.[22]

Within the department, however, Peacock knew that some officials regarded the JCFAD investigations as a nuisance which not only meant more work, but threatened their foreign policy monopoly. Moreover, he was aware that some bureaucrats were uncomfortable with the very idea of democratic participation in foreign policy, and the emergence of community groups "lobbying" politicians. For them, the growing Soviet Jewry campaign was a prime example.[23]

But Peacock had told officials that they had to learn to live with parliamentary committee hearings, at the time a relatively new feature of the Australian Parliament's interest in foreign policy issues, much as the United States State Department had done with Congressional hearings. In response to his JCFAD presentation, Beazley thanked Peacock for his assurances, but emphasised that nobody should "suppress the truth for reasons of diplomacy".[24]

The Inquiry's first public witness was a Jewish dissident, Professor Alexander Voronel, who had emigrated to Israel after a three-year struggle to leave marked by hunger strikes, arrests and harassment. A distinguished physicist, Voronel had lost his high-level position and membership in Soviet academic societies after applying for an exit visa.[25] His four hours of testimony combined a moving personal account with an informed analysis of Soviet anti-Semitism.[26]

After a fortnight of hearings, and against advice from Foreign Affairs, the JCFAD subcommittee decided to widen the inquiry's terms of reference so that it would not consider Soviet Jews in isolation from other Soviet citizens.

The inquiry's original terms of reference were:

> The status of Soviet Jewry – whether or not Jews in the Soviet Union are the victims of adverse discrimination in citizenship, in rights to religious practice, in rights to publish, communicate, travel and emigrate and organise, as alleged in the petition presented to the House of Representatives by the Hon W C Wentworth on 2nd November 1976.[27]

But as the new title "Human Rights and the Soviet Union" made clear, the inquiry would now also consider other minority groups. The Parliament, however, which had accepted Wentworth's original petition unanimously, was less ready to agree to the new proposal. An intense debate followed. Some senators argued that the changed brief was too broad; others opposed targeting only the Soviet Union. But Cormack's strong support for the change, and his praise of Labor's Beazley as "a man of the highest and utmost integrity", eventually won bipartisan agreement.[28]

When Fraser called an election for 10 December 1977, which again he won convincingly, the inquiry suspended its hearings until

March 1978. It resumed under a new chairman, Senator John Murray Wheeldon. Like Beazley, Wheeldon was from Western Australia, Labor, and an intellectual politician with an interest in international affairs. But unlike Beazley, Wheeldon was on the ALP's Left. He had strongly opposed the Vietnam War, supported independence for East Timor, and vehemently criticised apartheid.

A well-connected member of the International Socialist Movement, Wheeldon had a special interest in the pre-World War II Austrian Social Democrats, a party that became a model for the democratic Left. On a visit to Melbourne during the inquiry, Wheeldon sat late into the night at the "Scheherezade", a Jewish restaurant in Acland Street, St Kilda, discussing the Austrian party with Bund leader, Bono Wiener.

Wheeldon's deputy chair was a Victorian Liberal, Barry D Simon, and the subcommittee's other members were Senator Kerry W Sibraa (Labor NSW), Senator D B Scott (National NSW), Ralph Jacobi (Labor South Australia), J D M Dobie (Liberal NSW) and Dr Richard E Klugman (Labor NSW). The inquiry's secretary, Klaus Ducker, played a major role in organising the subcommittee's research, testimony, and final report.

As inquiry chairman, Wheeldon brought a sharp tongue, keen wit, and a forensic questioning technique to his role.[29] He dismissed opposition to the inquiry from the Soviet embassy, and from "certain officers in the Department of Foreign Affairs whose interests lay in making their lives easy".[30]

Viewed from Foreign Affairs, however, the inquiry had made their lives anything but easy. Quite apart from the added research and investigation which the inquiry had demanded, and at which some officials had baulked, there was a more basic difficulty. As they saw it, they had an ongoing dilemma: how to balance the Soviet Union's breaches of human rights against Australia's other interests in the bilateral relationship. This was often reflected in the distinction the resident diplomats in Moscow made between what was happening "on the ground", and their recommendations as to how Australia should respond.

Thus when Canberra asked the Moscow embassy for a new

submission to cover the inquiry's extended brief into other minorities, the embassy's cable emphasised that there had been "no positive changes with regard to human rights ... since the signing of the Helsinki Accords in 1975". In fact the situation had deteriorated, the cable noted, because the individuals and groups who had tried to monitor the Accords had faced threats, arrests, detention without trial, heavy prison sentences, exile, expulsion and loss of citizenship.

But then the embassy recommended:

> A too robust public stand by Australia on human rights violations in the Soviet Union could hinder efforts to advance humanitarian interests by unpublicised bilateral diplomacy, e.g. family reunion and emigration cases. It could also impose penalties in other areas of relations such as meat purchases. Moreover, we should need to be sensitive to the interests of allies and other like-minded Western countries. In sum, we should look at the human rights issue in context of our overall relations with the Soviets and of wider Western interests.[31]

The inquiry continued its hearings and research through 1978 and into 1979. The Australian Committee for Soviet Jewry presented a written submission and its first two chairmen, Einfeld and Goot, gave oral evidence.[32] In October 1978, two months after visiting the Soviet Union for the first time, Leibler also appeared. In a lengthy presentation, partly in camera, he distinguished between the Jews who were calling for the right to emigrate, and other national groups and minorities such as the Ukrainians, who were advocating internal reform.[33]

For their part, the Soviets continued their objections throughout the inquiry, and not just at ambassadorial level in Canberra. In September 1978, *Pravda* commented on the Australian proceedings:

> The Soviet Union will never permit anybody to act as a judge or an advocate in the matters that concern it alone. We do not need to adopt foreign laws or look for prophets in other countries.[34]

After nearly two years of hearings, 28 meetings, 25 witnesses, and a transcript of 1059 pages, plus much testimony in camera, extensive documentation and many folders of commissioned research, the inquiry's final report was tabled in Parliament on 8 November 1979. Among its witnesses, in addition to Voronel, the inquiry had heard from exiles with international reputations in their fields.

Pastor H G Grivans was a Lutheran minister from Latvia who had spent seventeen years in prison camps because he refused to stop preaching. The Soviet authorities had exiled him just a few months before he came to Canberra.[35] Leonid Plyusch, a Ukrainian mathematician and dissident, who still bore the signs of his torture in a KGB psychiatric prison, chain-smoked a packet of cigarettes through his evidence.[36] Pytor Grigorenko, a 70-year-old former Red Army general, told how the KGB had stripped him of his rank, imprisoned him repeatedly, and administered mind-warping drugs while he was kept in psychiatric hospitals where he had three heart attacks. His "crime" had been to call for the Crimean Tartars to be allowed to return to their homelands.[37]

In its 211 pages it demonstrated convincingly that the Soviet Union had systematically and repeatedly violated basic human rights such as the rights to emigrate, write, speak out and assemble freely, and protest. It had mistreated political prisoners, and had used psychiatric hospitals to silence dissidents. It was guilty of official anti-Semitism and suppressing the rights of nationalities and religions. And it had "failed to implement many of its formal commitments to human rights whether they be judged by the standards of the Universal Declaration of Human Rights, the International Covenant on Civil and Political Rights, the Final Act of the 1975 Helsinki Agreement or, indeed, the Soviet Constitution."[38]

It was a landmark document,[39] certainly in Australia. It was the first time that a parliamentary committee, or any official body at that level, had inquired with such authority on the Soviet Union and human rights in general, or Soviet Jews in particular. Similar inquiries had been held in the United States and some European democracies. But Australia was not a member of NATO or any overtly anti-Soviet alliance, and so for its parliament to publish such a bipartisan report was significant.

Wheeldon himself added to the report's international impact with the quality of his polemical and philosophical contributions. His preface to the report is a neglected masterpiece of Australian political writing which deserved greater recognition. It is a cogently argued statement as to "why the Committee should study the situation of human rights in one country, namely the Soviet Union, when … there are numerous countries … where human rights and civil liberties are denied".

Wheeldon proposed "three substantial reasons". First, the Soviet Union was one of two superpowers, and while there were sometimes deprivations of human rights in the United States, even its biggest pro-Soviet critics had to agree it was easier for Australian parliamentarians to obtain information about human rights in the United States than in the Soviet Union. Moreover, external scrutiny and diplomatic pressure aimed at improving treatment of individuals or groups often could be more successful than internal pressure, whether in one-party states or democracies.

Wheeldon's second reason was most telling. The Soviet Union was not merely a superpower, but a leading nation within a group of nations which believed every nation should adopt its ideological system. It was an "evangelical" power which pursued that belief with force and had imposed it on many of its East European neighbours. So it "must surely be helpful" to consider the consequences of that system in the country which was first to adopt it.

And third, Wheeldon noted, the Soviet Union had signed the Helsinki Accords which explicitly stated that good relations between nations were linked to agreed principles on human rights. The observance of the Accords was a matter of concern to the Australian Parliament.

The inquiry's report received favourable press coverage, and the movement's leaders welcomed it in Australia and internationally. Sydney University academics Peter King and Martin Krygier published a booklet summarising the evidence and main findings, pointing out that the inquiry's composition had been bipartisan "as was the parliamentary impulse which almost inadvertently set it up".[40] King and Krygier also noted that one commentator, Peter Samuel, writing in *The Bulletin*, had suggested the report was so significant that the Australian government should sell hundreds of thousands of copies overseas.[41] In the event, the Government Publishing Service printed only 2800 copies.

It was a lost opportunity. Although some key human rights groups associated with the Helsinki Accords and Soviet Jewry movements received copies, it could have had a far wider circulation. But the Australian inquiry had received some international media coverage, it had resonated within the international Soviet Jewry movement, and despite the barriers to receiving information, dissidents and refuseniks inside the Soviet Union had welcomed it.

CHAPTER 14

FROM MELBOURNE TO MOSCOW

In his political biography, *Bob Hawke*, Robert Pullan quoted Isi Leibler as saying that "any man with moral vision who was also in business had to be a schizophrenic". Pullan added: "Leibler, a slight, restless, chain-smoking man, believed he was himself such a schizophrenic, but also believed that the two Isis, the shrewd, implacable businessman and the ethical voice for Australian Jews, could live with the psychosis."[1]

In late 1977 the Australian Olympic Federation (AOF) invited Leibler's company Jetset, which had been the AOF's official travel agent for the 1976 Montreal Olympics, to undertake the same role for the 1980 Olympic Games in Moscow. Leibler had to decide whether the two Isis could indeed live with the psychosis he had identified.

Although the calls for boycotting the Moscow Games had not yet reached the crescendo which followed the Soviet Union's invasion of Afghanistan in December 1979, Jewish and human rights groups, parliamentarians and sections of the media had already begun to agitate. Leibler knew that if Jetset accepted the Olympic Games role, he would face accusations of conflict of interest and betraying Soviet Jewry. But subject to approval from Israel, he believed that the advantages he could win for Soviet Jewry would justify his AOF involvement. He also believed his track record of leadership and international standing on Soviet Jewry would help to minimise any criticism.

The Lishkah leadership, including Levanon and Zvi Nezer, agreed with Leibler that he should accept the AOF role because it would enable him to travel to Moscow and so meet Soviet officials and the refuseniks. Such access by a leading Soviet Jewry activist was not otherwise available. The Israel Ambassador to Australia, Michael

Elitzur, and the Israel Foreign Ministry's Head of the East European Division, Joseph Govrin, also supported Leibler's AOF appointment.[2]

Judged in realpolitik terms the Israelis believed the end justified the means, and their response was understandable. But Israel was a sovereign state whose officials made such judgments and compromises as a matter of course. Leibler, however, was an individual businessman and a leader in a community where Soviet Jewry had become a volatile and emotional issue, in good measure because his leadership style had made it so.

The Israelis and Leibler both underestimated how many Jews in Australia and beyond would therefore see a clear conflict of interest, or at least the appearance of one. Had he better foreseen that reaction, Leibler may well have spent more time preparing his own community and the media for the choice he made. As it was, Leibler's relationship with the still shadowy Lishkah proved a serious problem. It meant that he was unable to explain his choice fully, even within the Jewish community. Which meant that the media coverage about his dual role, when it came, had an even greater impact. Many of Leibler's friends and supporters never doubted that, faced with a choice between Jetset and the Jews he was trying to help, he would always chose the Jews. But they also believed, whatever the benefits of access his Olympic Games role would give him, that he should not have put himself in such a position.

Not surprisingly, the Soviets, who had long regarded Leibler as "persona non grata", strongly opposed Jetset's appointment. From the outset they tried to persuade, cajole and threaten the AOF to change to another agent. But Julius "Judy" Patching, the AOF's Secretary-General, remained resolute, consistently supporting Jetset and Leibler. On his return from Moscow after an early meeting about the Olympics, Patching told Leibler he was not "neutral" in dealing with Soviet officials, many of whom who did not hide their anti-Semitism. He showed Leibler his family tree. It included his Jewish grandmother who was buried in Ballarat's Jewish cemetery.

The ever impatient Leibler had to wait some six months before he had a chance to press a visiting Soviet tourism delegation to arrange his first visit to Moscow. After meeting the Soviet officials, and a "politically sophisticated" discussion about Soviet Jewry, an excited Leibler was confident that he and his wife Naomi would receive their visas.[3] But when the official invitations to Moscow arrived, they were addressed to other Jetset executives. Leibler was excluded. After making it clear that nobody from Jetset would travel to Moscow unless he did first, he and Naomi then received their visas.

Leibler was elated. For some fifteen years he had tried repeatedly to obtain a visa for the Soviet Union. Now he was going in a dual role: as a prominent Australian businessman to negotiate about the Olympics, a critically sensitive issue for the Soviets, and as an internationally recognised leader of the Soviet Jewry movement.

In Jerusalem en route to Moscow, the Israelis agreed with Leibler that it was premature to call for an Olympic Games boycott. The Soviets were looking for a reason to exclude Israel from the Games, but had not succeeded. An early call for boycott would give them one. Also, Israel was fighting against Arab trade and sporting boycotts. It would be difficult to target the Soviets while arguing against all boycotts.

From Israel to London and, at last, Moscow. On arrival, Leibler cabled his mother: "My previous involvement and contribution to the cause of Soviet Jewry is insignificant when compared to the momentum that has commenced with our visit to Moscow."[4] He was especially grateful that Naomi had accompanied him, noting in his diary: "She displayed a determination and resoluteness that would astound even her closest friends."[5]

The Leiblers divided their time in Moscow between meeting the refuseniks and Jewish apologists, and Isi's business sessions with Soviet Olympic and tourism officials. But even the business meetings included discussions, often heated and emotional, about Jewish emigration. As Leibler quickly discovered, at least one of the officials at every business meeting was knowledgeable about Jewish issues, and either represented the KGB, or reported to it.

During his first visit Gheeman Vladimirovitch Bulgakov, the Chief of Foreign Tourism, was the most senior KGB official that

Leibler met. Bulgakov dismissed the calls for boycotting the Games, noting that Lord Killanin, the International Olympic Committee (IOC) president, had said he would not allow politics to interfere with sport. On Jewish issues, Bulgakov said Zionism was "racist and made him want to vomit" and that Israelis were "cruel butchers who massacred women and children". When Leibler pointed out that he was hosting a Zionist, Bulgakov was visibly angry but somehow contained himself.[6]

Most meetings with the Soviet officials followed a similar pattern. Leibler would raise his concerns and suggest that the Soviet Union's image and standing in advance of the Games would improve if Jews were free to leave. A diatribe against "Western and Zionist slanders" would follow; Leibler would respond; and eventually the discussion would turn to the more mundane business of airfares, hotel bookings and seat allocations.

Leibler also met Peter (Piotr) Pimenov, who had succeeded Shelepin as the Soviet Trade Union chief, and who was not involved in the Olympic Games discussions. Bob Hawke had arranged the meeting for Leibler to discuss Soviet Jewry. It did not go well. Pimenov claimed that the refuseniks were being detained only because of security concerns and that they would be allowed to leave after five years. Leibler later described him as "a huge bear-like man who continuously makes crude jokes at which he alone laughs".[7]

Among the Jewish apologists whom the Soviets arranged for Leibler to meet, Zalman Litvin, an academic, denied that there was any discrimination, and blamed President Jimmy Carter for the breakdown of détente with his "idiotic human rights outbursts" which he said had hurt Soviet Jews.

Leibler also met Aaron Vergelis, the editor of *Sovetish Heymland* (*Soviet Homeland*), a regime-sponsored journal in Yiddish. Vergelis was a diehard Stalinist and an active anti-Zionist. Leibler's conversation with him in Yiddish ended in a shouting match when Vergelis sought an invitation to visit Australia. Leibler told him: "A Jew who brackets Zionism and Nazism is not welcome in our community or anywhere else."[8]

A less angry, but no less depressing meeting, was the Leiblers' visit to the Moscow Choral Synagogue, the only officially sanctioned synagogue in the Soviet capital. As an Orthodox Jew, Leibler was moved that the synagogue's lay leaders and Rabbi Yakov Fishman were trying to maintain some form of Judaism. But he was depressed that the KGB controlled their activities, and that Fishman had been made to testify against Natan Sharansky, the leading Prisoner of Zion.

In dramatic contrast, the meetings with many of the key refuseniks, although also tempered by a deep sadness, were exhilarating. Leibler described the experience:

> In the midst of stagnation, helplessness and gloom the incredible refuseniks stand out. Even today when most of their colleagues have already left, they still represent the salt of the earth, the last great Zionists, the torchbearers of Jewish heroism.
>
> We spent every moment of our free time with this colony. We talked, we listened, we learned and we cried. Their faces will continue to haunt us. They are unlike any Jews we have ever met. Once they are out, they change.
>
> We thought we knew all about them. We read and we thought we understood. One cannot. One must be there with them surrounded by the sullen, ugly anti-Semitic Russian people. They dream of Zion knowing it not to be a Paradise. They live from day to day with young families uncertain whether next month they will be in Jerusalem or Siberia.
>
> They have their fellow Jews. They love life. What they so desperately yearn for, we take for granted. I am not an emotional person, but as I write this the tears well into my eyes. In one short week they became members of our family.[9]

In his report on the week in Moscow for the Lishkah and movement colleagues, Leibler summarised the stories of eleven leading refuseniks, including Riva Feldman, 60, a widow; Maria Slepak, whose husband, Vladimir, was in exile on a charge of "hooliganism"; Alla Begun, whose husband, Yosef, was also in exile on trumped-up charges of receiving money from abroad; Vladimir Prestin, a former engineer working as an elevator operator who had been waiting for a visa since 1969; Professor Alexander Lerner, 65, a leading cyberneticist who had lost his job when he applied for a visa in 1971; and Ilya Essas, a brilliant mathematician who became a self-taught Talmudic scholar and teacher even though it was a crime to teach Judaism.

These and other refuseniks became enmeshed with the lives of Leibler, his wife Naomi and his family for the next ten years, until they were able to leave after Mikhail Gorbachev became president. Until then, however, most continued to live on what Litvinoff described as "the black side of the moon".[10]

Yet Lerner, the doyen of the refuseniks, could tell Leibler:

> Even if I am not able to realise my dream of returning to my homeland in our lifetime, we are still happy to take part in this biblical event. Don't be too concerned about us. Please remember that we are much happier today than prior to our application for emigration – despite the danger. We feel we are involved and dedicating ourselves to our people and our country.[11]

Leibler's Moscow euphoria did not last long. While he was away the *Sunday Observer*, a Melbourne weekly tabloid, published a report which questioned Leibler's commercial association with the 1980 Olympic Games. By the time Leibler returned, he was under attack from within the Melbourne Jewish community. Leibler had expected some criticism, but he was stung by its extent, and angry that some of his supporters and communal colleagues had not spoken up for him.

In his defence he pointed to his record on Soviet Jewry and said it was "outrageous" that some people, without waiting to hear his explanation, "were willing to believe that I betrayed the cause of Soviet Jewry for financial benefit". Leibler said he felt "ashamed and humiliated" that he had to explain that Australians, not the Soviets, had appointed Jetset, that Moscow had bitterly protested, and that he had only accepted "after consulting with Israeli and Jewish experts". The Olympic Games appointment had been "exclusively designed" to provide him with a visa to the Soviet Union "for Jewish interests".[12]

As the VJBD president, Leibler knew he would first have to convince his own executive. After an intense debate, the Board executive supported him. But it was not one of their more ringing endorsements. The resolution said: "The executive records its appreciation of the work done by Mr Leibler in the cause of Soviet Jewry during his recent visit to Moscow and looks forward to his continuation of such work on future visits."[13] Leibler promised that Jetset would not enjoy any financial benefits from the Moscow Games, and said he would open a trust fund for any profits.

Neither his promise nor the VJBD resolution ended the criticism. The Zionist Federation president, Sydney-based Alan Newell, said Leibler's commercial connection to the Games was "morally indefensible to say the least".[14] In an open repudiation of Leibler's views, the ECAJ called for a change of venue for the Olympic Games. Of greater concern for Leibler, Australian Jewry's roof body had censured him for "an unfortunate absence of consultation" and a "regrettable breakdown in discipline". Incensed, Leibler asked the ECAJ president Dr Joachim Schneeweiss to rescind the censure resolution, and VJBD vice-president Arnold Bloch criticised Schneeweiss for the resolution's wording.[15]

Under the headline "The Two Hats of Isi Leibler", *The Bulletin* ensured the controversy spread from the Jewish community to its national readership.[16] Television current affairs programs took up the issue and found that Frank Knopfelmacher, a long-time Leibler friend and supporter on Soviet Jewry, had turned against him. In a television interview the anti-Soviet academic responded to Leibler's dismissal of his criticism.

> Well, you see, at least Spinoza was ex-communicated by learned rabbis. I have been ex-communicated by a travel agent.

Knopfelmacher's attack, together with the continuing criticism in the Jewish community and the media coverage, upset Leibler deeply. But his immediate concern was that the controversy would endanger his assumption of the ECAJ presidency, due in December. He needed allies, and turned to international Jewish leaders for support. Blaming the Sydney-Melbourne "parochial politics" for the campaign questioning his "conflict of interest",[17] and arguing that it was undermining his work for Soviet Jewry, Leibler sought help from the World Zionist Organisation's president, Aryeh Dulzin, and the

Board of Deputies of British Jews, Greville Janner. Both wrote letters in support.

As the always simmering tensions between Melbourne and Sydney boiled up again, Robert Goot, the NSW Board president, became the mediator. Leibler flew to Sydney on 5 October for an ECAJ meeting, expecting a tense debate over his future role. But to his relief, Schneeweiss accepted a compromise resolution, and Leibler was assured of the ECAJ presidency. Although the criticism of his dual role continued in some quarters, Leibler now felt more secure about winning the ECAJ endorsement and began planning for his second visit to Moscow.

Meanwhile, an unexpected outcome from the first visit was the impact it had on John Halfpenny, a leading communist and trade union leader. Halfpenny and his wife Margaret, who worked for Jetset, had accompanied Leibler and Naomi to Moscow. Then 43, he was the powerful Victorian secretary of the Amalgamated Metal Workers Union, which he had built into one of the country's largest unions with a membership of 200,000. Fluent in Russian, which he had learned while in the Soviet Union for sixteen months when he had been head of the Communist Party's Eureka Youth League, Halfpenny had acquired a reputation in the Party and on the Australian Left for independence and speaking his mind.

Despite the Leibler connection, Halfpenny was confident that as a leading Australian communist, the Soviet authorities would welcome him. It did not turn out that way. The problems began on arrival at Moscow Airport when an official car met the Leiblers, but Halfpenny and his wife were left to find their own transport. The slight was deliberate.

Former Russian colleagues asked him what he was doing with "the Zionist Leibler". Pat Clancy, the president of the pro-Moscow Socialist Party of Australia (SPA), was in Moscow for eye treatment. He warned Halfpenny that the Leibler-Soviet Jewry association would destroy him. Both Halfpenny and his wife were shocked at the viciousness of the attacks from his Russian friends when he mentioned that he had been to Israel. Some refused to see him. Despite the warnings and abuse, Halfpenny met some of the refuseniks whose plight moved him.

On their departure at Moscow Airport, officials searched the Halfpennys' luggage, confiscated the Soviet Jewry literature and withheld their passports for an hour while two KGB officers interrogated a furious Halfpenny. During a stopover in Tokyo, Halfpenny called a press conference to condemn the Soviet trials of dissidents, the abuse of human rights, and the persecution of Jews. As a communist, he said it was his duty to condemn such "travesties of justice".[18] Back in Australia, Halfpenny came under attack not only from the CPA, but also from the ALP's Socialist Left who accused him of "selling out" to "Leibler and the Zionists".

The attacks left Halfpenny "bitter and demoralised" and hastened the disillusionment he already felt about the Soviet Union and his communist affiliations.[19] With good reason, Halfpenny's dilemmas reminded Leibler of Mortimer's agonising about his communism some fifteen years earlier.[20] Within a year after he had returned to Moscow, Halfpenny resigned from the CPA, and three years later joined the ALP. As a Labor candidate he ran unsuccessfully for the Senate in 1987, the same year he became the secretary of the Victorian Trades Hall Council. He died in 2003.

CHAPTER 15

THE GAMES RUSSIANS PLAY

The Soviets had opposed the AOF's choice of Jetset and Leibler from the outset. But after Leibler's first trip to Moscow in August 1978, and the widespread media coverage and controversy that followed, they redoubled their efforts. In October 1978 Vladimir Koval, the Moscow Games Organising Team's vice-president, visited Australia and demanded, publicly and privately, that the AOF should drop Jetset.

Koval extended his demands beyond the AOF as a sporting body. He warned the Australian government not to try to use the Olympic Games "for political advantage", and foreshadowed possible restrictions on Australian visitors. Foreign Affairs rejected the threat. A memorandum noted that the Soviet Union was trying to use the Games "to gain credit and international respectability, which in view of their recent record on human rights, it patently does not deserve".[1]

Koval also threatened AOF officials in his private meetings. Feeling the pressure, Patching, accompanied by the AOF president Syd Grange and vice-president David McKenzie, came to Melbourne to plead with Leibler to give up all his Soviet Jewry activities. Leibler was adamant that what he did in his free time in Moscow was his private business. He warned Patching that if Jetset was forced to resign the agency, he would create a "public scandal" about the AOF's surrender to pressure from the Russians.

In more conciliatory mode, Leibler pointed out he was campaigning both locally and overseas against moves to boycott the Games. Moreover, he was confident that in threatening to take the AOF to the IOC, Koval was only bluffing. At the meeting's end, Grange agreed it would be a mistake "to ditch" Jetset. It was clear to Grange and his colleagues that however unhappy they were with the

Soviet pressures, they could not move against Leibler.[2]

But as he wanted to maintain a positive relationship, Leibler wrote to the AOF and undertook not to say anything publicly which would link the AOF to his Soviet Jewry activities. Furthermore, he said he would not do anything to undermine the Olympic Games movement in Australia, and pledged he would not make any preferential ticket allocations to "fringe groups".[3]

Leibler copied the letter to Koval. But he had no illusions that it would placate the Soviets or hasten his application for a second visa. So he hinted to the Games officials that he might withdraw his company after all, but in a blaze of publicity. Shortly after, the Soviet embassy issued his second visa. Fraser asked Australia's overseas posts to give Leibler every assistance, and Peacock provided a letter of introduction.[4]

Despite the support from Fraser and Peacock, Foreign Affairs officials were reluctant about helping Leibler. They advised Ambassador Murray Bourchier, who was fluent in Russian and had been in Moscow for ten years, that "any assistance you may be able to provide is likely to be very limited indeed".[5] Bourchier should not meet Leibler at the airport, the Canberra officials advised, but Peacock was "concerned that so far as possible the embassy be seen to be helpful to him on what is admittedly a private, but very delicate mission".[6]

Bourchier told the Soviet Ministry of Foreign Affairs that Leibler's visit was private in character, but that Peacock was interested. So "it would be helpful for bilateral relations if Leibler was to receive an authoritative account of Soviet policy on Jewish emigration during his visit".[7] The Soviet diplomats advised that Leibler should pursue Jewish emigration matters through Intourist and the Soviet Olympic Games authorities.

Leibler arrived at Moscow's Sheremetyevo Airport for his second trip on 6 December 1978, accompanied by one of his managers, Lionel Landman, and Margaret Halfpenny.[8] In contrast to the official welcome he received on his first visit, Soviet officials began harassing Leibler as soon as he arrived. The immigration officer shouted questions at him and the customs officers turned his luggage inside out. At his hotel, Leibler found his room was sub-standard. It was not the spacious luxury suite which Intourist had allocated him and Naomi on his first visit.

At the Australian embassy, Bourchier confirmed that Leibler's first visit had created "significant waves". This time the Soviets would follow him everywhere and monitor every word. He should not go anywhere alone and avoid provocative situations, especially with women. Leibler soon found Bourchier's warnings were not exaggerated; the surveillance was ubiquitous.[9] But the Soviets did not prevent him from meeting the refuseniks.

In the opening meeting with the Games' officials, and also unlike his first visit, the Soviets refused to discuss Soviet Jewry. One official read out a Ministry of Foreign Affairs statement warning Leibler that if he continued his Soviet Jewry activities, they would not cooperate with Jetset.[10] At a lunch that followed, Leibler argued that he was not motivated by anti-Soviet hostility but by concern for his co-religionists. Many problems would be solved, he suggested, if Moscow allowed the refuseniks to leave, released Jewish prisoners, and re-established Jewish culture. The majority of Jews wanted to remain in the Soviet Union, and they should not be punished because some wanted to leave.

As for his own role, Leibler said he was firmly opposed to a Games' boycott, and pledged that Jetset would be an efficient service provider. He was not trying to put pressure on the Soviet regime but was rather trying to find a conciliatory way to resolve the problems.

But the Soviets did not accept Leibler's efforts at reassurance. In retrospect, it might seem that Leibler was either naive to believe they would, an unlikely explanation, or whistling in the dark in the hope that they might. His second visit to Moscow confirmed that trying to balance his role as the AOF's agent against his role as a leading Soviet Jewry activist was a highwire act. It demanded *chutzpah* and a willingness to take immense risks.

He found this out at the very next meeting, attended by Patching and other AOF officials, where the Soviets accused him of breaching his pledge not to say anything which would undermine the Moscow Olympics. They produced an extract from the *Canberra Times*, quoting Leibler as saying that "anti-Semitism in the USSR was obscene and permeated all sections of the news media under the pretext of representing anti-Zionism".[11] The officials insisted that Leibler's statement was blatantly anti-Soviet. Leibler tried to argue that he had spoken as the Jewish community's president, not as Jetset's head. He did not convince them, nor did he expect he would. He knew, however, that somehow he had to continue his highwire performance while in Moscow.

During his second visit, Leibler again met the refuseniks he had come to know, including Riva Feldman, Vladimir Prestin, Alla Begun, the Abramoviches and Professor Lerner. Afterwards he wrote:

> With all of them I felt as if I was reuniting with close family after a lengthy interval. Each meeting started with hugs and kisses. Whatever else I may have achieved, the knowledge of the comfort and contact I had with these wonderful people more than justified the other traumas I was to undergo.[12]

On departure at the airport, Soviet officials subjected Leibler to a humiliating search of his luggage, confiscated his notes and papers, and took him into a side room for interrogation. Landman, Patching and the other Australians had passed through the screening without problems. As Leibler's interrogation dragged on, he became increasingly uneasy that he would be detained not only until after his flight left, but arrested. It was then that he recalled an interview with a senior KGB official shortly after arrival in Moscow who had warned him that he was "playing with fire" and endangering himself if he continued his efforts for Soviet Jews. But the official had also given him his card. Leibler produced it for his airport interrogators. The ploy worked. The airport officials released him with an apology, and he was allowed to catch his plane.

In his report on the second visit, Leibler concluded that he had achieved his main objectives. Interestingly, a more independent observer, Australia's Ambassador Bourchier, whose confidential assessment was made available to Professor Suzanne Rutland only 30 years later, tended to agree. The Australian Ambassador wrote:

(Leibler) seems to have played his cards cleverly with due regard for the limits of his situation. His contacts in Moscow were limited to Intourist and Olympic Games officials who, though suspicious and critical, afforded him a serious hearing.

Bourchier summarised Leibler's message as a warning that Moscow should release the 2000 hardcore refuseniks, or face Jewish extremists demonstrating during the Games. Bourchier concluded:

Leibler's message would have been most unpalatable to the Soviets. He will need to persist if his efforts are to have effect, and to demonstrate that he can deliver if some kind of accommodation can be reached.[13]

Whatever Leibler thought he had achieved in Moscow, however, did not prevent further criticism from within the Jewish community. Among the most vocal critics was Melbourne's Rabbi Ronald Lubofsky, a Leibler family friend, who wrote to Rabbi Dr Israel Porush. The former Sydney rabbi, now living in Melbourne, was quick to defend his son-in-law. But Lubofsky had reiterated concerns about the conflict of interest which had persisted, especially in Melbourne's Orthodox Mizrachi community, the Leiblers' immediate social circle. It was an especially painful time for Leibler and and his wife. Close friendships came under severe strain; some did not survive.

Adding to Leibler's troubles was the hostile reaction from the Lishkah leadership after he criticised their organisational failures. Leibler had complained at length about the inaccurate information he had received about the refuseniks, and the lack of coordination between Israel, the refuseniks and the international movement's activists. In response, Zvi Nezer defended the Lishkah's activities, and another Lishkah operative, Yitzhak Rager, wrote a scathing rebuke.[14] Naomi read Rager's letter to her husband on the phone while he was travelling overseas. The letter angered Leibler, and by the time he reached Israel some three weeks later he was even angrier.

Leibler's Israeli friends, however, persuaded him to meet the Lishkah leadership, including Rager. After assuring Levanon and Nezer that he did not wish to undermine them, he lashed out angrily against Rager. For his part, Rager only agreed to put his criticism of Leibler aside after some of the more prominent refuseniks backed Leibler and threatened to go public against the Lishkah if the Israelis penalised him. For Leibler, the angry exchange had cleared the air, and he and the Israelis agreed to put their differences behind them.

It was the differences and personal animosities among the refuseniks themselves who had made it to Israel which now engaged Leibler's attention. After speaking to Professor Benjamin Fein, Victor Polsky and Alexander Voronel (who had been in Australia for the parliamentary inquiry into Human Rights in the Soviet Union), Leibler urged them to put their jealousies aside and to try to cooperate on key issues. In his notes, Leibler wrote that even if the refuseniks who had come to Israel might sometimes be problematic, they were still entitled to respect and recognition.

> These were the heroes who paved the way for the Aliyah movement. Yet there is an ugly element (of personal rivalry) creeping into our movement. Whatever problems they may create, however, we have no right to forget so quickly who they are.[15]

Although Leibler believed that his second visit to Moscow had achieved his main objectives on the Jewish issues, the Soviets were even angrier and more determined to retaliate. They told the Australian embassy again that Moscow might have to protest about Jetset and the AOF to Lord Killanin and the IOC. They also hinted that they would cut back Australia's seat allocation. To back up their threats, they allocated only 60 first-class hotel rooms to Jetset, while giving 1000 rooms to two small travel agents, Palanga in Sydney and Sputnick in Melbourne, which represented the Soviet communist youth movement. When Leibler objected vehemently, the Soviets adjusted the allocations, but stepped up their pressure on the AOF even further to drop Jetset.

The AOF faced a crisis. A Foreign Affairs memo summed up their dilemma:

> Clearly Soviet pressure is resented but equally they are not entirely happy [with] Jetset's behaviour … [The] AOF may

wish to put Australian games and attendance interests well
ahead of Mr Leibler's political interests. This does not mean
that AOF are not fully sympathetic to Leibler's cause, but that
they have no interest in becoming bogged down in human
rights issues or the undue politicisation of the Games.[16]

Grange told Leibler that Australia was facing problems with
ticketing and that he had asked the Australian IOC representative,
Kevan Gosper, to intervene. At the IOC meeting, the Soviet representative, Vitaly Smirnov, told David McKenzie that Australia was in
deep trouble and that the "Soviet government at the highest level was
incensed with Jetset and the past activities of its Managing Director,
Isi Leibler".[17]

Even more telling, Ignati Novikov, Deputy Chairman of the
Presidium, Council of Members of the USSR, and a member of
the CPSU Central Committee since 1961, described Leibler as a
"criminal" and lodged formal complaints against Jetset with both the
AOF and Lord Killanin.[18] Leibler's Soviet Jewry activities had now
reached the Politburo.

After the IOC meeting in Montevideo in April, McKenzie,
Patching and Grange met Leibler and Landman to tell them that
Novikov, speaking for the Soviet government at the highest level,
had advised them that "under no circumstances would Leibler ever
again be issued with an entry visa and should Leibler come to the
Soviet Union, he would be arrested".[19] Grange said this was "a battle
imposed upon them which they could not possibly win".[20]

Leibler responded aggressively. Jetset had lost $120,000 at the
Montreal Olympics as the AOF agent, he claimed, and had already
invested close to $100,000 in overheads for the Moscow Games.
He warned that if the AOF reneged on his contract, they would
face bipartisan condemnation for having capitulated to the Soviets,
and Fraser could initiate "drastic action as he has no love for Soviet
blackmail".[21]

Leibler's reference to "drastic action" implied that he somehow
knew the government would cut AOF's funding if they gave in to
Moscow. If the AOF held firm, however, he was confident that would

solve all the problems. After further discussion, it appeared that Leibler had made his case. The AOF officials agreed to telex Moscow reaffirming Jetset's appointment as the official travel agent, noting also that Jetset was the trade union movement's travel agent, and repeating their main concern that Australian visitors should receive satisfactory accommodation. They also proposed that the Soviets should send a representative to Australia at the AOF's expense to finalise the contract.

Despite the AOF's confirmation that Jetset would continue its role, Leibler remained sceptical. He was worried that the AOF would eventually placate the Russians. And despite knowing that his efforts were probably futile, Leibler continued to try to secure a visa to accompany Bob Hawke to the Soviet Union.

By May 1979, Grange was totally demoralised. He told Leibler that he could not understand why the AOF had become involved with Jetset and what "a tragedy it was for Australian sportsmen".[22] Yet Grange also pleaded with Leibler not to ask for help from Hawke or Fraser. Lord Killanin, Grange explained, opposed any governments or politicians who interfered with the IOC's independence. Grange acknowledged that Killanin was desperate to please the Soviets, and that the IOC executive was stacked with pro-Soviet members who would press the AOF to accept Soviet demands.

Foreign Affairs followed the Games' problems closely, noting that the Soviets were trying to drive a wedge between Leibler and the AOF. But the diplomats advised against any government involvement. Their main concern was how to keep the more serious issues from becoming public.[23]

CHAPTER 16

HAWKE'S MISSION IMPOSSIBLE

In Bob Hawke's memoirs he wrote that the only time that he had contemplated suicide was when he realised, in black despair, that Soviet duplicity had led him to give false hope to a group of Russian Jews.

> I have never experienced such a sense of utter desolation. That I had been played for a sucker by the Soviets was of no moment. That I had, albeit in good faith, raised and then dashed the hopes of these great human beings brought me to a point of desperation that I questioned the value of continuing my own life. I have never seen anything to match the joy in their eyes, and the thought of their despair tormented me.[1]

That was in 1979. Hawke also records how eight years later, as Australia's Prime Minister, his appeal to the Soviet Union's President Mikhail Gorbachev led to the freedom of those Russian Jews and others. But the story of Hawke's involvement with Soviet Jewry begins a decade before his disastrous visit to Moscow in 1979.

Hawke was aware of Soviet Jewry's problems even before his first visit to Israel in July 1971. As the Australian Council of Trade Unions (ACTU) president, he had signed a protest letter in December 1970 against the death sentences which the Soviet authorities had imposed on the would-be Leningrad hijackers. In May 1971, during the campaign against the impending rugby union tour by the Springboks, South Africa's all-white team, he said the ACTU would also bar Soviet sporting teams if they deliberately excluded Jews.[2]

But it was his first visit to Israel which enhanced his awareness. It created a profound emotional and intellectual identification with the Jewish state. It established a close bond of affection and respect with Golda Meir. And it made him a key player in the Australian and international Soviet Jewry campaign for the next two decades.

Ironically, given the Cohen Affair in 1962, and Senator Cohen's controversial views about Soviet Jewry, Hawke visited Israel as the inaugural Sam Cohen Fellow. Senator Cohen had died suddenly while campaigning in South Australia during the 1969 election. As a tribute, Cohen's widow, Judith (later Justice Judith Cohen), Clyde Holding (at the time Victorian ALP leader), and Walter Lippmann, a Jewish community leader, had established the fellowship to enable trade union officials to visit Israel and, on their return, to give the Sam Cohen Memorial Lecture.

Tellingly, Hawke entitled his lecture, "Masada, Moscow and Melbourne". Israel was an inspiration for Australia, he said. It was a small lone democracy in the Middle East facing attack and the world's survival was tied to its survival. As he told his audience:

> There is a powder keg there in the Middle East. Every decent human being must be committed to the viability of Israel. If the bell tolls for Israel, it won't just toll for Israel, it will toll for all mankind.[3]

Although Hawke spoke about the Soviet Union's role in the Middle East, hence the reference to "Moscow" in the lecture's title, he said nothing about his secret talks on Soviet Jewry with high-ranking officials in the USSR after his Israel visit. Those meetings had come about after he had told Michael Siew, his Israeli escort, that as an Australian trade union leader who had access to his Soviet counterparts at the International Labor Organisation (ILO) in Geneva, he wanted to help Soviet Jewry. The offer led to a meeting with Israel's Prime Minister Golda Meir which, in Hawke's own terms, was a life-changing event.

Reflecting on the meeting in Meir's Tel Aviv office some 40 years later, Hawke recalled that Susan, his fourteen-year-old daughter who had travelled with him to Israel, had accompanied him.

> Golda was this marvellous combination. A tough intelligent lady. And then this loving grandmother who came dashing around (the desk) to comfort Susan when my poor daughter knocked her drink over and broke something. It was a beautiful juxtaposition. I became a fan.
>
> Golda spoke with strength and vigor, passion and conviction, about the issues confronting Israel. And she talked

about Soviet Jewry ... I [said] I was going to the Soviet Union
as the ACTU president and I'd be happy to help.[4]

Meir arranged for Hawke to meet Israel's foreign minister, Abba
Eban, and the Lishkah briefed him on their reading of Soviet Jewry.
After attending an International Labour Organisation (ILO) meeting
in Geneva, Hawke flew back to Israel to pick up his daughter, and
then on to Palanga, the Baltic Sea resort where Alexander N Shelepin,
then the Soviet trade union movement's president, was holidaying.

A former head of the KGB, Shelepin was ranked fifth in the
Politburo hierarchy. He and Hawke had formed a friendly working
relationship and, using interpreters, they talked without a break for
sixteen hours "through morning, lunch and dinner and well into the
night, while the vodka flowed".[5] But Hawke had no illusions about
Shelepin, as he recalled 40 years on:

> He was a small man. Short and tough. You could just imagine
> him pressing the buttons and dispatching people. But he was
> intelligent and listened to argument. I put the argument to
> him not only in terms of morality, but as always, by trying to
> see the person's self-interest in acting the way I wanted him
> to act.[6]

The talking ranged over international trade union affairs, the
Middle East and Arab-Israeli relations, Soviet Jewry and the
invitation from the Secretary-General of the Histadrut, Ben Aharon,
for Shelepin to visit Israel.[7] On the Arab-Israeli conflict, Hawke told
Shelepin that the Soviet Union was "backing the wrong horse". The
Soviet Union and Israel were both 20th century creations; both had
suffered great losses in World War II; and both were deeply concerned
with territorial security.

On Soviet Jewry, Hawke said it would be in Moscow's interest to be
more liberal because it would improve their international standing.
Shelepin responded that the Soviets had to consider the effect on
other national minority groups if they let the Jews emigrate freely.
Moreover, while Jews made up only 2 per cent of the population they
constituted 15 per cent of the scientific community. So how could
Moscow let them go, especially if they had access to state secrets?

Hawke argued that most of the visa applicants did not work in sensitive positions, and that if those who did were allowed to leave, their fellow Jews might be more loyal.

Hawke later told the Australian embassy in Moscow that he believed the meeting would bear fruit in due course, and that Shelepin had promised to maintain contact through the Australian Ambassador in Moscow.[8] Hawke agreed not to publicise the Shelepin meeting, but he sent a full report to Eban in Jerusalem.

In the months that followed, the numbers of Jewish emigrants increased from 13,000 in 1971 to 32,000 in 1972, and 35,000 in 1973. Some Israeli officials believed that Hawke's intervention with Shelepin had contributed to the increase. One Australian diplomat even suggested that the Soviets were so influenced by their own anti-Jewish propaganda about Jewish power controlling the world, that they believed that Hawke was a representative of a "mighty and devious foe".[9] But the evidence is that the significant increase in emigration was mostly due to the Nixon-Kissinger policy of détente which, in turn, enhanced the international protest movement's impact on Moscow.

Hawke visited Israel again in November 1973, immediately after the Yom Kippur War. As the first non-Israeli visitor to the Golan Heights, barely days after the ceasefire, he was appalled at the carnage of war, the stench of death, and the debris of battle. In Jerusalem he wept with Golda Meir as they looked at photos of young Israeli soldiers, shot by the Syrians, hands tied behind their backs.

It was a wrenching emotional meeting. As he had done at his first meeting with the Israeli Prime Minister, Hawke wanted to help. He offered to return to Moscow. The Israelis asked him to convey a double message to the Soviet leadership: they were determined to defend themselves even if it meant nuclear war between the superpowers, and they were determined to continue the campaign for Soviet Jewry.

Hawke flew to Moscow on 22 November 1973, and again met Shelepin. Talking through the night, Hawke "had the sense that this was one of the biggest moments of [his] life";[10] that somehow he had to make Shelepin understand the extent of the Syrian and

Egyptian defeat, the enormity of the Soviet Union's loss in weaponry and wealth, and how close the conflict had come to war between the United States and the Soviet Union. Nor would the shock of the Yom Kippur War, and the serious losses Israel had suffered, change Jerusalem's campaign to free Soviet Jewry.

By late 1973, however, Shelepin had lost much of his influence in the Kremlin. Although still a Politburo member, his KGB past and security connections had aroused Brezhnev's distrust. Hawke did not meet his Soviet trade union counterpart again, and in 1975 Shelepin was dropped from the Politburo.

The Yom Kippur War, however, had certainly strengthened Hawke's already serious commitment to Israel. When Whitlam announced his policy of even-handed neutrality during the war, Hawke was scathing: "Oil is a murky substance and it has, I believe, blurred the vision of men of goodwill."[11] In an address to the Zionist Federation's Biennial Conference in January 1974 he repudiated "even-handedness" as morally repugnant and inconsistent with ALP policy.[12] Hawke was the ALP's president, and his open conflict with Whitlam on Israel led to calls within the party for his resignation. But Hawke refused to resign, and his popular appeal as the 1974 election loomed, ensured he could resist the pressures.

Hawke's consistent defence of Israel against Labor Party critics, and his outspoken denunciations of Bill Hartley, a leading member of the ALP's Socialist Left, endeared him to Australian Jews.

Hartley, who represented the Iraqi News Agency, became increasingly hostile to Israel after the Yom Kippur War. He described it as "a huge ghetto founded on a monstrous injustice".[13] In response, Hawke declared that he represented the ALP's policy, and that Hartley had breached it. And it was he who spoke for most Australians on Israel, while Hartley was an extremist who represented a fringe minority. Despite a drop in support for Israel and a growth in pro-Palestinian views after the Yom Kippur War, Hawke's public popularity and trade union standing were significant in maintaining a majority pro-Israel public opinion.

In 1979 Hawke made his third visit to Moscow for Soviet Jewry.

Officially it was to meet the Soviet All Union Council In Moscow (AUCTU). But his real purpose was to try to win the release of twelve Prisoners of Zion and gain permission for the refuseniks to emigrate.

Hawke had been very supportive on Soviet Jewry since before his first meeting with Shelepin in 1971. But he had become more involved in the issue as his business and personal relationship with Leibler grew after the ACTU-Jetset agreement in September 1978. Leibler had built Jetset from a small travel agency, in which he had invested in the 1960s to help his friend and political colleague Bono Wiener, into the largest travel and tour operator in Australia and the Asia-Pacific region. When the ACTU-New World Travel partnership failed, Leibler approached Hawke to establish ACTU-Jetset and the "Leisure Club Subsidy" scheme. It became a commercial success for Jetset and a rare financial one for the ACTU.

By March 1979 Leibler had visited the Soviet Union twice, first in September 1978, and again in December. As Moscow had previously declared him "persona non grata", and had refused to grant him a visa, Leibler had only been able to enter the Soviet Union because the AOF had appointed Jetset as its official travel agent for the 1980 Olympic Games in Moscow. But the Soviets refused to issue a visa for Leibler to make a third trip so he could accompany Hawke. Leibler was aware, however, that Hawke's meetings in Moscow could be critical, and arranged to meet him in Israel beforehand for the Lishkah's briefings.

Leibler also prepared his own briefing for Hawke, summarising details about the refuseniks he would meet, including Riva Feldman, the group's key coordinator, Vladimir Prestin, Elya Essas, Professor Alexander Lerner, Pavel Abramovich, Professor Victor Brailovski and wife Irina, Alla Begun, Maria Slepak and Lev Ulanovsky. His message to Hawke was upbeat:

> You are going into the Soviet Union at the most opportune time for achieving results. Your presence, your role, and the high regard in which you are held by the Soviets could make you the catalyst to bring about a favourable policy determination to one of the Jewish people's greatest and historic tragedies.[14]

As might be said in retrospect, "no pressure". Leibler tried to reassure Hawke further by telling him that he was "brilliant, intelligent and respected by the Russians".[15] But, in hindsight, it was an exuberantly optimistic expectation for Leibler to think that Hawke, for all his famed success at negotiating conflicts, could achieve in a totalitarian regime what heads of government and international leaders had failed to achieve: the release of the refuseniks.

Although Hawke's relationship with his wife Hazel was at a low ebb, the couple agreed that they should travel to Moscow together. Leibler and his wife Naomi would meet them first in Israel and then wait for them in Rome.[16]

In Israel, Hawke met Prime Minister Menachem Begin, who hugged him enthusiastically. But Begin was less enthusiastic about Hawke's peace plan for the Arab-Israeli conflict. Israel should give up the territories occupied in 1967, Hawke proposed, and go back to the prior borders. If the Arabs reneged on the agreement and attacked, Israel would be free to conquer, retain and annex the territories. Begin listened, politely at first, then bemusedly, until he changed the subject.

The Israeli Prime Minister was much more attentive, however, when Hawke and Leibler discussed their hopes for freeing the refuseniks and Prisoners of Zion. As a young Zionist in Vilnius when the Red Army occupied Lithuania in 1940, Begin had been imprisoned and tortured by the NKVD, the KGB's predecessor. The experience had left its mark, literally, on the Israeli leader. Hawke's mission mattered to him, and he prayed that it would succeed.[17]

CHAPTER 17

HOPE AGAINST HOPE

On his first night in Moscow, Hawke's Soviet hosts took him to dinner at the trade union-owned Orbit Hotel where he was staying. Hawke invited Australia's Ambassador Bourchier and the Commercial Counsellor John Tinney to join him. Bourchier's diplomatic report to Canberra on the dinner, and on Hawke's five-day visit, together with Leibler's private journal kept while waiting for Hawke in Rome, are contemporaneous accounts. Both are hitherto unpublished, and shed new light on the events which led to Hawke's time of despair.

Of special interest is that Bourchier asked Foreign Affairs officials in Canberra not to file his report on Hawke's visit in the usual way, i.e. "not file the text in registry". This was to ensure that Peacock, as the Liberal government's minister, would not have access to his frank account. Hawke had made it clear he was preparing to enter parliamentary politics, and Bourchier did not want his potential opponents to read his personal, more colourful comments on the Moscow visit. He added: "I do not think the Minister would quarrel with this point of principle." Bourchier's colleagues in Canberra agreed. They hid the report in another folder and buried it under a pile of documents dealing with United States Congressional hearings – where it remained for the next 25 years, until co-author Suzanne Rutland came across it in her archival research for this book.

Bourchier's "lost" report begins with "the usual bibulous" round of toasts at the Orbit Hotel dinner, and the Soviet efforts to force liquor on the Australians. After dinner, Hawke asked Bourchier and Tinney up to his room, only to find that two of his Russian hosts had followed them, and had burst in clutching bottles of vodka. They took beer from Hawke's refrigerator and settled down for a long night. But Hawke turned on them:

"I don't remember inviting you bastards to my room for a drink, so why don't you piss off?"

"You think we better piss off, do you Bob?"

"Yes!" said Hawke.[1]

They left.

Hawke was not only tired and unwilling to keep drinking; he told Bourchier that the refuseniks were waiting for him to telephone, which he could not do until his Russian hosts had left. Over the next two days Hawke and Hazel had three emotional meetings with the refuseniks which he later described in his memoirs.

> My commitment to these people was reinforced by meeting them in their miserable apartments. Their nobility of spirit overwhelmed me. Here were professors, engineers, men and women of outstanding talent relegated to menial occupations, prevented from freely practising their religion, their children denied access to university. They were pariahs in a squalid society.
>
> Yet through all this, their indomitable faith imbued their sadness with a warmth and optimism which moved me beyond measure. I felt a personal convergence with them and was determined to do everything in my power to honour that faith and justify their hope in me.[2]

But the Soviet authorities had other ideas. On 23 May Hawke had a four-hour lunch meeting with Aleksei Shibaev, the trade union chief who had replaced Shelepin, and three senior trade union officials, Peter (Piotr) Pimenov, Vsevolod Mozhayev, and Vladimir Kirillov. Hazel took shorthand notes.

Hawke told Bourchier about the meeting two days later. Bourchier wrote:

> I found (Hawke) in a very excited state of mind. He said that there had been dramatic developments which he felt amounted to a real breakthrough, although he found it difficult to take it entirely at its face value …[3]

Hawke recounted his exchanges with Pimenov and Shibaev, especially after Shibaev said the All Union Council of Trade Unions of the USSR (AUCTU) Presidium was in session at the time and that he would like them to consider Hawke's arguments about letting the refuseniks leave. When he returned from the AUCTU meeting, he announced: "The [AUCTU] Presidium has totally accepted your arguments."[4] But what did that mean?

The next day, Kirillov and Mozhayev returned to Hawke's hotel and invited him to a bar – without Hazel – where Pimenov joined them. The Russians plied him with "the compulsory vodka and cognac". Some 30 years later, Hawke told me that that was the standard Soviet technique in any negotiation, but that they always played "dirty pool". As hosts, he said, they would always cheat. Some drank water instead of vodka; some would not fill their glasses, and they would always pace themselves, taking it in turns to offer toasts, while trying to get their guests drunk.[5]

But in an account which he had not given before, Hawke told me he "got even" with Pimenov. He wanted to slow down the alcohol consumption and decided the only way was to switch from vodka to beer.

> So I said to the interpreter who had served in the Soviet Embassy in London: "You've heard about cricket?"
>
> "Yeah, yeah," he said.
>
> "So tell them I've been playing on your wicket. Now you're going to play on mine. No more vodka. Beer."

Hawke said they couldn't refuse, but the only available beer was Egyptian. So the Russians wanted to continue the toasts in vodka. Hawke insisted on beer, and told the Russians he held the world's speed record for beer drinking. To demonstrate:

> I just opened the bottle and gulled it down. Pimenov, a great hulking brute of a man, was in awe. Now he had to drink his beer. He got it down somehow, and proposed the next toast in vodka. No, I said. Another beer. Bob, he said, you're a bastard. And they all knocked off.[6]

When the drinking session ended, Pimenov and his associates told Hawke again that officials at the highest levels had considered his requests and had agreed to them. The next morning, 25 May 1979, Hazel called Leibler to report the good news. She said: "What has happened is absolutely unreal, the success we have achieved is beyond all expectations."

In his diary, Leibler wrote:

> Then Hawke comes to the phone. He sounded loaded but wasn't. He was emotionally drained and the man was crying like a little child. "We've done it, Isi. We've done it. We've achieved the unbelievable." "What?" I asked him. He said, "We had a long session and what has happened here is totally unreal. I have been given an unqualified guarantee that all prisoners will be released and that every refusenik of five years standing and over will also be released."[7]

Finding the news hard to believe, Leibler kept asking Hawke if the Soviets had not conned him. But Hawke, still crying, said it was the most important thing in his life.[8] Former refuseniks Victor Polsky and Alexander Voronel were with Leibler and heard the conversation. Leibler's diary note reflects his uncertainty at the news.

> It would appear that our operation has been successfully or near successfully concluded. I just can't believe it. Where on earth do we go from here, is it really true? I am in a state of shock and stunned. I refuse to permit myself to believe that we have achieved such an outstanding success. I want to remain sober and calm.[9]

Bourchier's account written from Moscow reports that Hawke believed he had received assurances that "the whole thing was wrapped up, that a policy change was on its way, and even that the signs of change would be seen in two weeks time".[10] That belief was strengthened when Kirillov, who had admitted to Hawke that he was himself Jewish and had previously begged him not to press his case so hard, had broken into tears of joy at Shibaev's news.

Bourchier described Hawke's mood as a mixture of "euphoria combined with recurring misgivings".[11] The Australian Ambassador told him that he thought Soviet policy on Jewish emigration would only be decided at Politburo level and "not all of a sudden" as the result of ideas a visiting Australian had put to trade union leaders. If the Soviets, however, had decided to use Hawke as the vehicle for such a change in policy, it would only be because they saw a special advantage. Bourchier advised Hawke to let the refuseniks make any press announcements, and that he should take a conservative approach.

When Hawke met the refuseniks that evening he was surprised that they were far more cautious about the news than he had expected. Hawke told Bourchier later that he could not be as precise as they wanted him to be, because he himself was somewhat confused.

After speaking to Leibler, Hawke met the key refuseniks again, and they drafted a statement welcoming "the position which we believe has been conveyed ... to an Australian trade union official Mr Bob Hawke ... on behalf of the Soviet authorities in regard to the emigration of Jews from their country ..."[12] The refuseniks referred to three issues which they believed had been resolved. Applicants who had had visas denied for more than five years would be granted exit permits. The twelve Prisoners of Zion in jail or in exile would be released. And in future, five years would be the maximum period for refusal of visas, consistent with the need for state secrets and security.

At the Orbit Hotel on the morning he left Moscow, Hawke showed Pimenov the refuseniks' statement. He read it and, without comment, put it in his pocket. When Hawke asked what he could do with the statement, Pimenov replied he could do with it as he wished. Which Hawke took to mean that he could go public with it.[13]

Hawke and Hazel then left for Moscow Airport accompanied by Pimenov whose anti-Semitic remarks, unheard by Hawke, shocked Hazel. There were 105 nationalities in the Soviet Union and only the Jews were unhappy, he told her. As for the Jews who were burnt and gassed in the death camps, their fellow Jews had sent them there and had betrayed them. "These are the people that your husband is trying to promote."[14]

At Rome Airport, Leibler and an Australian embassy car were waiting for the Hawkes. Leibler was shocked to see that Hawke was so emotionally drained that he was unable to walk. As Leibler wrote at the time:

> Hawke had blanks in his memory. He was unable to sit up in the car, and ... the combination of alcohol, physical stress in both Australia and Israel combined with the emotional impact of meeting the refuseniks has made him fall apart. I am terribly concerned.[15]

Hawke was due to speak to a Soviet Jewry Presidium meeting in Rome shortly after his arrival. But Leibler covered for him, saying he was exhausted, and arranged for a day's delay. But he made no mention of Hawke's intoxication and his need for medical attention. Meanwhile, as the Hawkes were flying to Rome, three refuseniks – Alexander Lerner, Victor Brailovsky and Vladimir Prestin – had released the statement in Moscow. As a result, some journalists were waiting at Rome Airport. But Hawke said only that there might be "good news".[16] The next day Hawke elaborated and the news agency AAP-AP reported:

> Bob Hawke said here today that Moscow might take some time before implementing promises to release Jewish prisoners and ease visa regulations for Soviet Jews, but he was confident they "will do it". Those decisions have been taken in principle but I think it will take some time before they are carried out. But once it has been done in principle it seems to me it is a case of mechanics now.[17]

The Australian and international press reported the news prominently.[18] As ECAJ president, Leibler wrote to Soviet Ambassador Basov in Canberra within days to thank him for the Soviet undertakings. Although others might hesitate to express their appreciation until the undertakings had been realised, Leibler said, he had no such reservations.[19]

After Hawke had partially recovered, he met some of the Soviet Jewry movement's leaders who were in Rome for a conference. He reported on his Moscow visit, but cautioned that implementing the agreements might take time. Together with Bourchier, however, Western diplomats in Moscow were more sceptical.[20]

From Rome, Hawke flew to Geneva for the ILO meeting where Pimenov was due to give him a list of the refuseniks who would receive exit visas. But Pimenov, who was fluent in English, refused to speak to him except through an interpreter.[21] Angry and distressed, Hawke telephoned Leibler. Pimenov was accompanied "by a huge hood that he had never seen beforehand" that Hawke assumed was a KGB official because Pimenov refused to see him privately. Through the interpreter, Hawke told Pimenov that he was puzzled and saddened. What was going on? He thought that he had received unqualified guarantees about the refuseniks and prisoners. Pimenov told Hawke that he had misunderstood and that the matter was still being considered. It was as far as Pimenov was prepared to go. He ended the conversation and Hawke did not see him again.[22]

In Moscow, Isai Goldshtein, a refusenik since 1971, told journalists that the Soviet Passport and Visa Office (OVIR) director, General Vladimir Borisenko, had confirmed that the trade union council was not authorised to decide on exit visas, and that Hawke had not received permission to make any statement. Naum Meiman, who chaired the Helsinki Human Rights Monitoring Committee in Moscow, said that he feared that "Hawke had been duped into a disinformation scheme", and Yelena Bonner, wife of the dissident leader, Andrei Sakharov, said that Hawke was "suffering under an illusion because of inexperience in dealing with Soviet negotiators".[23]

In Geneva, after Pimenov had left, a KGB official contacted Hawke and said that implementing the undertakings on refuseniks was linked to the SALT II agreement. Carter and Brezhnev had signed it in Vienna a few days before, but the US Senate still had to approve it. Moscow wanted Hawke to use his influence on the American Jewish community to lobby the Senate to ratify SALT II without amendments. The KGB official told Hawke he would confirm this either before he left Geneva or by a message from the Soviet embassy which said simply, "Go on, Bob". Hawke never received the confirmation and Moscow did not fulfill the promises he had received.[24]

His mission's failure had a devastating impact on Hawke. Even after he overcame his initial despair, the Moscow experience tormented him. He told friends that if the opportunity ever arose he was determined to make amends. As Leibler later wrote to Begin, Hawke's greatest concern was that having raised their expectations, he had let the refuseniks down.[25]

Why did it happen? There is no question that the Soviet trade union officials who met Hawke made him a series of specific promises about the prisoners and refuseniks. There is a question whether the promises were made subject to ratification by higher authority or whether, as Hawke understood them, higher authority had approved them and they were unqualified guarantees. There is no question that Hawke's Russian interlocutors used alcohol to try to manipulate him, and that Hawke's long record of heavy drinking made him susceptible. There remains a question about the extent to which Hawke's susceptibility to alcohol explains why he may have misunderstood what Pimenov and the trade union officials told him.

Bourchier's diplomatic report, however, provides a possible answer to one puzzling aspect: why did the refuseniks, long used to their hopes being raised and dashed, agree to go public this time with a press statement? As he had acknowledged, Hawke was confused and had not been able to provide the answers they wanted about the AUCTU promises. According to a conversation Bourchier had some weeks later with the *Christian Science Monitor*'s Moscow correspondent David Willis, Professor Lerner had told Willis on 6 June that the refuseniks had made their statement at Hawke's insistence on the morning he departed so that he could show it to Pimenov.[26]

What remains very much a matter of speculation is whether the Soviets set out deliberately, at KGB level or elsewhere in the hierarchy, to deceive Hawke and so punish him for his involvement with Soviet Jewry, or whether it was a breakdown of communication between government departments, a regular occurrence even in the Soviet totalitarian regime.

Leibler later told a Hawke biographer:

> The Soviets did not, I think, anticipate a head-on confrontation with Hawke, and they initially gave in to him. That's a theory, but I think it's probably pretty right. But when the hiccups started with SALT all the concessions were frozen.[27]

Hawke himself wrote:

> The Soviets may have thought it desirable to get a message of hope for the refuseniks out of Moscow before the Carter-Brezhnev meeting to prevent possible protests by Jews in Vienna.[28]

As for the KGB approach to Hawke in Geneva, that may have been an attempt to prevent him from using the ILO meeting as a forum to attack the Soviets. But that, too, is speculation.

Hawke returned to Australia in June 1979. After months of indecision, he decided in September to leave the ACTU and stand for parliament. He won the Melbourne seat of Wills at the October 1980 election and went on to defeat Malcolm Fraser in the 1983 election. For the next four years, until November 1987 when he met the Soviet President, Mikhail Gorbachev, in Leningrad, Prime Minister Hawke maintained his interest in Soviet Jewry and the refuseniks. And his fellow Cabinet ministers were very much aware of his views.

In 2010 Hawke recalled:

> The Cabinet knew my position [on Soviet Jewry] and they respected that. It was never an issue at the cabinet level. One interesting point was that Keating came in one time and he said: "Alright for you, and your Jewish mates in Israel. But I've got a whole lot of Muslims in my electorate and it doesn't help me." And I said, "Well, Paul, I'm sorry about that, but that's the way it is, mate."[29]

CHAPTER 18

SOME OF MY CLOSEST FRIENDS ARE KGB

In the lead-up to the Moscow Olympics, George Zoubkov held the title of Intourist vice-president. But he was also a senior KGB agent. After Liebler reported on his meeting with Zoubkov in Singapore in August 1979, Emmanuel Litvinoff summed him up:

> Zoubkov is a character out of classical Russian literature – boastful, bullying, indiscreet yet cunning, almost certainly a cowardly *toochus-lecker* (arse licker) in appropriate circumstances, and no doubt one of the Great Leader's hangmen.[1]

The meeting with Zoubkov was a last-ditch effort to pin down the agreement between Jetset, the AOF and the Moscow Games' organisers.

From the late 1950s to the late 1980s, Litvinoff, the editor of the newsletter *Jews in Eastern Europe,* was Leibler's most important and consistent confidant. Over three decades, they exchanged thousands of letters, reports and publications. Throughout, Leibler relied heavily on the documentation about Soviet Jewry which Litvinoff published in his newsletter, a vital source in the international movement's campaign. But, especially at times of great pressure, Leibler relied even more on Litvinoff's moral and emotional support. The roller-coaster ride Leibler experienced in the lead-up to the 1980 Moscow Games was certainly such a time, and Leibler welcomed Litvinoff's often pungent commentary.

Litvinoff was a study in contrasts to Leibler. A poet, novelist, essayist, journalist and researcher, he was best known in the literary world for his biting verse denunciation in verse of T S Eliot's anti-Semitism. But Litvinoff had a deeply personal connection to the 20th century drama of Soviet Jewry which served as a psychological spur to his involvement. Born in London's Whitechapel in 1915 to parents who had fled Czarist pogroms in Odessa, he was two when his father returned to fight for the Bolshevik Revolution, never to be heard from again. Litvinoff's trilogy *The Faces of Terror* explored in fiction the tragedy of a generation of idealistic Jews who were seduced by revolution and then betrayed by Stalinist repression and anti-Semitism.

The shared historical perspective on Soviet Jewry between Litvinoff and Leibler lent an extra dimension to their correspondence. Of their many exchanges, the story of Leibler's long night in Singapore with Zoubkov has a special place.

Leibler met Zoubkov during a Pacific Asia Travel Association (PATA) meeting. The Soviets saw Singapore as "neutral ground" and had agreed, albeit reluctantly, to talk to Leibler there.[2] In mid-1979, with the Olympics scheduled just twelve months away, and despite eighteen months of threats, warnings and haggling, Moscow had still not finalised the agreement with the AOF and Jetset. The Soviets were still hoping to force the AOF to drop Jetset, and were using smaller Australian travel agents to create confusion. This added to the AOF's ever-increasing worries that Leibler's Soviet Jewry activities would jeopardise the chances of Australian visitors attending the Games.[3]

But Zoubkov and Leibler concluded the Jetset negotiations fairly quickly, and agreed on all the contentious travel issues. Zoubkov, however, was not only a senior KGB appointee within the Intourist organisation; he had been the KGB resident in the Soviet Union's Tel Aviv embassy for six years in the 1940s and 1950s. He spoke Hebrew, and was well informed about Soviet Jewry, Israeli politics and the World Jewish Congress. Not surprisingly, travel issues concluded, the conversation turned to Soviet Jewry.

Over dinner and many vodkas, Zoubkov claimed that Hawke was Leibler's puppet, boasted about his Kremlin connections, and said that while he admired Leibler as a Jewish nationalist, "if he had his way" he would hang all the Jewish nationalists in the Soviet Union from lamp posts.[4] At the same time he assured Leibler that he would try to arrange a visa for Leibler's third visit to Moscow, and even for some of the refuseniks, whose names he cited. In return, however, Leibler had to agree not to see the refuseniks when visiting Moscow, and to ensure that Jewish spectators would not infiltrate the Games' venues and stage protests. If at any stage he felt that Leibler was "double-crossing" him, he had ways to cause him physical harm. But by the early morning hours, the endless vodka toasts were too much for Zoubkov. He became ill and Leibler had to call a doctor.

By now, after two visits to Moscow, Leibler had had some experience with meeting senior KGB officials. But Zoubkov was in a class of his own. Britain had denied him a visa four times and the United States had banned him permanently. When Leibler's Israeli connections heard that he had met Zoubkov, and that he planned to meet him again, they warned him to take special care. In their assessment, Zoubkov had "a licence to kill", and a record to prove it.[5]

Reporting on the meeting, Leibler wrote that it was surreal to be drinking with "a brutal anti-Semitic Stalinist … who [has] a bloody record … babbling away in Hebrew and toasting me with *L'Chaim* (To Life). Or when he telephoned me and [began]: '*Shalom Chabibi, ma nishma?*' (Hullo my dear friend, what's new?)[6]

Having reached what he assumed was an agreement with Zoubkov, and while waiting for the documentation to come from Moscow for signature, Leibler was taken aback by a report in *The Age*.[7] The newspaper quoted Soviet officials as saying that his pro-Jewish activities could jeopardise the chances of many Australians getting tickets. *The Age* also reported that Moscow was unhappy about Hawke's efforts to press for the refuseniks' visas.

When Leibler phoned the Soviet embassy in Canberra to complain about the report, Yuri Pavlov, the acting ambassador, agreed to meet him. Pavlov came to Melbourne on 16 October for the launch of the Hermitage Soviet Art Exhibition by Australia's Jewish Governor General, Sir Zelman Cowen. After a meeting at the Jetset offices, Pavlov had dinner at Leibler's home. The discussion continued until 2 am, but unlike the Singapore meeting, it was sober. And Pavlov was a sharp contrast to Zoubkov.[8]

Pavlov's father had been persecuted during the Stalin era, which

Leibler believed made him more open to concerns about Soviet Jewry. Unlike other Soviet apparatchiks, Pavlov did not deny that Jews experienced discrimination, but said it was due to the Middle East conflict. Also, Jews were seen as clannish and refused to assimilate.

Pavlov was confident, however, that Moscow would release many of the refuseniks before the Games, although the Soviets were concerned that "the more they gave in on these matters, the more the Jews, and particularly the Israelis, interpret this as a sign of weakness and escalate their demands".[9] As for Leibler himself, Pavlov said the Soviet authorities had turned against him so strongly because he was too impatient and too emotional. His shouting match on his first visit with Aaron Vergelis, the Yiddish editor and Soviet apologist, had created a bad impression. Moscow had accepted Jetset as the Australian travel agent, but was wondering what "new Machiavellian tricks" Leibler was plotting.

Pavlov offered Leibler some advice. The Australian Jewish leader was neither President Carter nor Senator Ted Kennedy. He did not have the political clout of a single United States senator. So he had better choose between silent diplomacy or public meetings with the refuseniks. But he could not do both. Nor should Leibler expect too much from any help he might receive from the Australian government. The Soviets, Pavlov said, did not trust either Fraser or Peacock. They regarded Fraser as a Chinese supporter who had rebuffed their invitation to visit the Soviet Union. By comparison, they thought highly of Whitlam.

In agreeing to Pavlov's insistence that, if he received a visa for a third visit, he would not meet the refuseniks, Leibler had Professor Lerner's support. It was more important, Lerner believed, that he should meet the Soviet leadership. But Levanon, the Lishkah/Nativ's head, was not impressed. He told Abraham Kidron, the Israel Ambassador to Australia, that Leibler would be "the first Jew in history to accept conditions such as that laid down by the Russians ..."[10]

Levanon's criticism of Leibler, which he raised with the WJC's president, Phillip Klutznick, marked the most serious difference Leibler had had with the Lishkah/Nativ since Shaul Avigur had recruited him 20 years earlier. But Klutznick assured Leibler that he considered him "a moderate and responsible leader" and that he had the WJC's support.[11]

A few weeks later, President Carter nominated Klutznick to be the United States Secretary of Commerce. When Leibler, still pressing for a visa, met Pavlov again in Canberra with the new KGB resident, Genandy Nayanov, the Soviet officials asked him to persuade Klutznick to overturn the Jackson-Vanik amendment and grant Moscow Most Favoured Nation (MFN) status. The Soviets were especially angry that the Americans had just granted China MFN status, while denying it to Moscow. As the Soviets saw it, Pavlov said, they were consistently making concessions to the Jews on emigration and receiving nothing in return. Leibler was non-committal.[12]

Since their first meeting in mid-October in Melbourne, Pavlov's relationship with Leibler had been cordial, at times even friendly. But their last meeting, by chance at Canberra Airport, was anything but. The Parliamentary Inquiry into "Human Rights in the Soviet Union", with its devastating indictment of Moscow's systematic abuses, had been released on 8 November. Pavlov said the KGB, rightly or wrongly, blamed Leibler for the Inquiry and was determined not to give in to him. Were it to do so, it would be giving in to international anti-Soviet pressures.[13]

On his visits to Moscow, Pavlov claimed further, Leibler had handed out cards as ECAJ president, rather than business cards as Jetset's chairman. By "flaunting" his Jewish interests, he had humiliated some very important officials. Now they were making sure Leibler would not receive a visa. Barely a fortnight later, however, Nayanov called from Canberra to tell Leibler he could expect an invitation from Moscow.

But major international events intervened. On 24 December 1979 the Soviet Union invaded Afghanistan, and everything changed. Hopes for continuing détente were dashed; Carter was angry with Brezhnev who had misled him; the Cold War had made a comeback. The West's initial reaction over boycotting the Moscow Games was mixed, as was that of the international Soviet Jewry movement.[14]

On 17 January 1980 the Brussels Presidium met in London to grapple with the new dilemmas. Were it not for Soviet Jewry, Israel and the Jewish leading organisations would have supported a Games' boycott. But concern for the refuseniks took precedence. Leibler argued against a boycott because he feared that Moscow would use the refuseniks as scapegoats and retaliate against them. Instead, he proposed that the movement should take a low profile, yet be ready for a massive public campaign in the lead-up to the Games.[15] The Presidium agreed.

While in London, Leibler met Levanon and resolved their differences. On the critical issue of having agreed not to see the refuseniks, Leibler made it clear that since the war in Afghanistan conditions had changed fundamentally. Even if they offered him a visa he would refuse it, if it meant no contact with the refuseniks. Which is what he told the embassy when the invitation came on 23 January.[16]

The same day Carter issued an ultimatum to the Soviet Union. If it did not withdraw from Afghanistan by 20 February, the United States would call for a boycott of the Moscow Games. Although as late as October, Fraser had considered attending the Games himself, the invasion of Afghanistan made a deep impact on his world view. He supported Carter's call, and the government began to wind down its support for the AOF.[17] Fraser said the government would pay the $500, 000 it owed as the balance for its contribution, but asked the AOF to pass on his pro-boycott statement to Lord Killanin. The AOF agreed, but announced it would not support a boycott unless the Olympic committees of other main sporting countries did so.[18]

Australian public opinion on a boycott was divided, mostly along party lines. A *Sydney Morning Herald* poll showed Liberal voters were 60 per cent in favour; ALP voters were 65 per cent against.[19] Hawke said that he strongly opposed the Soviet invasion, but it was "improper for the small and dedicated group of athletes to be asked to carry the burden".[20]

Publicly, Leibler continued to speak out against the boycott. But other Jewish leaders, mainly rabbis, supported it. In a sermon,

Sydney's Rabbi Raymond Apple, the Great Synagogue's senior minister, said participating in the Games was "immoral since ... it lent an aura of respectability to the actions and policies of the host nation".[21] Eve Symon, the editor of Sydney's *Australian Jewish Times*, called for a boycott, and added:

> It is hard to understand the loud silence of the Australian Jewish community on this debate. The single voice in the Sydney Jewish community calling for the boycott came from the rabbinate.[22]

In fact, the Sydney and Melbourne communities were not silent. There was significant debate in the Jewish press and at community meetings. But Symon was right to point to the division between the rabbis and the lay leadership.[23] NSW Board president Robert Goot, for example, supported Leibler's proposal that the Jewish community should maintain a low profile, "... [not to] endanger the lives of Soviet Jewry".[24]

Yet while he opposed a boycott publicly, Leibler took a very different position with Fraser privately. In mid-February he wrote to Fraser, anticipating a confrontation between Jetset and the AOF. Although he supported a boycott, he wrote he could not do so publicly because it would endanger the advantages for Soviet Jewry that came from his business relationship with the AOF.[25]

In response, Fraser invited him to a private dinner at the Lodge in Canberra.[26] Despite his adamant public opposition to the Moscow Games, Fraser encouraged Leibler privately to go to Moscow, maintain the links with the refuseniks, and to continue negotiating with the Soviets. When Leibler asked him to approve support for his visit from Ambassador Bourchier and the embassy staff in Moscow, Fraser readily agreed.[27] But translating the prime ministerial approval into practice initially proved difficult. Foreign Affairs officials advised Peacock against becoming involved, and he did not object when Bourchier refused to make his staff or an embassy car available for Leibler.[28] But Fraser overruled Foreign Affairs and made it clear to Peacock that he, in turn, had to overrule the Ambassador.[29]

Again accompanied by Landman, Leibler arrived in Moscow on 17

March for his third visit. An Intourist interpreter and the embassy's First Secretary, John Okeley, welcomed them, steered them through Customs without any questions, and escorted them to their deluxe hotel rooms – a marked contrast to the hostile reception and third-rate accommodation Leibler had received on his second visit. But the pleasantries did not last for long.

After a series of tense meetings with Intourist officials to resolve the still outstanding ticketing and accommodation problems, Leibler asked Koval about meetings with officials on Soviet Jewry.[30] In anger Koval switched to English and berated Leibler.

> You have once more exploited your visit here for ulterior motives. I thought you had learnt a lesson. You were supposed to come here for the Olympics yet you come here to indulge in dirty political intrigues.[31]

Koval then stormed out of the room.

The Soviets made sure Leibler did not talk to any high-ranking officials that dealt with Soviet Jewry. But during his five days in Moscow, Leibler arranged as many meetings as he could with the refuseniks. As he prepared to leave, Prestin and Abramovich asked him to arrange for the Australian embassy to send twelve folders of documents in the diplomatic pouch. They told Leibler that they did not trust either the Dutch or the American embassies, but they believed that Australian diplomats were reliable.

It was a problematic request. Sending sensitive material out of Moscow in any embassy's diplomatic bag was risky. But the refuseniks no longer trusted the Americans because their diplomats had breached assurances that they would not pass some materials to the CIA. The breach had compromised Anatoly Shcharansky – later Natan Sharanksy – and had contributed to his harsh prison sentence. The refuseniks felt they no longer had a reliable link to the international movement and hoped that Australia would fill the gap.[32]

When Leibler brought the documents to the embassy, Bourchier said it was unlikely that Canberra would give permission. Peacock would have to consult Fraser. After a tense wait of 24 hours, Bourchier asked Leibler into the embassy's "cage", the soundproof room that was clear of bugs and wire-taps, to tell him that the Prime Minister had approved the use of the diplomatic bag. While in the "cage", Leibler asked Bourchier if the Australian diplomats could develop their contacts with the refuseniks who needed a reliable "listening post" because the Israelis often "misread the situation or had poor information".[33]

Bourchier admitted that his Minister and the Prime Minister had overruled his objections to the use of the diplomatic bags. With some bitterness, he commented that while Leibler would leave Moscow, he would have to stay on and bear the consequences of the Soviet hostility which Leibler had provoked.[34] As requested, however, Bourchier reached out to some of the refuseniks. But it was his successor, Ambassador Robert Edward "Ted" Pocock and his staff who went out of their way to develop close relations with the leading refuseniks and their families.

Unlike his uneventful arrival, Leibler's departure from Moscow Airport five days later was traumatic. Customs officers searched his luggage, and confiscated photos and trinkets. When a KGB official called him away for interrogation, Okeley, who had accompanied Leibler from the embassy, insisted on following. But other security officials pushed him away and, despite his diplomatic pass, barred his entry to the room where Leibler was being held.

Inside, the KGB officials told Leibler to strip. He refused, and declared he was not a criminal. When the officials suggested he was guilty of espionage, Leibler challenged them to charge him. They backed off and told him to empty his pockets. Leibler handed over his list of fifteen refuseniks and their addresses, but somehow managed to hide the rough notes of his meetings. After he caught his flight and had time to reflect, Leibler was both angry and exhausted. The KGB interrogation had been harrowing.[35]

On arrival in London, Leibler's main message was that the refuseniks did not want to link their cause to Afghanistan or other Cold War issues. And they opposed the calls for boycotting the Games. They had told him: "It is easy for Jews to be heroes at our expense in the streets of London, Paris or Tel Aviv".[36]

Leibler reported that the refuseniks were disappointed when he told them that Israel might have to join the boycott if the majority of Western countries pulled out. In Jerusalem he conveyed the refuseniks' views to Prime Minister Menachem Begin, Begin's adviser Yehuda Avner, the newly appointed Foreign Minister Yitzhak Shamir, Professor Ya'akov Roi, an expert on Soviet Jewry, and Yosef Govrin, head of the Foreign Ministry's Soviet desk. Leibler came away from his meeting with Begin, who supported a boycott, concerned that "the man has a hatred of Russia, but a total lack of understanding and depth about the [Soviet] Jewish problem".[37]

By late May, with only six weeks to the Games' opening ceremony, it was clear that Moscow would not release the refuseniks as a goodwill gesture nor, at the very least, allow Jewish tourists to meet them. Journalists reported that the Soviet authorities planned to clear Moscow of dissidents who would either be sent to prison, exile, or allowed to leave voluntarily. Professor Lerner was quoted as saying that he and his wife planned to go to the Ukraine:

> If I did not go by myself, I am sure the authorities would send me away somewhere of their own choosing and maybe I wouldn't be able to come back at all … The climate has changed. While our leaders were interested in détente with the West, public support in America and Europe for our cause helped us. Now it only makes the Soviet authorities more determined to do as they want with us, no matter what the West thinks.[38]

CHAPTER 19

IT'S ABOUT THE REFUSENIKS

In 2008, as some Australian politicians called on athletes to boycott the Beijing Olympic Games and protest against China's human rights abuses in Tibet, Malcolm Fraser disagreed strongly. For the first time publicly, he also claimed he had been wrong to support the boycott campaign against the Moscow Olympics in 1980. Looking back, the former Prime Minister said it had been a bad and divisive policy.

At the time, however, he had pursued it vigorously.[1] By the time the AOF met on 24 May 1980 to decide whether to go to Moscow, Fraser had told his Cabinet that President Carter and all the European leaders he had met favoured a boycott; he had issued scores of statements calling for it; he had authorised a booklet for national distribution and had lobbied the AOF strongly, sending it 37 telegrams.

Although Australia's IOC representative, Kevan Gosper, president Syd Grange and secretary-general Julius (Judy) Patching favoured a boycott, vice-president David McKenzie recruited enough votes (6–5) to defeat the proposal. Fraser had invested great effort, expense, and his political standing. But he had lost. It was seen as his first significant political defeat in five years. Comparing the Moscow Olympics with Hitler's 1936 Berlin Games he said: "I pray that the Soviet Union will not interpret this and other decisions of Olympic Federations as a weakening of Western will, as Nazi Germany did in 1936."[2] The Leader of the Opposition, Bill Hayden, supported the AOF's decision. But most Australian newspaper editorials favoured a boycott, as did a majority – 59 to 33 per cent – of public opinion.[3]

Australia's Jewish communities did not oppose the AOF's decision or call for a boycott. But they held a series of protests and rallies in Melbourne, Sydney, Brisbane and Perth, calling for the release of the Prisoners of Zion and all refuseniks who had been waiting for longer than five years. In a letter to the Soviet Ambassador Nikolai Sudarikov, Leibler warned that if Moscow did not respond positively, the international Jewish leadership might not be able to control extremists from disrupting the events.[4]

The Soviets, however, did not view Leibler's warning, echoed by some other Jewish leaders, as a credible threat. Nor did Leibler himself. Writing to the Lishkah/Nativ he lamented the lack of any coordinated international action during the Games, as each community "did its own thing".[5]

The Moscow Games, blanketed by heavy Soviet security, concluded without major disruption from Jews or human rights supporters. Despite the solidarity rallies to coincide with the Games, there was a sense among Jewish communities in Australia that they had done too little, too late. Goot summed up the widespread ambivalence: "Although we felt in our Jewish hearts that we should be calling for a boycott, our heads ruled."[6]

Fraser's views on Moscow meanwhile had won praise in the international Soviet Jewry movement. The WJC recorded their gratitude, and the Lishkah/Nativ commended his readiness to let the refuseniks send highly sensitive documents out of the Soviet Union via the Australian embassy's diplomatic bag. The Israelis told Leibler that the material was invaluable.[7] The most notable recognition for Fraser came from the International B'nai B'rith who awarded him their annual Human Rights Medal. Four American presidents, Nobel Prize winners and Israeli leaders were among its previous recipients. Fraser's citation referred to his "sustained opposition to discrimination on the basis of race, color or creed; his commitment to providing in Australia a refuge for the dispossessed from many parts of the world, and his contribution to the cause of freedom and peace".[8]

Foreign Affairs advised Fraser not to go to Washington to receive the award. But when he found he could not receive it in absentia, he flew to Washington with a retinue of staff and senior public servants, including the Foreign Affairs Secretary, Peter Henderson. Some Labor politicians derided Fraser's links to the Jewish community, as did some newspaper cartoonists.⁹ But the Melbourne commentator Douglas Wilkie, who noted that Fraser's mother, born Una Woolf, came from a Jewish family, said that Fraser shared a sympathy for "an embattled Israel" with Hawke.¹⁰ After discussion with Fraser, Leibler decided not to attend the Washington ceremony to avoid further suggestions that he and the Australian Jewish community had "orchestrated" the award.¹¹

In his acceptance speech, Fraser outlined his wider foreign policies and attacked the Soviet Union. He castigated America's NATO allies for failing to assist the United States sufficiently in Afghanistan, and referred to "the capacity for self-delusion as a critical factor in the West today". Soviet policy, Fraser said, had demonstrated again that Nazi Germany was its only rival in the 20th century for adding to the sum of human misery.¹²

Until his loss to Hawke in the 1983 elections, Fraser continued his criticism of the Soviets on Afghanistan and human rights. In February 1982 Alan Cadman, the Liberal MP for Mitchell, a north-west Sydney seat, asked Fraser in the House of Representatives about the Soviet Union's "harsh and cruel treatment" of Jews.¹³

Fraser expressed the government's concern. He noted the increased harassment of visa applicants and the growing numbers of rejected applications. Some refuseniks had also been tried on false charges and sent to prison and labour camps. He continued:

At a time when the Soviet Union is participating in international conferences dealing with the Helsinki Accords, this violation of human rights is even more noteworthy. There is a continuing suppression of Jewish religious and cultural expression. This occurs against a background of hostile propaganda in the Soviet media.

The Government is in full accord with the United States Government's strenuous efforts in negotiations with the Soviet Union to allow free emigration of Jews and others who wish to leave the Soviet Union.

The Soviet Government's actions in this regard are totally unacceptable to everyone concerned with human rights and, indeed, must be condemned. They are among the factors

inhibiting an improvement in relations between the Soviet
Union and the United States and its Western allies.[14]

It was the strongest statement from any Australian prime minister
about Soviet Jews. But it also reflected the deteriorating situation they
faced in the early 1980s, which became known as "The Dark Years".
During this period, the fate of Natan Sharansky, the best-known
Prisoner of Zion, reflected the pessimism within the Soviet Jewry
movement. Arrested on trumped-up charges of spying for the United
States, Sharansky was sentenced to thirteen years of forced labour
in a Siberian prison. Australian parliamentarians joined colleagues
throughout the West who took up Sharansky's cause. His wife Avital
pursued his cause tirelessly. Allowed to leave for Israel shortly after
their Moscow wedding, she lobbied government leaders and the
international media to press the Soviets for her husband's release.

During his visit to Israel in June 1982, Australia's Foreign Affairs
Minister Tony Street met Avital. She told him how the prison
authorities had confiscated Sharansky's prayer book and Jewish
calendar and had restricted access to his family. He had suffered
months of solitary confinement, he had gone on hunger strikes to
draw attention to his plight, and his health had worsened.[15] Street
promised Avital that the Australian government would try to help.[16]
In October, the former *Bulletin* editor, Peter Coleman, who became
the Liberal member for the Sydney seat of Wentworth, asked Street
about Sharansky. It gave the Foreign Affairs Minister opportunity to
outline the government's diplomatic interventions.[17]

A variety of factors had contributed to create "The Dark Years". In
January 1980 Moscow tightened the emigration regulations. All visa
applicants now had to have a certificate from an immediate family
member in Israel confirming "first degree kinship". This made it
almost impossible for Jews to receive exit visas, and its effects were
immediate. In 1979, 51,000 Soviet Jews left. The new restrictions
reduced the flow by 60 per cent in 1980.[18]

In the following years, the numbers declined even more
dramatically. By 1982 less than 3000 were allowed to leave. The
decline in emigration demoralised the Soviet Jewry movement,

already divided over *neshira*, the "drop-out" factor. The *noshrim* numbers had risen from around 60 per cent of emigrants in early 1980 to a high of 78 per cent by the year's end.

The *noshrim* debate, or as some dubbed it, the *noshrim* "war", divided into pro-Israel advocates and "freedom of choice" proponents. Writing about the "war" some 20 years later, Steven Windmueller, an American analyst, argued it went far beyond the emigration issue itself. It reflected "two definitions for the Jewish future that would continue to have significant implications [for] … the Israel-Diaspora connection."[19]

At the time, however, the "war" not only divided the movement, but also contributed to the decline in emigration. Evaluating the reasons for the decline, the Australian embassy in Moscow cited two other factors: the Washington-Moscow Cold War tensions, and Moscow's growing concern that the "brain drain" of Jewish scientists was hampering its efforts to compete with Western technology.[20]

At every opportunity, Leibler attacked the *noshrim* surge. He argued it betrayed the Soviet Jewish movement; that the *noshrim* would lose their Jewish identity in the West; and that the Soviet Jewish activists bitterly condemned the practice. He claimed that as long as the nationalist movement was "Zionist" and tied to Israel, Marxist/Leninist ideology could accept it as a movement of national reunification. As it had increasingly become a movement of free emigration, it had given Moscow the "excuse" to cut back dramatically.[21]

The "freedom of choice" proponents, mainly American leaders, argued that Jewish leaders in the West who did not make *aliya* i.e. emigrate to Israel, had no right to impose different standards on Russian Jews. And if the organised Jewish communities did not welcome and help the "drop-outs", then either non-Jewish organisations or non-Zionist Jewish groups such as Chabad would do so.

The heated debates on the issue at world forums were repeated in Australia. At a VJBD meeting the Board's acting president, Phil Symons, supported the Israeli position against the Jewish Welfare

Society's president, Walter Lippmann, who argued that the Jewish community had a duty to help Soviet Jews wherever they wanted to go. But the Australian Soviet Jewry campaign's new chair, Sam Salcman, and most Board delegates, supported the Zionist movement's view.[22]

As emigration declined significantly, the international movement increasingly focused on the Prisoners of Zion and the refuseniks. In the Soviet Union, they faced harassment, intimidation and arrest on false charges which included treason, espionage, anti-Soviet propaganda, "malicious hooliganism", draft evasion and "parasitism". The latter charge was especially unjust as it was usually made against those who had lost their jobs because they had applied to leave.

In October 1983 Australia's embassy reported that a Colonel Dragunski had formed an anti-Zionist committee which had official sanction. The new committee likened Zionism to Nazism and "Begin and his thugs" to the Nazis and their atrocities. The embassy said the new body's main purpose was to harass the refuseniks.

> Although of course the committee is not officially anti-Semitic, its establishment will allow an official vehicle for the expression of [suitably phrased] anti-Semitic views.[23]

The embassy's assessment proved all too accurate. In June 1984, the Minister for the Arts, Barry Cohen, met Litvinoff, who was visiting Australia. In an interview with the *Canberra Times*, Litvinoff said that conditions for Soviet Jewry had worsened since Konstantin Chernenko had become President after Yuri Andropov's death in February 1984. Explaining how it was no longer possible to telephone Soviet Jewish activists and that not all mail was getting through, Litvinoff described the bleak outlook:

> The Soviet authorities could not be more bloody-minded than they are at the moment. The brusque rudeness with which the West German Foreign Minister, Hans-Dietrich Genscher, was dismissed when he attempted to raise human rights issues with his counterpart, Andrei Gromyko, was amazing. You have to go back to the Stalinist days to find that behaviour.[24]

The *Canberra Times* reported that Australia's Foreign Affairs Minister Hayden had had a similar response from Gromyko during his visit to Moscow a few weeks earlier when he expressed concern about the health of dissident Dr Andrei Sakharov and his wife Yelena Bonner. Gromyko responded that the Soviet Union would not be told how to deal with the Sakharovs by other countries and then said: "The conversation on this subject ends here."[25]

The Dark Years and the loss of momentum from the decline in emigration posed a challenge to the Soviet Jewry movement: how to maintain the involvement of its grassroots activists and volunteers. When Goot stepped down after nearly ten years of leadership in Sydney, he contrasted the attendance of 60 at a protest rally in September 1981, with the nearly 3000 who had come to the Sydney Town Hall rally in 1970.[26] And when Melbourne's Sam Salcman succeeded Goot as chair of the Australian Committee for Soviet Jewry, Salcman's first public statement summed up the problem:

> Our task, however unproductive it may appear at the moment, must be to assure our Soviet brethren that we are aware of their plight and are using all our endeavours to shore-up their morale. [We have to remind the world and the Soviet authorities that our concern for our Jewish brothers in the Soviet will not abate.[27]

Under Salcman, the campaign added establishing relationships with Soviet Jews to holding protests and rallies. Volunteers sent educational and cultural materials. Schools, women's groups and synagogues were encouraged to send greeting cards to prisoners and refuseniks, especially for Jewish festivals. Salcman introduced a program which twinned Australian and Soviet children for their bar and bat mitzvah celebrations, especially the sons and daughters of refuseniks. Working with the Women's Campaign for Soviet Jewry in London, known as the Thirty-Fives Committee, Salcman's twinning campaign also caught on in Sydney's community. Sydney community leader Diane Shteinman expanded the program when she followed Salcman as the ACSJ chair in 1985.

As an active ALP member, Salcman had to deal with the Party's Socialist Left and Bill Hartley. In keeping with his extreme anti-Israel activities, Hartley praised an American Jewish anti-Zionist writer,

Alfred Lilienthal, who denied that there was any persecution of Jews in the Soviet Union. In a charged debate at a Victorian ALP conference, Salcman pointed out that the far-right and anti-Semitic League of Rights were the main distributors of Lilienthal's publications.[28] But in 1982, a year before Hawke became Prime Minister, Hartley and the Socialist Left still had enough influence to prevent the ALP's federal conference from passing Salcman's resolution to condemn Soviet anti-Semitism.

After Hawke defeated Fraser in 1983, however, the balance of power in the Labor Party shifted away from the Socialist Left to its more pro-American and pro-Israel elements. Prominent Jewish leaders and businessmen had supported Hawke during the election campaign and many in the Jewish community welcomed his victory. In one of his first acts after his election, he sent a message to the World Conference on Soviet Jewry in Jerusalem, which reinforced his widespread popularity.

Leibler wrote to Hawke:

> It was a very proud moment for me when 1500 Jewish leaders ... demonstrated their appreciation to the Prime Minister of Australia ... for [your] well known record of intervening on behalf of Soviet Jewry.[29]

But Hawke also sought to rebuild ties with the Soviet Union. Shortly after his election he renewed the cultural, sporting and trading links which Fraser had cut after the Soviet invasion of Afghanistan. Hawke argued that his predecessor's restrictions lacked consistency. While he had tried to ban athletes from the Moscow Olympics, Hawke said Australia had continued to export wool to the Soviet Union which included bales from Nareen, Fraser's property in Victoria's Western District. The government would continue to criticise the Soviet invasion and push for a withdrawal, but would not use it "for political purposes".[30]

Having replaced him as the ALP's leader just a month before the election, Hawke had offered Hayden the portfolio of his choice. Hayden became Foreign Minister and, given the tension between the two men, Hawke took care to intervene as little as possible. But the new relationship cut across Hawke's previous close friendship with Leibler. Combined with his prime ministerial responsibilities, it meant Leibler found access increasingly difficult. In July 1983, Leibler told Hawke that "he was harder to get at than his predecessor". Hawke responded that "he was worth waiting for".[31]

In September 1983, Leibler met John Bowen, Hawke's adviser on Eastern Europe, and other officials in Canberra to discuss policy on Soviet Jewry. Foreign Affairs had proposed that Hawke should write to President Yuri Andropov, but Leibler warned that would be too confrontationist, and advised working instead through the new Soviet Ambassador, Evgeni Samoteikin. Despite the rapport he established with Foreign Affairs officials, Leibler found his relationship with Hayden remained tense. In 1980, when Hayden was Leader of the Opposition, Leibler had had angry exchanges with him, urging the ALP leader not to meet the PLO's Yasser Arafat. Yoram Dinstein, an international law professor at Tel Aviv University who worked with Leibler on Soviet Jewry, met Hayden during his visit to Israel and found him "totally unsympathetic". Dinstein reported that Hayden so resented the pressure that Leibler had put on him not to meet Arafat, that Hayden went out of his way to meet him.[32]

The tensions between Hayden and the Jewish community's leadership increased in October 1983, after he approved the establishment of a PLO office in Canberra. Leibler again sought to meet Hawke to express his concern at the government's "tilt against Israel". After an ECAJ meeting with Hawke on 6 October, he asked Leibler to stay behind for five minutes. The two men embraced, and Hawke assured Leibler that he would not let Hayden act again against Israel. Nor had he forgotten Soviet Jewry.[33]

Hayden was more sympathetic on Soviet Jewry than on Israel.[34] Whether in his talks with Soviet Foreign Minister Andrei Gromyko in Moscow, where Gromyko refused to discuss human rights issues at all, or in promoting Australia's role after being elected to the United Nations Commission on Human Rights, Hayden spoke out. When Leibler asked him to raise Soviet Jewry, Hayden could reply that Australia had already expressed its concern "over the repressive measures used against minority and ethnic groups seeking, by non-violent means, to assert their cultural and religious identities, and over the difficulties faced by Soviet Jews who wish to emigrate".[35]

CHAPTER 20

GORBACHEV, GENEVA AND *GLASNOST*

By the time they visited Australia in 1999 for a joint lecture tour, Mikhail Gorbachev and General Norman Schwarzkopf had been out of the news for a decade. But they had each made history. So they attracted audiences, some willing to pay $1000 for the best seats. Of the two men, Gorbachev had not only made history; he had changed it. But when he spoke to Australian audiences in Russian, with an interpreter translating every few minutes, it made him seem pedestrian. Away from the dramatic television images of the late 1980s and early 1990s, the man who had presided over the collapse of the most powerful empire in history appeared reduced in stature, more like the friendly visiting uncle from Moscow.

During their Melbourne lectures, the two men were guests at a reception at Raheen, the home of Richard and Jeanne Pratt. My wife Aura and I knew that Gorbachev's policies of *glasnost* and *perestroika* had eventually led to the great exodus of a million Soviet Jews. We had visited the refuseniks in his early years as President, and my wife had been in the Soviet Union again just two years later when "the gates were open". When we had a chance to do so at Raheen, we told him that the Jewish people would always remember what he had done.

Gorbachev listened carefully, and for a moment I thought the purple patch on his head had turned darker. Then he answered through his interpreter:

> Thank you, but I never wanted them to leave. They were our most educated people. We had invested so much in them. We needed them. I wanted them to stay. We lost so much when they left us. But I had no choice. The world wouldn't let us keep them.

Explaining himself in 1999, Gorbachev was being consistent. When he succeeded Chernenko in 1985 as President, Gorbachev believed that if he wanted "to reconstruct" the Soviet economy – *perestroika* – his country could not afford to lose the "human capital" represented by the disproportionately high numbers of Jewish scientists and technologists.

In the short term, therefore, the Gorbachev regime reduced emigration even further, and clamped down harder on religious and cultural activities. It took until mid-1987 before Gorbachev realised that he could not reconstruct the Soviet economy without the West, and that he could not win the West unless he changed Moscow's policies on human rights. But when it came to letting Jews go, he did so reluctantly.

Gorbachev had taken over in Moscow in 1985, just weeks after Ronald Reagan had begun his second term in the White House. The new Washington-Moscow relationship offered the international Soviet Jewry movement new hope. It was ten years since Moscow had signed the Helsinki Accords, but Soviet Jewry's plight had not improved. Reagan, however, had increasingly shown he was prepared to confront the Soviets on human rights, and Britain's Margaret Thatcher had concluded that the West and the new Soviet leader "could do business together". There were prospects for change.

Leibler had always understood that the main game was between Washington and Moscow. As he wrote to Morris Abram, the chairman of the National Conference on Soviet Jewry:

> It is via the United States and not the backwoods of Australia that the destiny of Soviet Jewry will be resolved.[1]

Leibler's relationship with Abram, conducted mainly through extensive correspondence, proved invaluable to both. During the five years (1983–88) that Abram led the mainstream American Soviet Jewry movement, he facilitated Leibler's access to the highest levels of the United States government. This enhanced his already strong reputation as an international Jewish leader.

For his part, Leibler provided Abram with an informed and independent sounding board. Leibler knew the refuseniks first-hand, he had travelled regularly and widely in the Jewish world for 25 years, and as an Australian, he stood outside the in-fighting that beset American Jewish politics. Leibler also encouraged Abram's pro-Israel stance, especially in the debates over the "drop-outs". Abrams strengthened Leibler's hand in dealing with the World Jewish Congress and its president Edgar Bronfman, whose approach on Soviet Jewry too frequently reminded Leibler of Nahum Goldmann's.

For all that they shared on Soviet Jewry, however, Leibler and Abram were markedly different in personality, style, political background and involvement with Judaism. Abram had not had a bar mitzvah[2] and his first wife was initially not Jewish, although she later converted within her Reform congregation. By contrast, Leibler had grown up Orthodox, had been a Bnei Akiva youth leader, married a rabbi's daughter, and was steeped in Jewish observance and tradition. In January 1984, Abram wrote to Leibler:

> Getting to know you has been one of the pleasures of this new
> role for me. I just wish you weren't so far away for I would
> enjoy seeing you as a steady diet.[3]

Leibler reciprocated the expression of new-found friendship. His earlier and long-standing relationship with Litvinoff reflected a similar "Odd Couple" quality. Despite the tyranny of distance, perhaps also because of it, Leibler found he could be much more open with his international correspondents about his fears, failures and anxieties than with his Australian friends and colleagues. The total face-to-face time Leibler spent with each man – in five years with Abrams and in 30 with Litvinoff – could be counted in days or, at most, weeks. But their letters amounted to hundreds of pages in Abram's case, and thousands in Litvinoff's.

By the time Leibler first met Abram in 1983, the "small-town boy from Georgia" was already one of the outstanding public figures of his generation. A brilliant law student with degrees from the universities of Georgia, Chicago and Oxford, his work as a civil rights activist had led to major changes in Georgia's voting system. He had been president of the American Jewish Committee, and in 1964 had chaired the founding meeting of the American Jewish Conference on Soviet

Jewry (AJCSJ). In 1971 it became the National Conference on Soviet Jewry (NCSJ), and Abram returned as chairman. While heading the NCSJ in 1986, Abram became Chairman of the Conference of Presidents of Major American Jewish Organisations. By then he had also been the President of Brandeis University and had served four American presidents. From 1989–93, he served the fifth, President George Bush Snr, as the United States Ambassador to the UN in Geneva.[4]

After his death in 2000, one of his obituaries described him as a giant among leaders:

> Yet one of the most remarkable things about Morris Abram was his ability to enter these arenas with southern graciousness, a military sense of rectitude and a Jewish sense of justice all at once.[5]

It was these qualities that Abram brought to the Soviet Jewry movement after 1983.

In September 1985, the Soviet Jewry Presidium met in Washington, and Leibler joined a delegation of seven Jewish leaders in which he was the only non-American to meet Reagan in the Oval Office. For the Australian, the White House meeting was an emotional high point in the 25 years since he had immersed himself in the campaign. As Reagan posed for the "photo opportunity" with Leibler, he told him to keep protesting to him and other Western leaders.

> The more noise you make, it's easier for me to tell the Bolshies that I'm under tremendous pressure and that they should do something about the Jews.[6]

In his presentation to Reagan, Abram said that while the United States should not make Soviet Jewry's "right to leave" a precondition to arms limitation agreements, the issue of trust was critical. If the Soviet Union could not be trusted to grant basic human rights to Soviet Jewry, as undertaken in the Helsinki Accords in 1975, then the world could not believe its readiness to keep agreements on disarmament.

In his response, Reagan made it clear he did not trust the Soviets unless he could monitor any agreement. While he expressed his personal support for Soviet Jewry and promised to deliver, he said that discretion was better than public confrontation. He would not make any public statements either during or after the Geneva summit, but he would tell the Russians that the Jews were applying great pressure.[7]

The next day, another leadership delegation testified before a Congressional Subcommittee, and again Abram invited Leibler to join them. In his presentation, Leibler told the Subcommittee that Soviet Jewry had to be on the agenda at the Reagan-Gorbachev summit, because "it is a critical benchmark for measuring real progress towards the improved relationship between the super powers". He concluded:

> The renaissance of Soviet Jewry is one of the great inspirational sagas of the 20th century. After 60 years of Communism, Stalinist repression, and systematic discrimination, the rebirth of Jewish identity in the Soviet Union has been a triumph of the human spirit and a testament to the persistence of faith, tradition, and civilisation over tyranny, ideology, and the police state. It is the only movement since the Russian Revolution to force real and fundamental change, albeit temporary, in the Soviet system.[8]

The first Reagan-Gorbachev summit was held in Geneva in November 1985. With 4000 other journalists, I also came to Geneva for *The Bulletin* and the Channel Nine Network. Leibler was already there, attending WJC meetings, protest rallies, and giving radio interviews. More than I had expected, the summit had attracted the Soviet Jewry movement's activists, especially university students. They distributed press kits, lobbied American officials and any Soviet counterparts who would speak to them, and staged demonstrations. The larger organisations took full-page advertisements in the *International Herald Tribune*. Soviet Jewry may not have been high on the Reagan-Gorbachev agenda, but it was high on the news media's agenda. During a summit where news of the mostly secret summit talks was hard to come by, Soviet Jewry helped to fill the gap.[9]

In February 1986, Soviet Jewry not only made the news but also captured headlines internationally. Sharansky was released as part of an East-West prisoner exchange. As the most famous Prisoner of Zion, he had become a heroic figure within the movement. The pictures of him walking towards freedom on Glienicke Bridge, where the border between East and West Germany ran through the bridge's middle, created widespread celebration in Israel and the Jewish world. His reunion with his wife Avital featured in Jewish media everywhere. All through 1986 many Jewish parents, my wife and I among them, named their daughters Avital in her honour.

Sharansky's release had a wider significance. He was also the first political prisoner whom Gorbachev had freed in response to Reagan's insistent demands. Just a month later, Australia's representative at the UN Commission on Human Rights expressed concern about the repression of minority ethnic groups, especially in the Baltic area, and the ongoing violations of human rights, especially in Afghanistan. Although Australia welcomed Sharansky's release, he said the Soviet Union still needed "to adopt a more flexible and humane approach to Soviet Jews wishing to emigrate, a fundamental right of all citizens".[10]

The Australian government continued to raise the issue at the UN. But Foreign Affairs officials nevertheless advised a ten-member all-party parliamentary delegation, led by House of Representatives Speaker Joan Child, not to raise the subject on their visit to the Soviet Union. Child decided to ignore the advice.

An impressive parliamentarian who only months earlier had become Australia's first woman Speaker, Child was known for her outspoken dedication to social justice. After the sudden loss of her husband at age 46, she had raised five boys as a single mother by working as a cleaner, electorate secretary and trade union official. The Melbourne south-eastern electorate of Henty, which she had won for the Labor Party, had a large Jewish population, and many of her supporters, including Salcman and Magid, were Jewish community leaders. By the time she led the delegation to Moscow she had been to Israel, had talked about Soviet Jewry in parliament, and had spoken at protest rallies.[11]

In Moscow, Child and her delegation tried to raise Soviet Jewry with former Foreign Minister, Andrei Gromyko, now Chairman of the Supreme Soviet Presidium. But he launched into a diatribe for 45 minutes and did not allow questions. When he finished speaking and stood up to leave, Child stopped him:

> You said you would give us an hour. We all have questions for you. You will give us another cup of coffee and then give us equal time for questions and discussion.[12]

Despite his protestations, Child insisted that he remain. He did, for two hours. The Speaker told him that Soviet Jewry was a matter of international importance which transcended national boundaries. Gromyko replied: "You did not cross the world just to free a few Jews." Child asked: "Isn't it better to light a candle than to be in the darkness?"[13] When he tried to question her further, she told him that he was interrupting her, that he had had his time, and now it was her turn. Before he could leave, Child made sure Gromyko had an updated list of refuseniks and a list of Soviet citizens seeking family reunion to Australia.

The Child delegation also visited Professor Lerner, and met with 20 refuseniks. Child conveyed Hawke's greetings, especially to those he had met in 1979, as well as messages from Australian Jewish leaders. Impressed with their courage, Child promised that Australia would do its best to help them. But she explained that its influence was limited.[14] Back in Australia, Child continued to campaign.[15] On 31 December, to mark the New Year, she publicised the plight of two Prisoners of Zion, jailed for teaching Hebrew.

In March 1987, when the Soviet Foreign Minister Eduard Shevardnadze landed at Fairbairn's Royal Australian Air Force base, he became the highest ranking Soviet official to visit Australia. But he did not expect the NSW Jewish Board of Deputies president, Professor Graham de Vahl Davis, to be in the official welcoming party. Nor did anybody else. Flashing his driver's licence at the RAAF guards and Federal police, de Vahl Davis had evaded security and joined the line of dignitaries. When it was his turn to greet Shevardnadze, he asked why there were Jews imprisoned in the Soviet Union. The Foreign Minister was taken aback, and the news media had a field day.[16]

Hawke and Hayden also raised the Soviet Jewry issue with

Shevardnadze, and after their meeting, Hawke called Leibler to brief him. He said he had spent half an hour discussing Soviet Jewry and human rights with Shevardnadze, and had made clear his own strong feelings. The Soviet Foreign Minister listened "without responding with any heat or anger", Hawke said, and explained that Moscow was reviewing its nationalities policies. But he had rejected Hawke's claim about freedom of religion and teaching Hebrew. Hawke passed on lists of refuseniks and Shevardnadze promised to review them. Summing up the meeting, Hawke told Leibler that he could be "warily optimistic". He added that "having burnt his fingers" previously, he would not make any predictions. But he was hopeful.[17]

Hawke and Hayden were not the only Australian politicians to question Shevardnadze about Soviet Jewry. When he visited New South Wales, Labor's Premier Barrie Unsworth also raised the issue. When Shevardnadze denied that Jews were prevented from leaving the Soviet Union, Unsworth asked pointedly: "Then why are the people downstairs demonstrating?"[18]

A parliamentary delegation, comprising Liberal Senator Robert Hill, Labor MHR Alan Griffiths, and Australian Democrats Senator Michael Macklin tried to present Shevardnadze with a petition signed by 131 federal parliamentarians, calling on Moscow to allow free emigration. At first he refused to accept it. By the time he changed his mind, the three parliamentarians had left Canberra. So the Soviet embassy offered to meet the parliamentarians when they returned.[19] It was a sign that change was in the wind. Soviet embassy officials had never been as accommodating on Soviet Jewry before. Within months the signs of change grew even stronger.

CHAPTER 21

TEN DAYS IN MOSCOW

The "three room deluxe suites" at Moscow's Hotel Intourist in September 1987 promised more than they delivered. A travel brochure on the bedside table offered package tours to "Marvellous Siberia – Land of Attractions". But hot water, toilet facilities and lighting were all uncertain. Breakfast was an unvarying buffet of boredom: cold peas, coleslaw, shredded beetroot, boiled eggs, weak tea and stale bread. But at least our floor's "babushka", the matronly lady who monitored the guests' comings and goings for the KGB, was happy. She was certainly proud of her full set of gold teeth.

My wife Aura and I were staying at the Hotel Intourist with Isi Leibler and his wife Naomi. Just weeks earlier, Leibler had received an unexpected invitation to come for Rosh Hashanah – the Jewish New Year – from Boris Gramm, the Moscow Synagogue Community Centre's president. This followed Leibler's meeting with Gramm in Budapest in May 1987, the first World Jewish Congress meeting in an Eastern Bloc country. Leibler had asked Gramm about returning to Moscow, but did not expect a positive answer.[1] The Gramm invitation telex in mid-August was a complete surprise. Leibler asked me to join him, document the meetings, and report on the visit. It was a dream opportunity. As it was for Aura, a professional singer who had sung in demonstrations for Soviet Jewry in Sydney and Melbourne all through the 1970s and 1980s.

But our excitement paled by comparison to Leibler's. As he saw it, he was on the most important mission in three decades of campaigning. Arriving in Moscow for the first time since 1980, after repeated refusals and a devastating visa revocation, he was a mix of agitation and anxiety, determination and suspicion. He had had his hopes dashed before. In 1986, he had received visas for himself and wife Naomi, but a week before departure, the Soviets revoked them without giving any reasons.[2]

Adding to his emotional determination was the encouragement he had received from Prime Minister Bob Hawke. In a lengthy Melbourne meeting, Hawke had enthusiastically endorsed the visit and confirmed that Ambassador Ted Pocock would provide the Moscow embassy's resources – car and driver, diplomatic escorts and interpreters – to support Leibler's mission.[3]

Ambassador Pocock had already earned the refuseniks' respect and affection. A senior Australian diplomat with a reputation for independence and forthrightness before his Moscow post, Pocock had shown his support from the time he arrived in 1984. In the three years that followed, he became one of the Australian diplomatic service's unsung heroes for his contribution to the refuseniks' cause and human rights. During our visit to Moscow we heard much about the personal concern which Pocock and his wife Meg had shown for the refuseniks and their families. Their warm feelings for the Pococks in turn were obvious at the Ambassador's farewell party, which we attended in Moscow. Leibler was so impressed that he nominated Pocock for an international Jewish award, only to hear from Foreign Affairs that Australian diplomats did not receive awards for doing their duty.[4]

But as noted in his *Sydney Morning Herald* obituary after his death in 2013, Pocock had always done more than his duty:

> Together with two or three other Western missions, he provided protection for refuseniks and other dissidents by ensuring that the Russian authorities knew they were watching over them.[5]

The refuseniks regarded Pocock as unique. He had reached out to them beyond the friendship shown even by the American and Dutch ambassadors. Only Pocock had held an end of the year party to which he had invited 25 refuseniks – officially enemies of the state – to drink Australian wines alongside the most senior, and discomfited, Soviet Foreign Ministry officials and their Kremlin colleagues.[6]

In August 1986, when the prospects for leaving the Soviet

Union were especially bleak, and at the risk of incurring Moscow's displeasure, Pocock hosted a lunch at the Australian embassy for the leading refuseniks, Alexander Lerner, Alexander Joffe and Vladimir Prestin.[7] Some four months later, Pocock invited all the refuseniks on Speaker Joan Child's list to the embassy. (Child had presented her list to the Soviets during her visit in July 1986.)

After a third lunch for refuseniks in June 1987, Pocock's assessment was not optimistic.

> Soviet Policy on Jewish refuseniks continues to be arbitrary and opportunistic. Two of the 17 families on the list passed to the USSR Supreme Soviet by Madam Speaker in July 1986 have been given permission to leave, but another has been told not to reapply until 1993, and we have heard of other husbands but not wives being given visas. The refusenik leaders remain convinced that they would continue to be "hostages until the price is right".[8]

When Leibler learned in late July 1986 that the Soviets had revoked his visa, Pocock asked the Soviet Foreign Ministry to reconsider, but without success.[9] Now, after the Soviet embassy in Canberra confirmed that Moscow had endorsed the latest invitation, Leibler still hovered between elation and anxiety. Something could still go wrong.

Even during a stopover in London, where he met leaders of Britain's Soviet Jewry movement, he remained nervous and edgy. Only after the officials at Moscow's Sheremetyevo Airport had finally waved him and Naomi through, and the Australian embassy's Second Secretary, Rakesh Ahuza, had welcomed him, did Leibler begin to believe that the "surrealistic" had become "real".[10]

In our ten days in Moscow, the four of us only slept a few hours each night. During the day Leibler and I met Soviet officials and had follow-up briefings at the Australian embassy. The long sessions with refuseniks, for which Naomi and Aura joined us, began in the evenings and continued to the early morning. And the two emotional days of Rosh Hashanah in the synagogue began each evening before, continued through the day into the late afternoon, and resumed at night.[11]

Most of the meetings we had with Soviet officials were frustrating. They dutifully referred to *glasnost* and *perestroika*, but the changes had touched very few of them or the policies they administered. Mostly we heard only the official line on Soviet Jewry, Israel and the West. At worst it descended into crude anti-Semitic propaganda, and the conversations ended. At best it was a somewhat more sophisticated Sovietspeak. The meetings only became interesting, and sometimes tense, when Leibler confronted the surprised and usually less informed officials with his knowledge of Soviet law and Marxist-Leninist ideology.

Two of our meetings, however were more encouraging and, as the next few years were to show, harbingers of things to come.

When we met him in September 1987, Melor G Sturva was *Isvestia*'s leading political columnist. As the paper's former head of bureau in the United States for 30 years, his office walls were jammed with photos of him alongside virtually every Hollywoood star and big name in American public life since President Eisenhower. He said he supported *glasnost* and Gorbachev because at last he and his colleagues could do their job as journalists, albeit Soviet journalists still operating within the Communist Party's constraints.[12] But that was an advance on being a party hack.

At *Isvestia* that mattered. The paper was printed in Moscow and in 48 cities across the Soviet Union. It had a daily circulation of nine million. The paper's largest department was the letters to the editor section where 70 people were employed to handle the torrent of readers' mail running at 400,000 letters a year. I asked him if he had heard the old Russian joke: "*Pravda* means 'Truth' and *Isvestia* means 'News'. But there is no truth in *Pravda* and no news in *Isvestia*." Sturva agreed that until recently it had been no joke, but an accurate critique. He was insistent, however, that the press was changing dramatically.

The other positive meeting was with Uri Reshetov, the Soviet Foreign Ministry's Deputy Head of the Humanitarian Department. Reshetov, who spoke relatively free of propaganda, had been in the United States during talks between the United States Secretary of State, George Shultz, and the Soviet Foreign Minister Eduard

Shevardnadze. He had also met Robert Schifter, the United States Assistant Secretary for Human Rights, who had become the State Department's point man on Soviet Jewry. Reshetov told us that all the long-term refuseniks would be permitted to leave very soon. This was welcome news.[13] But from long and bitter experience, the refuseniks treated it cautiously.

Nevertheless, Reshetov's more optimistic forecast, coming just hours before the Jewish New Year, added a sense of hope as we arrived at the Moscow Choral Synagogue that evening. The police had closed off Arkhipova Street, and uniformed militia and plain-clothes KGB watched the crowd of about 1000, mainly youngsters, which had formed outside. They sang along with the Hebrew and Yiddish music on their cassette players. Inside the synagogue, where NBC News had been allowed to film the service, a crowd of 1200, mainly old Jews, overflowed into the aisles and women's gallery.

The Choral synagogue was one of only three left in Moscow in 1987 with an estimated Jewish population of 500,000. Since the 1960s, Arkhipova Street had become the symbolic centre of protest by thousands of young Jews. In some years as many as 20,000 came on the festival of Simchat Torah, not to pray, but to sing, dance and express their solidarity.

Very few young people, however, were in the synagogue this Rosh Hashanah for the morning prayers. A lead cantor and six accompanying cantors led a long choral service which ran for seven hours and finished at 3.30 pm. A haunting anachronism, the cantorial performance was designed for a vanished audience: the Jews of Eastern Europe in the 1920s and 1930s. Somehow this museum piece had survived.

In the synagogue gallery, a few old women, sometimes weeping into their prayer books, watched the congregation below – old men in their seventies and eighties. Some were returned soldiers, decked out in their clusters of Red Army medals and ribbons. Yet their faces told of defeat, not victory. Some tentatively wished us *A gut Yohr* – "Happy New Year" – in Yiddish. Others shook hands silently. Still others shuffled behind Leibler and me as we followed Chief Rabbi

Adolf Solomonovich Shayevich in the Torah procession. When they felt safe they whispered in Yiddish: "Do not trust any of them. They work for the KGB."

Sadly, they were right. Shayevich and Gramm were compliant and token religious leaders. As one of the first two rabbinical students whom Moscow had allowed to go to Budapest for ordination, Shayevich routinely had to oppose the Jewish protest movement as "a Zionist conspiracy". Yet both men had spoken to Leibler at the WJC Budapest meeting four months earlier, where they had also met Dr Joseph Burg, an Israeli Cabinet member.[14] Shayevich's balancing act only ended some fifteen months after our visit, when he resigned from the notorious Soviet Public Anti-Zionist Committee and began to build some credibility among Russian Jews.

Aware of Shayevich's compromised role, Leibler nevertheless believed that his closeness to the Communist Party leadership could help. It was the synagogue, after all, which had invited an internationally known Soviet Jewry activist to Moscow. So Leibler welcomed Shayevich's invitation to speak from the pulpit on the Sabbath after Rosh Hashanah. After some brief remarks in English, Leibler continued in Yiddish. For at least some of the worshippers, it was the language still remembered from their childhoods.

> When I see you here in Shul; when I think of the Jews I have met … here, who, in difficult circumstances, are studying Torah, learning our holy language, and singing songs of the synagogue, then I know that "Am Yisrael Chai! The Jewish people live".[15]

For Leibler, it was a peak experience to be the first international lay leader to speak from the Arkhipova Street pulpit in many decades. Reminiscing about it 25 years later, he regarded it as one of the most moving days of his life.

The three days in the synagogue, deeply stirring as they were, had left us saddened and depressed. As a still photograph of the tragedy of Soviet Jewry after 70 years of communist persecution and repression, it was hard to take. With relief, we resumed our meetings with the refuseniks. None of them had come to the Arkhipova

Street synagogue for the festival. The secular Zionists did not attend synagogue anyhow. And the emerging group of Orthodox refuseniks, virtually all self-taught in Hebrew and classical Jewish texts, held their own services in carefully chosen premises.

Being with the refuseniks, secular or Orthodox, and speaking Hebrew or English or Yiddish to them, was uplifting. No matter how poignant it was to hear of the disappointments, rejections and cruelties they had faced, their determination and persistence were awe-inspiring and inspirational. We had come to offer them our support. But they offered us hope and optimism.

Each story was moving, multi-layered, and a profound testament to the human spirit. I had often heard "ordinary people who came to lead extraordinary lives". But when I met these remarkable men and women, it rang true.

Each of their stories was familiar, sometimes vividly so, from the Jewish movement's documentation which I had followed closely for three decades. I had grown up with Russian Jews in Melbourne, and I knew something of their rich and emotionally charged milieu. I had read the great Russian-Yiddish writers, and the poets and novelists of Russian dissident literature. As a journalist writing about the Cold War since the 1960s, who had worked in Washington and had reported from Eastern Europe, I thought I had some understanding of Soviet politics and Soviet society.

Yet despite the sense of familiarity on meeting the refuseniks, nothing prepared me for the details of their lives. They then became remote and mysterious, as if their accounts came from a land which lay beyond the geography of human understanding.

Of the many refusenik stories, four made a special impact and remain with me: those I heard from Yosif Begun, Pavel and Marta Abramovich, Vladimir and Maria Slepak, and Alexander Lerner. More than 25 years later, they resonate as if I had heard them yesterday.

Yosif Begun first applied to emigrate to Israel in 1971, and immediately lost his job as a senior research worker at the Moscow Institute for Economic Planning. He could only find menial work.

When he tried to register as a Hebrew teacher in 1977, he was arrested, charged with parasitism and sentenced to two years exile in Siberia. A further sentence of three years exile followed when he tried to return to Moscow.

In 1983 Begun had tried again to register as a Hebrew teacher. The KGB charged him with anti-Soviet propaganda and agitation, tried him in a closed court and sentenced him to seven years imprisonment plus five years of internal exile. In the Ural Mountains' Chestopol Prison, the harshest in the Soviet Union, Begun landed in solitary confinement after a hunger strike. For nearly three years the prison authorities did not allow any family visits, and restricted him to cells measuring two metres by one metre. As his health deteriorated, Begun continued to insist on his "rights" to receive a Hebrew Bible and a Russian/Hebrew dictionary. After refusing to conform to the "accepted code of attire" because he stubbornly wore a *yarmulkeh*, the Jewish ritual skull-cap, the prison cancelled a family visit already approved.

When we met him, Begun had only recently received his exit visa, but he was delaying his departure until his son's emigration status was clarified. As we talked over tea, the man's intellect, unquenchable will and enormous courage shone through. When I asked him how he had survived the prison's "strict regime", he smiled: "My faith as a Jew. Without it, I would be a dead man." But there was a disconcerting playfulness about his answer. He also had a flair for the dramatic gesture. Just as we rose to leave, he brought out some old clothing which he handed to a somewhat bewildered Leibler. It was Begun's fur-lined cap and the prisoner's jacket he had worn in Chestopol prison, marked with his name in Russian on the pocket. He gave them to Leibler. "While I was in prison," he said, "you were outside fighting for my freedom. My hat and coat are yours." For once Leibler was lost for words.[16]

Pavel and Marta Abramovich's apartment was tiny. Yet somehow more than 50 friends and refusenik families crowded into it for a joyously sad farewell party for their only son, Felix, 23. He had received his exit visa and was leaving for Israel the next day. But his parents did not know when, or even if, they would join him. Pavel and Marta had been in refusal for more than sixteen years. Their ordeal had begun in 1971 when Pavel, a radio electronics engineer, applied to leave and was refused on grounds of "state secrecy". After Pavel began teaching Hebrew, the KGB put him under house arrest, regularly raided and searched his home, took away his books and possessions, and disconnected his phone. Pavel was dismissed from every job, even as a cleaner of toilets.

At Felix's bitter-sweet farewell party, Aura somehow found a guitar and, singing along with Naomi, led a medley of Hebrew songs which continued for an hour. All the familiar favourites, heard at every bar mitzvah and wedding in the Jewish world, took on new meaning that night in Moscow.[17] Singing loudly and defiantly in a language the Soviets still banned, the refuseniks voiced their own distinctive protest. Just two months later, after Hawke met Gorbachev, the Abramoviches received permission to emigrate.

But when we met them, Vladimir and Masha Slepak were still waiting for their exit visas. Known as the "Father of the Refuseniks", Vladimir and his wife had not seen one of their sons for nearly ten years. The couple had first applied for a visa in 1970. An aviation engineer, Vladimir was dismissed from his job, as was Masha, a doctor. But they attracted international attention in 1978 when they hung a banner across their Moscow apartment balcony which read: "Let us go to our son in Israel." (A son had married a United States citizen and had been able to leave.) KGB agents smashed their door down, prosecuted them for "malicious hooliganism", and exiled Vladimir to Siberia for five years, where Masha joined him.

After they were eventually allowed to leave, the Slepaks' story became the subject of films and books, most notably Chaim Potok's *The Gates of November*. But even in 1987, while still in refusal, they had become internationally known heroes.

Leibler and I met Vladimir on the second night of Rosh Hashanah in the Archipova Street synagogue. We walked with him to his apartment more than an hour away. Although he and Masha had been waiting to leave for more than seventeen years, Vladimir was surprisingly optimistic. As we walked past the KGB's infamous Lubianka prison, he told Russian jokes. ("Do you know why the Lubianka is the tallest building in Moscow?" he asked. "Because from the basement you can see Siberia.")

At their apartment, however, Masha's mood was in sharp contrast. That morning she had farewelled yet another refusenik couple, and the strain was showing.

> How many more times can I go out to Sheremetyevo Airport? How many more times can I say goodbye? After seventeen years I just can't any more. I just can't do it.

During the dinner, which she had taken great pains to prepare according to the festive ritual, she brightened up. But it was her sister-in-law who told us the story that turned us cold. "Do you know very much about Stalin?" she asked. She saw our puzzled looks, and explained.

Her father had been Comrade Rubinstein, a Polish communist from Warsaw. After the Russian Revolution, he had risen to be Lazar Kaganovich's deputy. Kaganovich, a Jewish Politburo member, became one of Stalin's closest henchmen, and was involved in many atrocities. In the 1936–37 purges, he denounced Comrade Rubinstein and forced him to "confess" his crimes against the state. Many years later, when Moscow agreed to rehabilitate Rubinstein, his widow learned that the NKVD had tortured him by playing recordings in the cell next to him of children crying. The cries, the secret police told him, were those of his own children. He lost his mind before the NKVD shot him.

We sat silently. There was nothing to be said. Except to wish Comrade Rubinstein's daughter well in her bid for an exit visa for which she said she had "only" been waiting for three years. A month to the day after our Moscow dinner, Leibler and I heard the wonderful news in Melbourne: the Slepaks were out, and on their way to Israel. Shortly after, so was Comrade Rubinstein's daughter.

Our last night in Moscow began, as earlier nights had begun, at Alexander Lerner's apartment, no. 322 at 4 Dmitria Ulyanova. It was an address that acquired its own place in 20th century history.

If Slepak was known as the "Father of the Refuseniks", Lerner was their patriarch. A cyberneticist with an international reputation, he had applied for an exit visa in 1971, aged 57. As with many of the refuseniks, Israel's victory in the 1967 Six-Day War had inspired him, as much as the growing Soviet anti-Semitism had appalled him. Although dismissed from his high-level position, designated an enemy of the state, and harassed by the KGB, Lerner's international reputation and networks which gave him some protection.

Unable to continue his work at the institute which had employed him, Lerner began a series of weekly scientific seminars at his apartment for his refusenik colleagues. The meetings continued for nearly ten years. His natural talent for leadership turned the apartment into a centre activism and dissent. It was here that many international leaders, Hawke among them, had come to support Lerner and highlight the Soviet Jewry cause.

This last evening, the atmosphere in Lerner's apartment was emotionally charged. We had come there to go with him to meet the eminent Soviet scientist, Nobel Peace Prize winner and dissident, Dr Andrei Sakharov and his wife Yelena Bonner. First we had to farewell Slepak, Yuli Kosharovsky and Alexander Yoffe. There were embraces and tears. When and where would we see each other again?[18]

Meeting Sakharov an hour later was less emotional, but no less inspirational. It was only ten months since Sakharov had returned to Moscow after serving a six-year sentence of "internal exile" in Gorky. Arrested in 1980 after public protests against the Soviet invasion of Afghanistan in 1979, Sakharov had been subject to constant KGB surveillance and harassment, force-fed after he went on a hunger strike, and held in isolation for four months. After years of international protests and petitions calling for his release, Gorbachev telephoned Sakharov in December 1986 to tell him that he and his wife were free. After their release, the Sakharovs were assigned an additional apartment in their Moscow building on the floor immediately below.

With Lerner who introduced us, we met over tea and cake in their kitchen. Tall and somewhat stooped, Sakharov appeared tired and frail. He looked older than 66. But after a few minutes of conversation, his strength, conviction and clarity of thought were palpable.[19] To Leibler's delighted surprise, Sakharov agreed to be quoted in a news article about his views on the refuseniks, Soviet Jewry and human rights. Apart from the interviews which he had given shortly after his release, he had not spoken to the international or Soviet press on any subject for many months. But very much aware of the Gorbachev-Reagan summit scheduled for Washington some two months later, and out of the high regard in which he clearly held Lerner, Sakharov spoke freely about his views.

In an extended report published in *The Australian* and the *Jerusalem Post*, and picked up by news agencies internationally, I wrote that Sakharov had called on Gorbachev and Reagan not to allow arms reduction agreements to relegate human rights to a secondary place at the Washington summit. On Soviet Jewry, Sakharov said there was an urgent need to allow long-time applicants to leave, that Soviet law should guarantee the right of free emigration for all Soviet citizens, and that Jews who wanted to study and teach Hebrew should be able to do so freely and legally.[20]

Despite Gorbachev's personal intervention and numerous invitations, Sakharov was still not allowed to leave the Soviet Union. The given reason was his access to "classified information" when he had worked on research projects as a nuclear physicist some 30 years earlier. The day we met him, he had learnt that he could not attend a conference in Sydney to which the Australian Human Rights Commission had invited him. Despite the restrictions on his own freedom, Sakharov was still prepared to speak out on behalf of freedom for Soviet Jews. It spoke to the man's decency and courage.

Our last day in Moscow began in the Australian embassy in the "cone of silence", the debugged meeting room, with a final discussion with Ambassador Pocock. At Sheremetyevo Airport, the official who supervised our luggage spoke unusually articulate English and went out of his way to be helpful. Leibler was impressed and gave him a $10 tip. The Australian embassy's Rakesh Ahuja, who had escorted us throughout our visit, explained to Leibler that he had just tipped a senior KGB official.[21]

For all the signs of change, however, the Soviet Union was still a grim place and a police state. A reminder came as the British Airways flight left the runway and the plane's passengers burst into spontaneous applause.

On his return to Melbourne, Leibler's book-length report on the visit predicted that Moscow would soon allow the long-term refuseniks to leave. But Leibler doubted that the Soviets would allow full-scale Jewish emigration, or direct flights to Israel.[22] He was right on the first count. Within eighteen months some 12,000 refuseniks left the Soviet Union.

But in common with Israeli and world Jewry leaders, Leibler was too pessimistic about the second prediction. Just three years later, Gorbachev approved direct flights to Israel, an initiative he had vigorously opposed. And three years after that, with flights landing at Tel Aviv Airport almost hourly on some days, more than a million Soviet Jews had come to Israel in one of the greatest mass migrations of the 20th century.

In late 1987, however, despite some of the encouraging signs we had seen in Moscow during our visit, many of the leading refuseniks still did not know their fate, and large-scale emigration seemed a distant dream.

In Australia, buoyed by his Moscow visit, Leibler stepped up his lobbying of Hawke and the government. Re-elected in November as the ECAJ president for his third term, Leibler asked Sydney-based Diane Shteinman, who had served as Chair of the Australian Campaign for Soviet Jewry under Leslie Caplan, to continue the Australian campaign's day-to-day work as its Convenor.

With the Gorbachev-Hawke summit just a week away, Leibler met Hawke and John Bowan in Canberra in late November to agree on a priority list of refuseniks which the Australian Prime Minister would present to the Soviet president.[23] For Leibler and the refuseniks, hope beckoned. For Hawke, redemption.

CHAPTER 22

THE FULL CIRCLE

Across the facade of the Grand Kremlin Palace sit five double-headed eagles, the centre-pieces in the Russian coat-of-arms. But on 1 December 1987, when Hawke met Gorbachev in the Palace's Catherine Hall, the Cyrillic letters CCCP (Union of Soviet Socialist Republics) still took pride of place.

Each man came into the ornate reception hall through golden doors embossed with Tsarist emblems, a reminder that this was once the Tsar's residence in Moscow.[1] They were due to meet for fifteen to 20 minutes, but ended up talking for three and a quarter hours. Foreign Minister Hayden and Foreign Minister Shevernadze joined them for the last hour. They continued the discussions on trade, technology transfer, East-West relations, arms reduction, sporting relations, medical research and human rights. Hawke presented his list of refuseniks and Gorbachev promised to investigate, but he made no commitments. The Soviet leader said he was concerned that the large numbers of Jews wanting to leave posed a serious brain drain problem.[2] Hawke said later that there was no animosity in their "vibrant" discussion on human rights.[3]

Along with other Western leaders who had met Gorbachev, Hawke was impressed. He described him as "an engaging human being, warm, enthusiastic, quick to understand and appreciate points being made … [it had been] a stimulating and rewarding discussion."[4] Hawke believed he had met "a man of destiny … the indispensable man for closing down the Cold War".[5]

The next day, as he prepared to leave the Soviet Union, Hawke joined 20 of the refuseniks at the Australian embassy. He had met some of them in 1979. Acutely aware of the depressing events eight years earlier, Hawke was cautious: "It was sad to see these fine people [still] in a position where they can't leave … I was careful not to be too optimistic."[6] Hazel Hawke, who had been with him in Moscow on the earlier visit, had her own memories. She met separately with Jewish Women Against Refusal, and was equally careful not to raise expectations.

But as they were due to board the Prime Minister's plane in Moscow, Hawke heard that Gorbachev had approved exit visas for two families: Pavel and Marta Abramovich, in refusal since 1971, and Alexander and Rose Ioffe and their daughter Anna, in refusal since 1976. As soon as he arrived in Tokyo, Hawke phoned Leibler with the good news. In turn Leibler phoned Pavel. But as it was 3 am in Moscow and he had not yet heard the news, he was wary.[7] After the exit visas were confirmed, Australian radio stations interviewed an overjoyed Pavel, as well as Hawke and Leibler.

Although Gorbachev had only agreed to release five of the 20 refuseniks on Hawke's list, the two leaders had met at a propitious time for the Soviet Jewry movement. Just days later Gorbachev was due in Washington for his first United States summit with Reagan. In their reaction to the release of the Abramovich and Ioffe families, the National Conference on Soviet Jewry, the campaign's leading American organisation, reflected the mounting pressure on Gorbachev.

> While welcome, such individual gestures, even to the Australian prime minister, do not satisfy the need for a radical improvement in emigration procedures. This continuing violation of the rights of Soviet Jews is one of the primary reasons why we are demonstrating in Washington DC on Summit Sunday on December 6.[8]

The mass rally for Soviet Jewry on Sunday, 6 December, held on the Mall in the American capital, drew 250,000 demonstrators, mostly Jews from communities across the United States. It was the largest Jewish rally ever held in Washington. Calling on Gorbachev to "Let My People Go", the demonstrators made history and the front pages. In his compelling history of the American campaign, Gal Beckerman noted that "… in the closing moments of the rally, with all the people who had given years of their lives to a struggle that felt historic to them – even biblical – there seemed to be a strong feeling of victory".[9]

At the summit, however, Reagan made only passing reference to Soviet Jewry. But by then, the Reagan administration was confident that Moscow was preparing for a major policy change.[10]

As Gorbachev met Reagan in Washington, Hawke told Parliament in Canberra that Gorbachev understood human rights were important to help the Soviet Union's economic development, and that Australia would continue to press for every refusenik's freedom.

On 22 December, Professor Lerner phoned an excited Leibler to tell him that he had received his exit visa.[11] When he finally arrived in Tel Aviv in late January, Lerner heard that Speaker Child was visiting Jerusalem at the invitation of Knesset Speaker Shlomo Hillel. In an emotional reunion at the King David Hotel, Child recalled the last time she had seen him in Moscow in 1986.

> He was in a tiny flat … where the kitchen, bathroom, and loo were in an area six feet by six feet, and there were two other rooms each ten by eight. The Russians called it an upgraded flat.[12]

Leibler's own reunion with Lerner, Begun, Abramovich and the other refuseniks came in Jerusalem in February 1988. As he had done hundreds of times for nearly three decades, Leibler shared his feelings with Litvinoff.

> The last few months … have proved to be the most exciting and gratifying period. After so many years of effort and frustration, I find myself, together with Naomi, among those fortunate to witness the happy finale of decades of struggle by modern-day heroes of the Jewish people.[13]

In fact, it was not the finale, but the penultimate chapter. Most of the refusenik heroes had indeed won their struggle. But there was much more to come. Not only for the remaining refuseniks, but most importantly, for the millions of Soviet Jews.

For Leibler, the last chapter began in May 1988, when he flew fifteen refuseniks to Melbourne and, together with Hawke, welcomed them at the Melbourne Concert Hall to a jubilant audience of 3000

Australian Jews. The last chapter's finale came after one last visit to Moscow – to open the Solomon Mykhoels Cultural Centre.

Throughout Soviet Jewish history, names resonated with their own special poignancy. Few, however, as powerfully and tragically as Mykhoels. Solomon Mikhailovich Mykhoels was born Shloyme Vovsi into an Orthodox Jewish family in Dvinsk, Latvia, in 1890. After making his name as an actor, singer and director with the Moscow State Yiddish Theatre, Stalin appointed him Chair of the Jewish Anti-Fascist Committee in 1941 after the Nazis invaded the Soviet Union. The Committee, which brought together the leading intellectual, literary, and cultural Jewish figures, was set up to win political and financial support for the Soviet war effort, especially in the United States. Mykhoels travelled internationally and was widely praised for his successful promotion of Stalin and the Soviet Union.

In January 1948, however, an increasingly obsessed, paranoiac and Jew-hating Stalin ordered Mykhoels' murder and instructed the NKVD to portray it as a truck accident. It became the precursor for more murders, arrests, imprisonment and exile to the Gulag for many leading Jews, and the closure of nearly all Jewish institutions. Mykhoels' death marked the beginning of the next 40 years of the Soviets' official anti-Semitism.[14]

The Mykhoels Centre's opening ceremony on 12 February 1989 combined powerful symbolism with real progress in Soviet Jewish life. This was the first authentic centre of Jewish culture in Moscow for 50 years. Working over the previous twelve months with some remaining refuseniks and activists, Mikhail Chlenov and Velvel Chernin, Leibler had used the Australian government's support for expanded cultural contact to win a far-reaching agreement with Moscow.

Finalised in Moscow in October 1988,[15] it legitimised the Hebrew language and Hebrew culture, and enabled the teaching of traditional Jewish texts.[16] These activities had been criminal offences, punishable by prison terms. More broadly, the new agreement reflected a fundamental and historic ideological change by the Soviet communists towards Zionism.[17] Given traditional communist policies on nationalities and culture, such a revolutionary change could only have happened after the highest levels of the Kremlin's leadership had sanctioned it.

So when Leibler dedicated the Centre in February 1989 by affixing a *mezuzah* to the Centre's door – the small case of parchment inscribed with Hebrew texts which marks a Jewish residence – it was a moment of historic vindication. More than 70 leaders representing Israel and a dozen leading Jewish communities who had flown to Moscow for the event attested to its significance. As did messages from Israel's Prime Minister Yitzhak Shamir, Foreign Minister Moshe Arens, Britain's Prime Minister Margaret Thatcher, and the newly appointed United States Secretary of State, James Baker. But as Leibler knew only too well, and as the message from Australia's Prime Minister Hawke underlined, it was also a distinctively Australian moment.

The Mykhoels Centre opening had partly had its origins over a dinner in Melbourne a year earlier. Leibler had invited the Soviet embassy's Valeri Zemstov and his wife to join him and Naomi before the Zemstovs returned to Moscow. Originally sceptical about Zemstov, nominally the First Secretary, but whom he regarded as the KGB station chief in Canberra, Leibler had found him more open to discussion as Soviet policy changes gathered pace. Over dinner the conversation turned to the new Human Contacts agreement which Hawke and Hayden had begun negotiating during their meetings with Gorbachev some three months earlier.

Leibler asked Zemstov whether this could allow Australian Jewish cultural and artistic groups to visit the Soviet Union as part of a reciprocal relationship. Somewhat to Leibler's surprise, Zemskov was enthusiastic about the idea. He suggested that Leibler should work with Michael Edgley, the Australian impresario who had specialised in bringing Soviet ballet, theatre and circus companies to Australia.[18]

Leibler seized upon Zemskov's response and saw an opening for something much larger than bringing Australian Jewish artists to Moscow. In the meetings that followed during 1988 with Edgley's representatives, visiting Russian Jewish theatrical producer Michael Gluz,[19] and visiting officials from the Soviet Ministry of Culture,

Leibler proposed a joint venture between the Australian Jewish community and the Soviets to establish a Jewish cultural centre in Moscow. It would house a library, museum, art gallery, coffee shop, kosher restaurant and theatre. He emphasised that building such "cultural bridges" could only happen if Moscow released all the remaining refuseniks. Moreover, he explained that he had won the World Jewish Congress' support for the proposal.

Which turned out to be short-lived. Although the Soviet authorities welcomed Leibler's idea, it ran into opposition from Jewish quarters. The WJC, although initially supportive, became increasingly unhappy with Leibler's activities because they had their own plans for a cultural centre at the Arkhipova Street Synagogue.[20] In addition, the WJC president Edgar Bronfman had met Shevernadze in March, and had asked that the ban on Hebrew be dropped. Now it appeared that Leibler was moving with the Australian government's help to conclude a separate agreement.

The World Zionist Organisation's Chairman Simcha Dinitz shared the WJC's resistance and suspicions about Leibler acting independently.[21] As significantly, David Bartov, the Nativ/Lishkah head, claimed that "the Soviets are just currying favour with the Western Jewish organisations ..."[22] At home, some sections of the Australian Jewish community led by Michael Danby, later a Labor MP, criticised Leibler for making "pre-emptive concessions" to the Soviets.[23]

Leibler's main ally, however, turned out to be Hawke and the Australian government. After the angry rupture in their relationship in May, following Hawke's comparison between the refuseniks and the Palestinians, the two men had had little contact. Leibler had written a scathing personal letter to Hawke, but had not received a reply. But Hawke had asked mutual friends in the Jewish community to speak to Leibler and maintain contact. On 8 July 1988, to Leibler's surprise, Hawke telephoned him. An emotional conversation, in which Hawke told Leibler that his letter was "outrageous and offensive", helped to restore some of the broken connections.[24]

Although he welcomed his support, Leibler had lost much of his respect and admiration for Hawke. In a revealing note to Reuven Merhav, the Israeli Foreign Ministry's Director-General, Leibler wrote:

> Hawke has illusions of grandeur and is obsessed with a belief that he is destined to become an arbitrator to achieve a peace settlement in the Middle East.
>
> However, he and I have had an extraordinarily close personal relationship. Possibly in order to compensate for his negative attitude on the Middle East, he has given instructions to all Government departments to do everything possible to assist me in other areas.[25]

But Hawke's support on Soviet Jewry reflected more than a desire to help Leibler or to make up for the criticism he had received from Jewish leaders about his Middle East policies. The Hawke government as a whole had come to believe that under Gorbachev there was a "new" Soviet Union. Which is why Hawke described the Mykhoels Centre as "a concrete example of improved bilateral relations".[26] In the months that followed his phone conversation with Hawke, Leibler met regularly in Canberra with the Prime Minister's Department and Foreign Affairs officials to plan his visit to Moscow in October – his fifth in eleven years – to conclude the Mykhoels Centre agreement.[27]

In Moscow, Pocock's successor, Ambassador Robin Ashwin, ensured that an Australian embassy official accompanied Leibler to all his meetings with the Ministry of Culture. The message to Moscow was clear. The agreement to end the 70 year ban of Hebrew language and culture had the Australian government's support.[28] Along with the release of the refuseniks, Leibler described the Moscow agreements as climactic in his 30 years of involvement with Soviet Jewry.[29]

Although Leibler had won the Australian government's enthusiastic support, he was less successful with some international Jewish organisations, who were either sceptical or strongly opposed to his Mykhoels initiative. Some of this was due to Leibler's own "crash-or-crash through" style and his selective approach to consultation, a doctrine which he preached to others, especially at the WJC, but did not always practise himself. His successful pursuit of media coverage, often more prominent and extensive than some international leaders could gain for themselves, created its own jealousies and rivalries.

The Australian leader, however, had a critical advantage. He had developed his superior media awareness over three decades of dealing with the Australian press, and had learned that concrete results and direct relationships with reporters tended to win a "better run" than reams of news releases. This experience gave him an important edge in the internecine, and often petty, organisational conflicts within Diaspora Jewry, which often revolved around competing news releases.

Leibler's relationship with the WJC during the late 1980s was especially problematic. But in 1988, as Gorbachev began changing Moscow's policies, the WJC was a significant player. Leibler knew the WJC had to be involved. Bronfman and Singer had become increasingly adept at Jewish NGO diplomacy. A billionaire business leader, Bronfman used his private jet and international networks to promote the notion that the WJC represented Jewish communities in 70 countries and so spoke for Diaspora Jewry. This was only partially true. In practice, the WJC was just another American Jewish organisation, with even less of a constituency than most. Bronfman and Singer ran their own race and operated with limited accountability. But the WJC had become a strong "brand" in the American Jewish organisational alphabet soup. Building on large injections of Bronfman's personal wealth to create a professional arm, it had won recognition in Washington and Moscow.

As an Australian leader from a relatively small Jewish community, Leibler needed the WJC connection. So he manouvered around the inevitable tensions which periodically erupted into heated conflict with Bronfman and Singer. By now Leibler was a mature and recognised leader on Soviet Jewry But he remained concerned that the WJC was not always as militant as he thought was necessary, an echo from the rows he had had 20 years earlier with the WJC's founder, Dr Nahum Goldmann. In October 1988 the wheel turned full circle, and the WJC appointed Leibler a WJC vice-president, the first Australian Jewish leader to be so recognised.[30]

Leibler welcomed the appointment, but savoured the irony that someone Goldmann had once dismissed as an *enfant terrible* was now a WJC leader undertaking sensitive diplomacy in Moscow. In the last frantic months leading up to the Mykhoels Centre opening, and after resolving his differences with Bronfman, at least temporarily, he used the WJC connection to full advantage.[31] And reconciled to Leibler's achievement, Bronfman made sure, for his part, to attend the opening ceremony and claim the credit for the WJC.

Much of the widespread international media coverage that followed the Centre's opening focused on the speech by writer and Nobel Peace Prize winner Elie Wiesel.[32] Recalling his first visit to the Soviet Union in 1965, and his book *The Jews of Silence* which followed, Wiesel reminded his listeners that the title had not referred to the Soviet Jews. It had instead described the Jews of the West, especially American Jewry, who in the mid-1960s had not yet taken up the Soviet Jewry cause.

Addressing Soviet Jewry Wiesel said:

> This Mykhoels Center is your doing. It has become a reality primarily because you have kept Jewish memory alive ...
>
> You who for years knew nothing of Jewish life ... turn out to be profoundly Jewish, eager to learn and to teach the immortal values of our common Jewish heritage. How can one fail to admire you? Jews of the Soviet Union, thank you.[33]

Wiesel's speech made the headlines. But the opening ceremony was replete with many "firsts". A Russian language exhibition on the Holocaust from the Simon Wiesenthal Centre in Los Angeles. Works by Israeli artist Yossi Stern openly displayed. Readings in Hebrew by Israel's unofficial poet laureate, Yehuda Amichai.

All this had been taboo just eighteen months earlier. Especially powerful was the return to Moscow by former refusenik Yuli Edelshtein. Just five years earlier he had languished in a Soviet prison. Now he came representing the Forum, the Israeli NGO of former Soviet Jews, and headed by Natan Sharansky, the most famous Prisoner of Zion. Seven years later the two were ministers in the Israeli government.

In addition to the Mykhoels Centre opening ceremony, Leibler had also arranged for concerts in Moscow and Leningrad (later reverting to St Petersburg) where Israeli and international Jewish performers joined Russian Jewish artists. At the first concert at Moscow's Tchaikovsky Centre, an audience of over 1000 filled the hall, while another 2000 followed it on screens outside.[34] Similar-sized audiences, many travelling from as far away as small Jewish communities in Siberia, came to the subsequent performances. They had lined up in the snow to buy tickets for celebrated Israeli singers Yaffa Yarkoni and musical theatre star Dudu Fisher, American folk-singer, Robyn Helzner, and Australian singer and composer Aura Levin.[35]

In 1987 Aura and the refuseniks had sung defiantly, but privately, in their small Moscow apartments. Now, barely eighteen months later, she and her colleagues were singing in Hebrew at concerts publicised in the Soviet media – for the first time since the Russian Revolution. An emotional Yaffa Yarkoni, an Israeli icon, told the cheering audience that her parents had come from the Caucasus. Dudu Fisher, who was also a cantor, won repeated encores for his traditional presentations.[36]

The week of concerts ended the Mykhoels Centre celebrations on a high note. Leibler had wanted "a spectacular show" for the Centre, and it had happened. Among the many messages of congratulation was one from Shoshana Cardin, who had succeeded Morris Abram as the Chair of the National Conference on Soviet Jewry. Cardin said she hoped the dedication would be a precursor for "many positive developments". Her hope was fulfilled.[37] The "positive developments" came within months, faster and more dramatically than anybody predicted.

On 9 November 1989, the Berlin Wall came down. On 30 September 1990, Gorbachev agreed to direct flights from Moscow to Tel Aviv, and so opened the gates to emigration even wider. In August 1991, Gorbachev lost power. And the Soviet Union, the most powerful empire in history, dissolved itself. But in the previous two years some 500,000 Soviet citizens had arrived in Israel, and they kept coming. By 1996, the figure was more than a million. Another 300,000 left for the United States, Germany and Australia. Over the next 25 years the new Exodus changed Israeli society, and made a significant impact on the Diaspora Jewish communities wherever the new immigrants settled.

At the Mykhoels Centre opening in February 1989, those momentous events still lay in the future. But enough had happened for Isi Leibler to look back 30 years to a meeting in Tel Aviv's Dan Hotel with Shaul Avigur. In the summer of 1959, Israel's legendary spymaster and the founder of the small clandestine liaison office for Soviet Jewry had recruited Leibler. He had asked him to work for Mission Improbable: to bring the Soviet Union's imprisoned and persecuted Jews to Israel. And to work for that goal from Australia, a relatively minor player in the Cold War, with a small post-Holocaust Jewish community of limited political influence.

In 1959 the signs were not all that propitious. But over the next 30 years, Australian Jews and their leaders worked with Australian governments, parliamentarians, diplomats, and opinion makers and took up the Soviet Jewry cause with growing fervour. They made a difference. It is a story worth telling.

ABOUT THE AUTHORS

Sam Lipski, following an extensive journalistic career in Australia and internationally, has been The Pratt Foundation's CEO since 1998. Among his varied media roles he was Foreign Editor, *The Bulletin*; Foundation Producer for the ABC's *This Day Tonight* and Executive Producer *Four Corners*; Washington Correspondent for *The Australian* and the *Jerusalem Post*; Australian correspondent for the *Washington Post*; and a columnist for *The Age*, the *Sydney Morning Herald*, *The Australian* and the Sydney *Daily Telegraph*. He also served as the Foreign Affairs and Media commentator on the Channel Nine Network's *Sunday* and *Today* programs. Sam was the *Australian Jewish News* editor-chief 1987–98, and in 1989 he was the *Jerusalem Report's* founding publisher.

In his community activities, he has served as the State Library of Victoria's President (2000–06), Chairman of Monash University's Advisory Board at The Centre for Jewish Civilisation, and Chairman of Melbourne University's Advisory Board at The Centre for Advanced Journalism. In 1993 he became a Member of the Order of Australia (AM) for his services to the media, and in 2008 Monash University awarded him an honorary Doctorate of Laws (LLD hon).

Suzanne D. Rutland MA (Hons) PhD, Dip Ed, OAM, is Professor of the Department of Hebrew, Biblical & Jewish Studies at the University of Sydney and the main lecturer in the program of Jewish Civilisation, Thought and Cultures. She founded, and continues to participate in, the Hebrew and Jewish Studies teacher education program in the Faculty of Education at the University of Sydney. She has published widely on Australian Jewish history, edits the Sydney edition of the *AJHS Journal*, and writes on issues relating to the Shoah and Israel. Her latest books are *The Jews in Australia* (Cambridge University Press,

2005) and *Nationality Stateless: Destination Australia*, co-authored with Sarah Rood (Melbourne: Jewish Museum of Australia and JDC, 2008). She shared a major government grant with the late Professor Emeritus Sol Encel to study 'The Political Sociology of Australian Jewry', was historical consultant for the Sydney Jewish Museum's major renovations to their Australian Jewish History section, and for the Jewish Museum of Australia, Melbourne. In January 2008 she received the Medal of the Order of Australia for services to Higher Jewish Education and interfaith dialogue.

ENDNOTES

CHAPTER 1: FROM RUSSIA WITH THANKS

1   *Australian Jewish News,* 20 May 1988, p. 5.
2   Blanche D'alpuget, *Robert J Hawke: A Biography,* Melbourne: Schwartz–Penguin Books, 1982, p. 285.
3   *Australian Jewish News,* 20 May 1988, p. 5.
4   All Prime Minister Hawke quotations are from his speech transcript – <pmtranscripts.dpmc.gov.au/transcripts/00007322>
    Cf. also the DVD by the Australian Institute of Jewish Affairs *From Russia with Thanks*, and the *Australian Jewish News* 20 May 1988, pp. 4–5.
5   *Australian Jewish News,* 20 May 1988, p. 4.
6   Bob Hawke, *The Hawke Memoirs,* William Heinemann Australia, 1994, p. 92.
7   ibid.
8   ibid.
9   ibid.
10 *Australian Jewish News,* 20 May 1988, p. 5.
11 *Australian Jewish News,* 27 May 1988 p. 3, and 3 June 1988, p. 13.
12 *Australian Jewish News,* 3 June 1988, p. 14.
13 *Australian Jewish News,* 3 June 1988, p. 15.
14 Stephen Mills, *The Hawke Years,* Viking 1993, p. 179.
15 Sam Lipski, interview with Bob Hawke, 2011, Sydney (Transcript available).
16 ibid.
17 Hawke transcript.

CHAPTER 2: THE SPYMASTER AND THE RECRUIT

1   Ami Isseroff, "Biography of Shaul Avigur", "Zionism and Israel – Biographies", http://www.zionism-israel.com/bio/Avigur_biography.htm, Accessed 30 Sep 2009.
2   Henry L. Feingold, *Silent No More: Saving the Jews of Russia, the American Jewish Effort, 1967–1989*, Syracuse, NY: Syracuse University Press, 2006.
3   Nehemiah Levanon, "Israel's Role in the Campaign" in Murray Friedman and Albert D Chernin, (eds), *A Second Exodus*, Brandeis

University Press, 1999, p. 71.

4   Pauline Peretz, "The action of Nativ's emissaries in the United States: A trigger for the American movement to aid Soviet Jews, 1958–1974", Translated by Julie Wayne and Pauline Peretz, Bulletin du Centre de recherche français de Jérusalem, 14: printemps 2004, pp. 112–28, http://bcrfj.revues.org/index270.html, accessed 30 September 2009.

5   Isi Leibler, email correspondence, 31 December 2010.

6   Isi Leibler, email correspondence, 15 September 2009.

7   Peretz, "The action of Nativ's emissaries in the United States".

8   Suzanne D Rutland interview with Nehemia Levanon, Kfar Blum, Israel, 10 December 2000.

9   Peretz, "The action of Nativ's emissaries in the United States".

10   NSW Jewish Board of Deputies Minutes, 20 May 1958.

CHAPTER 3: THREE LEADERS, THREE VOICES

1   Notes not dated re Sam Cohen's position, October 1961, IJLA-Jer.

2   Suzanne D Rutland interview with Vivianne de Vahl Davis, Sydney, 1988.

3   Kevin Anderson, Fossil in the Sandstone: The Recollecting Judge, Melbourne, 1986, p. 154.

4   Zelman Cowen, "Ashkanasy, Maurice (1901–1971)", Australian Dictionary of Biography, Volume 13, Melbourne University Press, 1993, pp. 78–9.

5   Cowen, "Ashkanasy", pp. 78–119.

6   Suzanne D Rutland interview with Billie Einfeld, Sydney, 1988.

7   Curriculum Vitae provided by Sydney Einfeld.

8   See Suzanne D Rutland, "The History of Australian Jewry, 1945–1960", PhD thesis, University of Sydney, 1990, p. 171.

9   ibid.

10   See, for example, Ashkanasy to Einfeld, 5 October 1956, Einfeld's reply, 15 October 1956, "C/M Interstate and Press Releases", 20 August 1956 – 14 June 1957, Box E41, ECAJ Cores Files, Archive of Australian Judaica, Fisher Library, University of Sydney (AAJ).

11   Julian Phillips, "Cohen, Samuel Herbert (Sam) (1918–1969)", Australian Dictionary of Biography, Volume 13, Melbourne University Press, 1993, pp. 458–9.

12   Philip Mendes, "The Senator Sam Cohen Affair: Soviet Anti-Semitism, the ALP and the 1961 federal election", Labour History, No. 78, May 2000, pp. 179–97.

13   For a detailed history of the Melbourne Jewish Council to Combat Fascism and Anti-Semitism see David Rechter, "Beyond the Pale: Jewish Communism in Melbourne", MA (Hons) thesis, University

of Melbourne, 1987, and also theses by Allan Leibler and Sara McNaughton, "Liberalism and Anti-Communism in the Melbourne Jewish Community in the 1940s and 1950s", BA (Hons) Thesis, University of Sydney 1984, and Philip Mendes, "The Jewish Council to Combat Fascism and Anti-Semitism: An Historical Re-Appraisal" (Part One), *AJHS Journal*, vol. 10, part 6, 1989, pp. 524–51; and (Part Two), vol 10, part 7, pp. 598–615. Also Norman Rothfield, "Melbourne Jewry's Cold War: My Years with the Jewish Council to Combat Fascism and Anti-Semitism," *AJHS Journal*, Vol XI, Part 6, June 1993, pp. 956–84.

14 Suzanne D Rutland, "Nazis Unwelcome! The Jewish Community and the 1950s German Migration Scheme", in Emily Turner-Graham and Christine Winter (eds.), *National Socialism in Oceania: A Critical Evaluation of its Effect and Aftermath*, Frankfurth am Main: Peter Lang, 2010, pp. 219–34.

15 "Judah Waten", Department of Internal Security, CRS A6119/XR, item [101], National Archives of Australia, Canberra (NAA).

16 McNaughton, "Liberalism and Anti-Communism", pp. 77–8.

17 Sam Cohen to H. Wolfensohn, 3 October 1950, St Coms (Public Relations, Immigration, Congregational), 1950–51, Box E40, ECAJ Corres. Files, AAJ.

18 Victorian Jewish Board of Deputies Minutes, 4 June 1951.

19 Rechter, "Beyond the Pale", pp. 138–40.

20 McNaughton, "Liberalism and Anti-Communism", p. 88.

21 ibid.

22 ibid., p. 94.

23 Sanger to Joseph Redapple, explaining the reasons for his resignation from the JCCF&A, 20 April 1950.

24 Mendes, "Senator Sam Cohen Affair", p. 180.

25 Rechter, "Beyond the Pale", pp. 143–4.

26 "Moscow", *Encyclopedia Judaica*, Volume 12.

27 *Australian Jewish Herald* (AJH), 10 August 1962.

28 Peter Medding, *From Assimilation to Group Survival: A Political and Sociological Study of an Australian Jewish Community*, Melbourne: Cheshire Press, 1968, pp. 215–17.

29 Suzanne D Rutland interview with Sam Goldbloom, Melbourne, April 1988.

30 Medding, *From Assimilation to Group Survival*, p. 217.

31 See "Talking History Project", Australian Centre for Jewish Civilisation, http://www.arts.monash.edu.au/jewish-civilisation/resources/talking/index.php

32 Mendes, "Sam Cohen Affair", p. 184.

33   Rank and File Committee, "Labor Yes – Sam Cohen No", Australian Labor Committee, Victorian Branch, Pamphlet No. 5, "Soviet Jewry, 1950–June 1962", IJLA-Jer.

34   Mendes, "Sam Cohen Affair", p. 184.

35   *Daily Telegraph* (DT), 4 October 1961.

36   Mugga, "The Cohen Case", Sydney *Bulletin*, 14 October 1961.

37   Mendes, "Sam Cohen Affair", p. 184.

38   Board President's statement, 13 October 1961, in "Sam Cohen "Labor yes – Sam Cohen – no", one of five different pamphlets dealing with the election contest, IJLA-Jer.

39   Statement made on behalf of the Executive to the next meeting of the Board, 13 October 1961, "Soviet Jewry, 1950–June 1962", IJLA-Jer.

40   Research Brief no.11 2004–05, Parliamentary Library, Parliament of Australia.

CHAPTER 4: WENTWORTH ASKS, BARWICK ANSWERS

1   Commonwealth Parliament Debates, 3 April 1962.

2   Tony Stephens, "Firebrand style hid true substance", *Sydney Morning Herald*, 17 June 2003, http://www.smh.com.au/articles/2003/06/16/1055615731284.html, accessed 1 February 2013.

3   Letter from W C Wentworth's private secretary to Isi Leibler, 30 August 1960 and Isi Leibler's reply, 1 September 1960. 794.1/250, Isi Joseph Leibler Archive, Jerusalem (IJLA-Jer).

4   Leibler to Wentworth, asking the latter to keep Leibler's involvement "confidential", 2 April 1962, 794.1/250, IJLA-Jer.

5   Sydney D Einfeld, ECAJ President to the Soviet Ambassador, 12 September 1962 and his reply, 24 September 1962, 794.1/250, IJLA-Jer.

6   Ian Hancock, *Gorton: He did it his way*, Sydney: Hodder 2002, p. 160.

7   Wentworth to Leibler, 24 April 1962, IJLA-Jer.

8   Reported in the *Australian Jewish Herald* (AJH), 16 February 1962

9   *AJH*, 15 June 1962.

10   *AJH*, 15 June 1962.

11   Public relations Report, 11 June 1962, "Soviet Jewry, July-December 1962", 794.1/250, IJLA-Jer.

12   Philip Mendes, "The Senator Sam Cohen Affair: Soviet Anti-Semitism, the ALP and the 1961 Federal Election", *Labour History*, No. 78, May 2000, p. 186.

13   See *AJH*, 29 June 1962 and 7 July 1962.

14   A Beth Din is a rabbinical court that deals with matters of Jewish law.

15   *AJH*, 29 June 1962.

16   *AJH*, 7 July 1962.

17   *AJH*, 10 August 1962.

18 Isi Leibler, "The Sea of Soviet Jews – Not so different from Nazi Germany", "Forum", *The Bulletin*, 29 September 1962.

19 V. Gamazeichshikov, press attaché of the USSR Embassy in Australia, Letters to the Editor, *The Bulletin*, 20 October 1962, p. 30.

20 Commonwealth Parliamentary Debates, House of Representatives, Vol H of R 36, 3 October 1962, pp. 1133 – 1136.

21 Commonwealth Parliamentary Debates, House of Representatives, Vol H of R 36, 3 October 1962, pp. 1133 – 1136.

22 *Jewish Chronicle*, London, 12 October 1962.

23 Yaacov Ro'i, *The Struggle for Soviet Jewish Emigration, 1948-1967*, Cambridge: Cambridge University Press, 1991, pp152-153.

24 *Daily Telegraph*, Sydney, 10 October 1962.

CHAPTER 5: THE COHEN AFFAIR

1 Senate Adjournment Debate, Commonwealth of Australia Parliamentary Debates, 7 August – 6 December 1962, Vol 22, 24th Parliament, First Session, pp. 1003-5.

2 Mendes, "Sam Cohen Affair", p. 188.

3 Senator Sam Cohen, Senate Adjournment debate, Vol S 22, 18 October 1962, p. 1006.

4 Cohen, Senate Adjournment debate, Vol S 22, 18 October 1962, p. 1006.

5 Cohen, Senate Adjournment debate, Vol S 22, 18 October 1962, p. 1010.

6 Senator George Branson, Senate Adjournment debate, Vol S 22, 18 October 1962, p. 1010.

7 Branson, Senate Adjournment debate, Vol S 22, 18 October 1962, p. 1011.

8 Senator Pat Kennelly, Senate Adjournment debate, Vol S 22, 18 October 1962, p. 1015.

9 Kennelly, Senate Adjournment debate, Vol S 22, 18 October 1962, p. 1017.

10 Senator Lionel Murphy, Senate Adjournment debate, Vol S 22, 18 October 1962, p. 1018.

11 Murphy, Senate Adjournment debate, Vol S 22, 18 October 1962, p. 1018.

12 Senator John Gorton, Senate Adjournment debate, Vol S 22, 18 October 1962, p. 1018.

13 Senator James Arnold, Senate Adjournment debate, Vol S 22, 18 October 1962, p. 1020.

14 Senator Sir Alister McMullin, Senate Adjournment debate, Vol S 22, 18 October 1962, pp. 1006-8.

15   *The Age*, 19 October 1962.

16   Leslie Haylen, Representatives Adjournment debate, Vol 36, 7 August–18 October 1962, 24th Parliament, First Session, 18 October 1962, p. 1763.

17   Harold Holt, Representatives Adjournment debate, Vol 36, 18 October 1962, p. 1763.

18   "Mr Haylen and the Jews", "Plain English", Sydney *Bulletin*, 27 October 1962.

19   Sam Lipski, "J'Accuse", *Australian Jewish Herald*, 26 October 1962.

20   Philip Mendes, "The Senator Sam Cohen Affair: Soviet Anti-Semitism, the ALP and the 1961 Federal Election", *Labour History*, No 78, May 2000, p. 189.

21   Mendes, "Sam Cohen Affair", pp. 189–90.

22   *Sunday Telegraph*, 4 November 1962.

23   "Mr Calwell and Senator Cohen", editorial, Sydney *Bulletin*, 10 November 1962.

24   Mendes, "Sam Cohen Affair", p. 192.

25   *Sunday Telegraph*, 11 November 1962.

26   Mendes, "Sam Cohen Affair", p. 191.

27   Leibler to Coleman, 26 October 1962, IJLA-Jer.

28   Litvinoff to Leibler, 29 October 1962, IJLA-Jer.

29   "Persecution of Jews in Russia", Prime Minster's Department, A1209/111, item 62/963, 26 October 1962, National Archives of Australia (NAA).

30   Alexander Downer, "Australia and Europe: Sharing Global Responsibilities", The Schuman Lecture, 11May 2006, http://www.foreignminister.gov.au/speeches/2006/060511_schuman_lecture.html

31   Plimsoll sent two cablegrams to Tange in the Department of External Affairs strongly objecting to raising the issue, one on 28 October and the second on 29 October 1962, Prime Minister's Department, A1209/111, item 62/963, 29 October 1962, National Archives of Australia (NAA).

32   Plimsoll to Tange, 29 October 1962, Prime Minister's Department, A1209/111, item 62/963, 29 October 1962, National Archives of Australia (NAA).

33   "Personal for Plimsoll from Tange", Secretary of the Department of External Affairs, outward cablegram. 30 October 1962, "Persecution of Jews in Russia", Prime Minister's Department, Series A1209/111, Item 62/963, NAA.

34   "Soviet Jewry, Text of the Australian Statement, From Australian Mission to the United Nations, New York", dated 31 October, recd 1 November 1962, Dept of External Affairs, A1838/1, "UN Human

Rights/Anti-Semitism", Part 2, item 929/5/2, Part 2, NAA Canberra. The speech was reported in the Australian press. See, for example, "Russia anti-Jews, Aust. Tells U.N. Meeting", *The West Australian*, 3 November 1962. See also for the same date "Australia in U.N. Clash Over Jews", *Sydney Morning Herald*, and "U.N. Clash on Jew Question in Russia", *Canberra Times*.

35 *Herald*, 2 November 1962.
36 "We hit at Russia on Jews: UN Attack", *The Sun News-Pictorial*, Melbourne, 2 November 1962.
37 Ro'i, *The Struggle for Soviet Jewish Emigration*, p. 168.
38 Suzanne D Rutland interview with Isi Leibler, 12 January 2011.
39 Israel's thanks and request to Australia to continue its efforts were first raised by N. Astar, Charge D'Affairs, 23 May 1963, in a meeting with P. Shaw, Australian Department of External Affairs. The new Israeli Ambassador, David Tesher raised it again when he presented his credentials to Sir Garfield Barwick, 1 July 1963, Series A1838, item 69/7/5/2, Part 3, NAA.
40 Suzanne D Rutland, *Pages of History: A Century of the Australian Jewish Press*, Sydney: Australian Jewish Press, 1995, p. 187.
41 Garfield Barwick, *Australian Foreign Policy 1962: Thirteenth Roy Mine Memorial Lecture*, Canberra: The Australian Institute of International Affairs, 1962.
42 David Marr, *Barwick*, Sydney: George Allen & Unwin, 1980, p. 136.
43 Garfield Barwick, *A Radical Tory – Garfield Barwick's Reflections and Recollections*, Sydney: Federation Press, 1995.
44 Decter to Leibler, Jewish Minorities Research, 17 December 1962, IJLA-Jer.
45 ibid.

CHAPTER 6: CHANNELS OF COMMUNICATION

1 Isi Leibler, Point 16, "Report VJBD re Soviet Jewry", 29 December 1962, ILJA-Jer.
2 Isi Leibler, Point 20, ibid.
3 Isi Leibler to Emanuel Litvinoff, 16 November 1962, IJLA-Jer. Leibler made a similar claim to a letter to Alan Reid, Editor, *Daily Telegraph*, 2 November 1962, IJLA-Jer.
4 Rough notes for the VJBD meeting, June 1962, IJLA-Jer.
5 Leibler to Litvinoff, 16 November 1962, IJLA-Jer.
6 NSW Board of Deputies Plenum Minutes, 20 November 1962.
7 NSW B. Executive Minutes, 11 December 1962.
8 Pamela Ruskin, "Roundabout", *Australian Jewish News*, 2 November 1962.

9   Mendes, "Sam Cohen Affair", pp. 193–4.

10   Rodney Gouttman, "The Sam Cohen Affair: A conspiracy?", *Australian Jewish Historical Society Journal*, Vol XV, Part 1, November 1999, p. 78.

11   Isi Leibler to Alan Reid, Editorial Department, *Daily Telegraph*, Sydney, 2 November 1962, IJLA-Jer.

12   *Australian Jewish Herald (AJH)*, 15 November 1963.

13   Suzanne D Rutland, "Leadership of Accommodation or Protest? Nahum Goldmann and the Struggle for Soviet Jewry", in Mark Raider (ed.), *Nahum Goldmann: Statesman Without a State*, New York: SUNY Press, 2009, pp. 273–98.

14   Ashkanasy to Menzies, 22 October 1963, item 69//2/5/7, Part 2, A 1838, NAA.

15   "Record of Conversation", with Mr Adlai Stevenson, New York, 8 November 1963, D O Hay, Permanent Representative, and Hay to the Secretary, Dept of External Affairs, 12 November 1963, "UN Human Rights and Anti-Semitism", item 929/5/2, Series A1838/1.

16   *AJH*, 22 November 1963.

17   Patrick Shaw, First Assistant Secretary, Sept Ext Affairs, to Ashkanasy, 25 November 1963, item 69//2/5/7, Part 2, A 1838, NAA.

18   Leibler to Decter and reply, November 1963, ILJA-Jer.

19   "Anti-Jewish Propaganda", Questions without Notice, House of Representatives, 15 April 1964, *Hansard*, p. 1068.

20   Barwick served as Chief Justice from 1964 to 1981.

CHAPTER 7: FROM RIGHT TO LEFT

1   Philip Mendes, "A Convergence of political interests: Isi Leibler, the Communist Party of Australia and Soviet anti-Semitism, 1964–66", *Australian Journal Of Politics And History [P]*, vol. 55, issue 2, Blackwell Publishing, Australia, pp. 157–69.

2   Suzanne D Rutland interview with Bernie Taft, Melbourne, 30 August 1998.

3   See Mendes, "A Convergence of Political Interests".

4   Bernard Taft *Crossing the Party Line: Memoirs of Bernie Taft*, Newham: Scribe Publications, 1994, p. 148.

5   Mortimer and Waten, 3 August 1964, "Isi Joseph Leibler, 1964–1965", Part 1, NAA.

6   ibid.

7   ibid.

8   Taft to Mary Walker, 17 November 1964, "Isi Joseph Leibler, 1964–1965", Part 1, NAA.

9   Mendes, "A Convergence of Political Interests".

10   "Isi Joseph Leibler, 1964–1965", Part 1, ASIO file, A6119/90, item 2564,

National Archives of Australia (NAA).

11   Leibler to Bartholomew Augustine Santamaria, 1 April 1964, IJLA-Jer.

12   This letter to Victor A Leginow, Soviet Ambassador, was signed by Isi Leibler, as General Secretary of the ECAJ, 1 October 1964, ECAJ Archives, Archive of Australian Judaica, Fisher Library, University of Sydney (AAJ).

13   Leibler to Sam Cohen, 4 June 1964, "Isi Joseph Leibler, 1964–1965", Part 1, NAA.

14   Judah Leon Waten to Solomon Faktor, 4 August 1964, "Isi Joseph Leibler, 1964–1965", Part 1, NAA.

15   Waten to Platz, 14 August 1964, "Isi Joseph Leibler, 1964–1965", p. 23, Part 1, NAA.

16   Waten and Faktor, 1 December 1964, "Isi Joseph Leibler, 1964–1965", Part 1, NAA.

17   Marvan Jurjevic to Malcolm Frederick Salman, 15 April 1966, p. 76, "Isi Joseph Leibler, 1964–1965", Part 2, NAA.

18   "Soviet Anti-Semitism", *Dissent*, Melbourne: The National Press, 1964.

19   Leibler to Litvnioff, 6 July 1964, IJLA-Jer.

20   Litvinoff to Leibler, 28 April 1964, IJLA-Jer.

21   "Aust. Communists on Soviet Jewry", *Australian Jewish Herald (AJH)*, 27 November 1964.

22   Leibler to Litvinoff, 24 November 1964, IJLA-Jer.

23   "Communists: Jew-baiters", *The Bulletin*, 12 December 1964.

24   Leibler and Mortimer, 8 December 1964, "Isi Joseph Leibler, 1964–1965", Part 1, NAA.

25   Suzanne D Rutland interview with Isi Leibler, Melbourne, 28 August 1998.

26   Suzanne D Rutland interview with Bernie Taft.

27   For a more detailed discussion of the Bridge episode see Suzanne D Rutland, "Creating Intellectual and Cultural Challenges: *The Bridge*", in Marianne Dacy, Jennifer Dowling and Suzanne Faigan, (eds) *Feast and Fasts: Festschrift in Honour of Alan David Crown*, Sydney: Mandelbaum Publishing, 2005.

28   Report, original from CIS, Sydney, 14 May 1948, A6122 XRI, item 155, NAA.

29   *AJH*, 4 September 1964, in "Soviet Jewry, 1963-1964", 7941/250, IJLA-Jer.

30   Yehuda Reinharz and Eytan Friesel "Nahum Goldmann: Jewish and Zionist Statesman – An Overview", in Mark A. Raider (ed), *Nahum Goldmann: Statesman without a State*, New York: SUNY Press, 2009, p. 3.

31   Nahum Goldmann, "The Problem of Soviet Jewry", an article circulated

by Maurice Allen, Chairman, NSW Jewish Board of Deputies, Report to Committee for Overseas Jewry, November 1963 – N.S. No.3, Board of Deputies Archives.

32   For more detail re Goldmann and Soviet Jewry see Suzanne D Rutland, "Leadership of Accommodation or Protest? Nahum Goldmann and the Struggle for Soviet Jewry", in Mark Raider (ed.), *Nahum Goldmann: Statesman Without a State*, New York: SUNY Press, 2009, pp. 273–98.

33   Isi Leibler to Rex Mortimer, 23 July 1965, "Isi Joseph Leibler, 1964–1965", Part 1, ASIO file, A6119/90, item 2564, NAA.

34   "Highlights of the WJC Executive", June 1965, IJLA-Jer.

35   Lecture on World Jewry as reported in the *AJH*, 10 December 1965.

36   Statement by Dr Nahum Goldmann, President of WZO, Press Conference, 10 June 1965, "Press statements by Goldmann, 1964–1965", Z6/2079, Central Zionist Archives, Jerusalem (CZA).

37   Litvinoff to Leibler, 27 June 1965, and Leibler to Litvinoff, 6 July 1965, IJLA-Jer.

38   Notes on conflict with Goldmann, July 1965, IJLA-Jer.

39   Leibler's hand written notes on the meeting, 13 July, in IJLA-Jer.

40   *Australian Jewish News (AJN)*, 23 July 1965.

41   *Jewish Chronicle*, London, 16 July 1965.

42   Notes on conflict with Goldmann, July 1965, IJLA-Jer.

43   Notes for address to Victorian Jewish Board of Deputies, 2 August 1965, IJLA-Jer.

44   Handwritten notes, WJC Plenary Session, 31 July – 9 August 1966, Brussels, IJLA-Jer.

45   *JC*, 12 August 1966.

46   Isi Leibler, "Draft Memo on Soviet Jews", 22 December 1966, ILJA-Jer.

47   Goldmann to Ashkanasy, 14 November 1966, the Executive Council of Australian Jewry (ECAJ), Z6/1179, CZA.

48   Ashkanasy to Goldmann, 25 November 1966, "Jewry 1966", Z6/1176, CZA.

49   Goldmann to Ashkanasy, 10 December 1966, "Material on Clash between WJC and Australian Jewry, 1967", Z6/1179, CZA

50   Signed by M. Ashkanasy, M. Slonim and Isi J. Leibler, "Material on Clash between WJC and Australian Jewry, 1967", Z6/1179, CZA.

51   Easterman to Goldmann, 3 March 1967, "Material on Clash between WJC and Australian Jewry, 1967", Z6/1179, CZA.

52   Riegner to Ashkanasy, 7 March 1967, "Material on Clash between WJC and Australian Jewry, 1967", Z6/1179, CZA.

53   Ashkanasy to Prinz, 21 April 1967, "Jewry 1966", Z6/1176, CZA.

54   Hayes to ECAJ, 24 March 1967, IJLA-Jer.

55   MAOZ was the Israeli equivalent of the Conference on Soviet Jewry formed in the US.

56   Meeting between Taft and Leibler, March 1971. Leibler wrote that Taft had seen Goldmann as "a liability to our cause" and that he considered him to be "servile, naïve, and totally devoid of any understanding of the way the Russians tick". Notes after meetings, March and 21 April 1971. The latter meeting took place in Isi Leibler's home. IJLA-Jer.

CHAPTER 8: ITALIAN LINERS AND THE PARTY

1   Terence H Irving, "Mortimer, Rex Alfred (1926–1979)", *Australian Dictionary of Biography*, National Centre of Biography, Australian National University, http://adb.anu.edu.au/biography/mortimer-rex-alfred-11181/text19925, accessed 7 April 2013.

2   This endorsement was published as a letter at the beginning of the book, Isi Leibler, *Soviet Jewry and Human Rights*, Melbourne: Human Rights Publications, 1965.

3   As quoted in the *Jewish Herald*, 9 April 1965.

4   Leibler to Emanuel Litvinoff, 5 April 1965, "Soviet Jewry", IJLA-Jer.

5   Helen Palmer, "Review of Soviet Jewry and Human Rights", *Outlook: An Independent Socialist Journal published monthly by the Left*, Vol 9, No 3, June 1965.

6   "Soviet Jewry" in *Arena: A Marxist Journal of Criticism and Discussion*, No 7, Winter 1965, edited by Janet Hase, Rex Mortimer and Nonie Sharp. See also S Murray-Smith, *Overland*, No 32, Spring 1965 and Ian Cummin's Review, *Dissent*, April 1965.

7   Margaret Hearn and Professor Courtney Oppenheim, 18 April 1965, "Isi Joseph Leibler, 1964–1965", Part 1, NAA.

8   Mark Aarons, *The Family File*, Melbourne: Black Inc, 2010, p. 205.

9   Aarons, *Family File*, p. 207.

10   *The Bulletin*, 12 June 1965.

11   *Soviet Jewry – A Reply to I. Leibler*, June 1965.

12   *AJN*, 8 July 1965.

13   Bernard Taft, *Crossing the Party Line*, p. 149. Also quoted in Mendes, "A convergence of political interests".

14   "Summary of Discussion with CPA – Sydney, 15 September 1965", IJLA-Jer.

15   Summary Notes of Meeting 8 November 1965, Leibler's home. Laurie Aarons had come to Melbourne at the invitation of the Jewish Progressive Centre to give a lecture to mark the November 1917 Bolshevik Revolution, IJLA-Jer.

16   Notes of meeting between Eric Aarons and Leibler, 6 December 1965, IJLA-Jer.

17   Leibler to Mortimer, 13 December 1965, "Isi Joseph Leibler, 1964–1965", Part 2, NAA.

18   *The Australian*, 17 December 1965.

19 Leibler to Litvinoff, 21 December 1965. The statement was published in the *Tribune*, 13 December and republished in the *Guardian*, 16 December 1965.

20 Sam Lipski, Introduction, *Soviet Jewry and the Australian Communist Party-Documents*.

21 Maurice Ashkanasy, *Jewish Herald*, 27 May 1966.

22 See *AJN*, 3 June 1966 and 1 July 1966, when Einfeld commends the booklet. Einfeld wrote to Leibler apologizing for the delay in his statement due to serious eye problems which made reading difficult, 24 June 1966. IJLA-Jer.

23 *Catholic Worker*, No 134, June 1966 and *News Weekly*, 15 June 1966, 29 June 1966, and 6 July 1966.

24 "Leibler Questions on New Book", *AJN*, 10 June 1966.

25 Telephone conversation, Mortimer and Taft, 20 October 1966, "Isi Joseph Leibler, 1964–1965", Part 2, NAA.

26 *AJH*, 11 November 1966.

27 ibid.

28 ibid.

29 "Background Information", 11 November 1966, IJLA-Jer.

30 "At the Board", report, "Isi Joseph Leibler, 1964–1965", Part 2, p. 119, NAA.

31 Fred Coleman, *The Decline and Fall of Soviet Empire: Forty Years That Shook the World, From Stalin to Yeltsin*, New York: St Martin's Griffin, 1997, p. 95.

32 Leibler to Decter, 29 March 1966, IJLA-Jer.

33 Leibler to Mortimer referring to Mortimer's comment re Eric Aarons, 14 November 1966, IJLA-Jer.

34 These points were set out in a written document: "Communist Party of Australia – Directive and Statement", 18 November 1966, Victoria, Report No. 2922/66, 24 November 1966, in "Isi Joseph Leibler, 1964–1965", Part 2, p. 132, NAA.

35 John Alan Sendy to Mortimer, 6 December 1966, "Isi Joseph Leibler, 1964–1965", Part 2, p. 134, NAA.

36 John Sendy and Sol Faktor, "Isi Joseph Leibler, 1966–1968", Part 3, p. 10-11, NAA.

37 Leibler to Litvinoff, 30 November 1966, IJLA-Jer.

38 CPA State Committee Minutes, 11 December 1966, in "Isi Joseph Leibler, 1966-1968", Part 3, pp. 14–19, NAA.

39 ibid.

40 D B Waterson, "Turner, Ian Alexander Hamilton (1922–1978)", *Australian Dictionary of Biography*, Volume 16, Melbourne University Press, 2002, pp. 424–5.

41 *AJN*, 4 August 1967. See the ongoing debate in the *AJN*, 18 and 25 August, 1, 15 and 29 September.

42 Judah Waten, "Letters to the Editor", *AJN*, 29 September 1967.

43 Leibler to Litvinoff and Decter, 19 September 1967, IJLA-Jer.

44 Isi Leibler to Laurie Aarons, General Secretary, CPA, 14 September 1967, "Soviet Jewry", VJBD Archives, Box 73, La Trobe Section, State Library of Victoria.

45 ECAJ Press Release prepared for 7 November 1967, the actual anniversary, Victorian Jewish Board of Deputies Archives, Box 73, La Trobe Section, State Library of Victoria.

46 Lou Jedwab and Sol Faktor to Hyrall Waten, 6 November 1967, "Isi Joseph Leibler, 1966-1968", Part 3, NAA.

47 *AJN*, 5 April 1968.

48 See *AJN*, 17 and 24 November 1967.

49 Leibler to Litvinoff, 27 August 1968, IJLA-Jer.

50 *Bulletin*, 17 May 1969.

51 Leibler to Litvinoff, 20 May 1969, IJLA, Jerusalem.

52 Litvinoff to Leibler, 27 May 1969, IJLA, Jerusalem.

53 Memo on meetings with Bernie Taft, March 1971, IJLA-Jer. See also Mendes, "A convergence of political interests".

CHAPTER 9: EXODUS VIA *SAMIZDAT*

1 Mark Ya. Azbel, *Refusenik – Trapped in the Soviet Union*, London: Hamish Hamilton, 1982, p. 215.

2 Jenna Weissman Joselit, in a book review of *Leon Uris: Life of a Best Seller* by Ira Nadel, University of Texas, 2010, in *Commentary*, New York, December 2010, p. 62.

3 Azbel, *Refusenik*, p. 215.

4 Howard M Sachar, *A History of the Jews in the Modern World*, New York: Howard A Knopf, 2005, p. 722.

5 V. Rabinovich, "Whom do the 'Prophets' of Zionism Serve?", *Docent, Sovetskaya Rossiya*, 24 January 1969, pp. 2–3, USSR – "Political Nationalities – Jews", Part 4, 69/2/5/7/, A1838, NAA.

6 G. Plotkin, "The Mask and Real Aspect of Zionism", *Pravda*, 12 December 1969, Part 4, 69/2/5/7/, A1838, NAA.

7 Letter from Isi Leibler, 20 April 1972, Box 70, VJBD.

8 "The Leningrad trial", Memo, p. 3, January 1971, Part 6, 69/2/5/7/, A1838, NAA.

9 John Bowan, 7 October 1969, Part 4, 69/2/5/7/, A1838, NAA.

10 Speech by Isi Leibler, as reported in the *AJN*, 21 May 1971, IJLA-Jer.

11 Draft, Soviet Jewry, 1970, Part 6, 69/2/5/7/, A1838, NAA.

12 *The Age*, Melbourne, 12 March 1970.

13 As quoted from the underground Jewish publication, *Exodus,* No. 2. 1970), "The Leningrad trial", Memo, January 1971, p. 4, Part 6, 69/2/5/7/, A1838, NAA.

14 Leonard Schroeter, *The Last Exodus,* New York: Universe Books, 1974, p. 125.

15 ibid., p. 125.

16 ibid., p. 127.

17 Yehoshua A Gilboa, *The Black Years of Soviet Jewry, 1939–1953,* Toronto: Little Brown and Company, 1971, p. 318–19.

18 Simon Sebag Montefiore, *Stalin, The Court of the Red Tsar,* London: Weidenfeld and Nicolson, 2003, pp. 519.

19 Schroeter, *The Last Exodus,* p. 128.

20 William Korey *The Soviet Cage: Anti-Semitism in Russia,* New York: Viking, 1973, p. 171.

21 Resolution Adopted by the Knesset at its Special Session on 19 November 1969, Part 4, 69/2/5/7/, A1838, NAA.

22 See correspondence 17 December 1969, 8 January 1970 and 22 April 1970, Part 4, 69/2/5/7/, A1838, NAA.

23 Instruction from Doron Ur, 30 July 1970, IJLA-Jer.

24 Keynote address by Marcus R Einfeld, campaign chairman, at mass rally of protest and solidarity with Soviet Jews held in the Sydney Town Hall on Sunday 30 August 1970. Full text supplied by Marcus Einfeld.

25 This delegation consisted of Gerald Falk, Harry Goldstein, Walter Lippmann, E Horton, Marcus Einfeld and Isi Leibler.

26 "Red envoy refuses to meet Jews", Sydney *Daily Telegraph*, 2 September 1970.

27 As reported in *The Australian*, 2 September 1970.

28 C T Moodie, Acting First Assistant Secretary, Division IV, Memo, 22 September 1979, Part 5, 69/2/5/7/, A1838, NAA.

29 ibid., 23 September 1970, Part 5, 69/2/5/7/, A1838, NAA.

30 *The Australian*, 24 October 1970.

31 A copy of this statement was sent to Marcus Einfeld after the Sydney mass rally in 1970, ECAJ Boxes, AAJ.

32 "Aboriginal Rights", 8–9 October 1970, Part 5, 69/2/5/7/, A1838, NAA.

33 "General Assembly: Third Committee", inward cablegram, 8–9 October 1970, Part 5, 69/2/5/7/, A1838, NAA.

34 "Position of Jews in the USSR", Memo for the Minister, 2 September 1970, Part 5, 69/2/5/7/, A1838, NAA.

35 Gal Beckerman, "Hijacking Their Way out of Tyranny", *New York Times,* 17 June 2010.

36 "Points from Statement by Prime Minister Mrs Golda Meir in the Knesset on 25 December 1970 regarding the verdict in the Leningrad

Trial of Soviet Jews", submitted by the Israeli Ambassador, Moshe
Erell, 26 December 1970, Part 5, 69/2/5/7/, A1838, NAA.

37 Memo, 28 December 1970, Part 5, 69/2/5/7/, A1838, NAA.

38 ibid.

39 PM's Message to U Thant, UN Secretary-General, Canberra, 27
December 1970, Part 5, 69/2/5/7/, A1838, NAA.

40 Cable from Tel Aviv Embassy, 29–30 December 1970, Part 5, 69/2/5/7/,
A1838, NAA.

41 See *Adelaide Advertiser*, 19 December 1970; and *The Sun*, Melbourne,
the *Standard*, Narrambool, Victoria, *Border Morning Mail*, Albury, on
22 December 1970, IJLA-Jer.

42 Editorial, *Sydney Morning Herald*, 30 December 1970.

43 Editorial, "The Hijacker Plotters", *Canberra Times*, 28 December 1970.
See also *Courier Mail*, Brisbane, 28 December 1970, *The Advocate*, 29
December 1970, *West Australian*, 29 December 1970, *The Australian*,
29 December 1970, where the editor claimed it was "a political case …
the Russian authorities clearly decided to martyr a Jew or two as an
objective lesson to the rest (in the case 3m)".

44 Resumé of activities and texts of statements and telegrams concerning
the Leningrad Hijack Trials December 1970, ECAJ Corres Files, Box
70. On 30/31 December 1970, AAJ. See also ECAJ material, December
1970, IJLA-Jer.

45 Report on demonstration in Canberra by Mr H Shaw, Box 70, 1970–
72, AAJ.

46 *West Australian*, 19 December 1970.

47 "The Leningrad trial", Memo, p. 2, January 1971, Part 6, 69/2/5/7/,
A1838, NAA.

48 Draft, Soviet Jewry, 1970, Part 6, 69/2/5/7/, A1838, NAA.

CHAPTER 10: PRISONERS OF ZION

1 Mosher Decter, "The Terror That Fails: Anti-Zionism as the
Lietmotif of Soviet Anti-Semitism", 23 page document. See also S.
Ettinger, "Russian-Jewish Relationship Before and After the October
Revolution", and J. Miller, "Profile of Soviet Jewry", IJLA-Jer.

2 Handwritten notes at the Brussels Conference, 23–25 February 1971,
IJLA-Jer.

3 ibid.

4 ibid.

5 Diane Armstrong, "One morning the synagogue was closed", *SMH*, 24
April 1971.

6 Isi Leibler, "February 1971 Brussels Conference Report", IJLA-Jer.

7 Email information, Isi Leibler, 13 January 2013.

8   Memo from Mr F B Cooper with his wife, invited by Soviet Counsellor (V N Smirnov) to dinner at USSR embassy residence. Mr A F Ekimenko, third sec, also present, 26 Feb 1971, Part 7, 69/2/5/7/, A1838, NAA.

9   ibid.

10   *SMH*, 16 May 1971.

11   *Australian Jewish Times*, 3 June 1971.

12   Press release, "Soviet Embassy ignores plea by 5000", 7 July 1971, Box 70, 1970–72.

13   Copy of PM response, 9 June 1971, and also comment by Moodie, 23 June 1971, Part 8, 69/2/5/7/, A1838, NAA.

14   F B Cooper, "Trial of Soviet Jews", 18 May 1971, Part 8, 69/2/5/7/, A1838, NAA.

15   C T Moodie, First Assistant Secretary, Pacific and Western Division, 21 May 1971, 69/2/5/7/, A1838, NAA 69/2/5/7/, A1838, NAA Part 8.

16   Note from Moodie re his telephone conversation with Erell, 17 June 1971, Part 8, 69/2/5/7/, A1838, NAA.

17   F B Cooper, Memo, 19 October 1971, Part 9, 69/2/5/7/, A1838, NAA.

18   Handwritten note, no date, around 6 October 1971, Part 9, 69/2/5/7/, A1838, NAA.

19   Report of meeting with Director-General of Israeli Foreign Ministry, Gideon Rafael, and Sir Keith Waller, Sec FA and Mr C H Stuart, NAM Section, and Israeli Ambassador, HE Mr Moshe Erell. Main subjects ME, Indonesia, Soviet Jewry and Invitation to the Secretary. 30 April 1971, pp. 6–7, Part 7, 69/2/5/7/, A1838, NAA.

20   F J Blakeney, Ambassador, "Jewish Emigration from the U.S.S.R.", 27 May 1971, Part 8. Also included in Part 9, 69/2/5/7/, A1838, NAA.

21   David Sadlier, 28 March 1972, Series A1036 Foreign Affairs, 201/4/2 Part 11, Minorities and Nationalities: Jews in the Soviet Union, 1971/2.

22   "Assistance for Jewish Emigrants from the USSR", Meeting with Miss Isobel Klein and Mr Edward Mirvis of the International Committee for Soviet Jewry, and David Sadlier, Counsellor, Australian Embassy, Washington, 28 July 1972, Minorities and Nationalities: Jews in the Soviet Union, 1971/72 item 201/4/2 Part 11, Foreign Affairs, Series A1036, NAA.

23   Inward cable from the Australian embassy, Moscow, 21 October 1972, Part 11, 69/2/5/7/, A1838, NAA.

24   Text of Resolution Adopted by the Knesset (Israel's Parliament) on 23 August 1972 Concerning Soviet Jewry, Part 12, 69/2/5/7/, A1838, NAA.

25   Nathan Jacobson, ECAJ, to Right Hon. William McMahon, no date, Part 11, 69/2/5/7/, A1838, NAA.

26   Suzanne D Rutland, *If You Will It, It is no Dream: The Moriah Story,*

1943–2003, Sydney: Playright Publishing, 2003, pp. 229–31.

27   30 August 1972, Part 11, 69/2/5/7/, A1838, NAA.

28   Professor Julius Stone and Professor Noel S. Hush, University of Sydney, *SMH*, 27 November 1972, Part 11, 69/2/5/7/, A1838, NAA.

29   News Bulletin, No. 2, April/May 1973.

30   *Canberra Times,* 4 September 1972. This protest was reported widely throughout the Australian media.

31   Typed testimony from Professor Dori Parolla, IJLA-Jer.

32   Robert Goot, "Report of Campaign", September 1972 and Isi Leibler speech, Public Protest Meeting, St Kilda Town Hall, 1 October 1972, IJLA-Jer.

33   See Answer from Senator Wright to Senator Carrick, 30 August 1972, outward cable to Australian Embassies in Tel Aviv and Moscow, Part 11, 69/2/5/7/, A1838, NAA.

34   Prime Minister McMahon, 13 September 1972, Part 11, 69/2/5/7/, A1838, NAA.

35   Report of Bowen's meeting with Gromyko at NUN NYC – Sir Laurence McIntyre present– raised question of Soviet Jewry, 25 September 1972, Part 11, 69/2/5/7/, A1838, NAA.

36   Quoted in William Korey, *The Soviet Cage*, p. 319.

37   ibid., p. 320.

38   J G Powys, Second Secretary, Moscow embassy, to the Secretary, DFA, Canberra, 27 December 1972, Part 11, 69/2/5/7/, A1838, NAA.

39   ibid.

40   ibid.

41   ibid.

42   ibid.

CHAPTER 11: HENRY J AND HENRY K

1   Walter Isaacson, *Kissinger – A Biography,* New York: Simon and Schuster, 2005, p. 612.

2   ibid.

3   All quotes from Nixon and Kissinger are taken from JTA reports, 14 December and 26 December 2010; www. jta.org.

4   Dan Kurzman, *Soldier of Peace: The Life of Yitzhak Rabin*, New York: HarperCollins, 1998.

5   Jonathan S Tobin, "Contentions", in Commentary online, 14 December 2010, www.commentarymagazine.com.

6   Richard Perle, Proceedings of the Kennan Institute conference on "The Legacy and Consequences of Jackson-Vanik: Reassessing Human Rights in 21st Century Russia, 4 February 2010, Woodrow Wilson Center, Washington DC.

CHAPTER 12: "YOU PEOPLE ARE HARD TO PLEASE"

1   For a more detailed discussion of Whitlam's Foreign Policy and the Jewish community, see Suzanne D Rutland, "Whitlam's Shifts in Foreign Policy 1972–1975: Israel and Soviet Jewry", *Australian Journal of Jewish Studies* (2012) 26: pp. 36–69.

2   Isi Leibler, "Summary of Canberra Meeting", 1 September 1970, "Soviet Jewry", IJLA-Jer.

3   ibid.

4   Tamar Eshel, president, to Mrs H E Scotford, president National Council of Women of Australia, 13 September 1972. NCWA sent its letter to Whitlam on 10 February, and included a copy of the letter they received from Mrs Eshel in Israel, Part 12, 69/2/5/7, A1838, NAA.

5   E G Whitlam, to Rev. F G Engel, General Secretary, Australian Council of Churches, 18 January 1973, Part 12, 69/2/5/7, A1838, NAA.

6   Outward cablegram, Australian Mission to the UN, New York and Australian Permanent Mission, UN, Geneva, 11 December 1973, Part 12, pp. 238–9.

7   ibid.

8   Letter from J G Powys following a meeting with Lambert D'Ansembourg, First Secretary of the Netherlands, 1 March 1973, Part 12.

9   F R Dalrymple, Ambassador, Israel, 13 March 1974, Part 12.

10 Report of meeting with Moshe Erell, Israeli Ambassador, and B C Hill, 13 March 1973, Part 12.

11 Handwritten note, 15 March 1972 and Memo 22 March 1972, Part 12.

12 Reply to Mr Snedden, 25 Jan 1974, pp. 252–3, Part 12.

13 Question in the Senate from Senator Kane, Hansard, pp. 2621–2, Part 12.

14 Robert M Goot, "Report of the NSW Division of the Australian campaign for the Rescue of Soviet Jewry – 1973", ECAJ Annual Report, 1973/1974.

15 Transcript of speech, "Australian Jewry, ALP, Jews and Israel", Vol 78, 9 May 1974, p. 13, IJLA-Jer.

16 ibid.

17 Victorian Jewish Board of Deputies, Press Release, 9 May 1974, "Australian Jewry", "ALP, Jews and Israel", Vol 78, IJLA-Jer.

18 Memo re meeting with Whitlam, V P Suslov, Head, Second European Dept, Soviet Foreign Ministry, Y I Pavlov, Soviet Ministry of Foreign Affairs and R J Greet, Assistant Secretary, Europe Branch, 17 November 1974, Part 13, 69/2/5/7 A1838, NAA.

19 ibid.

20 Draft document, p. 55, Part 13, 69/2/5/7, A1838, NAA.

21 Outward cablegram to Moscow, 3 December 1974, p. 68, Part 13.

22   Memo, "For Publication After My Return", p. 84, Part 13.

23   Jacobson to Whitlam, 28 January 1975, Part 13.

24   "Terrigal Conference: The Soviet Union: Jewish Emigration, Political Prisoners, Dissidents", February 1975, "USSR Political Dissent – Political and Cultural", item 69/2/8/2, Part 1, series A1838, NAA.

25   *Commonwealth Parliamentary Debates,* 1976, pp. 2735–43.

CHAPTER 13: FREEDOM RIDE TO CANBERRA

1   *Canberra Times*, 3 November 1976, Part 13.

2   "Human Rights" Petition from Mr Wentworth (Mackellar), Representatives, *Hansard*, 2 November 1976, p. 2180.

3   W C Wentworth to Sir Magnus McCormack, 4 November 1976, Part 13, 69/2/5/7/, A1838, NAA.

4   Kim Edward Beazley, *Father of the House: the Memoirs of Kim E. Beazley*, North Fremantle, WA: Fremantle Press, 2009, p. 251.

5   ibid., p. 252.

6   See Wentworth's letter 1 February 1977 and department's memo, pp. 256–7, Part 13, 69/2/5/7, A1838, NAA.

7   Ian Sinclair, Minister for Primary Industry, answered on behalf of Peacock. Sinclair to Sultanik, 30 March 1977, Part 14, 69/2/5/7/, A1838, NAA.

8   "Passover Plan was thwarted", *Courier Mail*, Brisbane, 23 March 1977.

9   *AJT*, 22 June 1978.

10   *SMH*, 17 July 1978.

11   Peacock to Sultanik, 4 August 1978, Part 16, 69/2/5/7/, A1838, NAA, pp. 140–4. See also Memo, F B Cooper, 19 July 1978, "USSR – Australia: Political and Cultural Dissent", item A69/2/8/2, Part 8, series A1838; and "Rabbinical Delegation Proposals to Australian Government", item 69/2/8, Part 8, series A1838, NAA.

12   Memo, 8 August 1978, Europe, Part 16. See also Memo 19July 1978, "USSR – Australia: Political and Cultural Dissent", item A69/2/8/2, Part 8, series A1838, NAA.

13   Andrew Peacock to Rabbi E Sultanik and other members of the Rabbinical Delegation, 23 August 1978, item 69/2/8, Part 8, series A1838, NAA.

14   ibid.

15   Myrna Shinbaum, as quoted in Murray Friedman and Albert D Chernin, eds., *A Second Exodus – The American Movement to Free Soviet Jews,* Boston: Brandeis University Press, 1999, p. 176.

16   Arnold Bloch, 10 September 1978, IJLA-Jer.

17   Police report, 23 August 1977, Part 14, 69/2/5/7/, A1838, NAA.

18   Memo from Bourchier to Canberra, 23 February 1979, Part 9, File No. 69/2/8/2, A1838 NAA.

19   For a detailed report of their presentation, see B. Welsly, East Europe Section, "Sub-committee on Human Rights in the Soviet Union of the Joint Committee on Foreign Affairs and Defence", 5 March 1979, item 69/2/8, series A1838, NAA.

20   DFA meeting with Mr A V Baslov, Ambassador, Mr I A Saprykin, Counsellor, and Mr Andrew Peacock and Mr K Chan, East Europe Section, Subjects: Bilateral Relations, Joint Com Enquiry into Soviet Jews; Chinese Delegation Visit, 20 September 1977, pp. 147–8, Part 14, 69/2/5/7, A1838, NAA.

21   Report of presentation to JCFAD Sub-committee, 7 October 1977, Part 15, 69/2/5/7/, A1838, NAA.

22   Minutes of Peacock's presentation, 19 October 1977, Part 15.

23   In a private conversation with a department officer, Cormack complained about the "present and prospective pressure he was receiving from the Zionist lobby". Notes re conversation with Cormack, 26 September 1977, Part 14, 69/2/5/7/, A1838, NAA.

24   Minutes of Peacock's presentation, 19 October 1977, Part 15, 69/2/5/7/, A1838, NAA.

25   "JFADC: Enquiry of the Sub-committee on the Petition Regarding Soviet Jewry", Professor Alexander Voronel: A Biographical Note, Part 14, p. 280.

26   See for example *The Canberra Times*, 8 October 1977.

27   Report of President, Dr J Schneeweiss, ECAJ Annual Conference, 4 December 1977.

28   "Joint Committee on Foreign Affairs and Defence", Senate Debate, *Hansard*, 26 October 1977, p. 1795.

29   Bob Carr, "Anti-Russian Lobby Gathers Strength Here", *Bulletin*, 25 July 1978.

30   See notes, 30 June 1978, Part 16, 69/2/5/7/, A1838, NAA.

31   Cable, "Human Rights in the USSR", 22 May 1978, p. 2. item 201/5, Part 3, repeated in Part 4, series A10136.

32   Robert Goot, hearing told: "It's hard for Russian Jews" *Telegraph* (Sydney), 12 April 1978.

33   Transcript of Isi Leibler"s submission to the Parliamentary Inquiry, 18 October 1978, with Senator Wheeldon (Chair), Senators Sibraa and Martin, and Dobie, Jacobi, Simon and Dr Klugman, IJLA, Jerusalem.

34   Pravda, "The Soviet Union will not stand interference in its affairs", 15 September 1978, English translation in full in Part 16.

35   *The Canberra Times*, 28 October 1977.

36   See articles in *The Canberra Times* and the *Sydney Morning Herald*, 15 April 1978.

37   *The Australian*, August/September 1978, newspaper clipping in "USSR

– Political Developments – Resistance, disaffection and émigré bodies dissidents", 27 July 1978 – 5 October 1978, item 69/2/8, Part 8, series A1838, NAA.

38   *Report of the Joint Committee of Foreign Affairs and Defence,* p. 137.
39   Suzanne D Rutland interview with Sam Salcman, Melbourne, 12 July 1998.
40   Peter King and Martin Krygier eds., *Human Rights in the Soviet Union: The Australian Enquiry* (sic), Sydney, Committee for Human Rights in the Soviet Union and Eastern Europe, 1980.
41   *The Bulletin*, 20 November 1979, pp. 54–5.

CHAPTER 14: FROM MELBOURNE TO MOSCOW

1   Pullan, *Bob Hawke,* p. 105.
2   Elitzur to Leibler, 15 February 1978, IJLA-Jer.
3   Isi Leibler, Report II, Visit to Moscow 6–13 December 1978, Second 8 day visit, p. 6, IJLA-Jer.
4   Cable to Rachel Leibler, 8 August 1978, IJLA-Jer.
5   Report of First Visit to Moscow, p. 8, IJLA-Jer.
6   Meeting with Organising Committee of the 1980 Olympic Games in Moscow, Vyacheslov Zhilin, Vladimir Ratinov, Gheeman Bulgakov, Sergey Nadzharov, Mde Nosakova and Alla Levitina, Report of First Visit to Moscow, p. 19, IJLA-Jer.
7   Report of First Visit to Moscow, p. 32, IJLA Report of First Visit to Moscow, p. 32, IJLA-Jer.
8   Report of First Visit to Moscow, p. 40, IJLA-Jer.
9   Report of First Visit to Moscow, p. 47, IJLA-Jer.
10   "To Moscow", Report of First Visit, p. 15, IJLA-Jer.
11   Report of First Visit to Moscow, p. 68, IJLA-Jer.
12   "Jetset and My Position", Report of First Visit, p. 14, IJLA-Jer.
13   *Sunday Observer*, 20 August 1978.
14   Letters were published defending Leibler from Newell's criticism, *AJN*, 1 September 1978.
15   Arnold Bloch to Dr Joachim Schneeweiss, 11 September 1978, IJLA-Jer.
16   "The two hats of Isi Leibler", *The Bulletin*, 12 September 1978.
17   Leibler to Dulzin, 25 September 1978, IJLA-Jer.
18   "The Role of John Halfpenny", Report of First Visit, IJLA-Jer. Reports about Halfpenny were published in *The Westralian*, 8 August 1978, *The Age*, 8 and 12 August 1978, *The Sun*, 12 August 1978, and *The Socialist*, 9 August 1978.
19   Leibler to Michael Elitzur, 17 August 1978, IJLA-Jer.
20   Note to Michael Elitzur, 6 September 1978, IJLA-Jer.

CHAPTER 15: THE GAMES RUSSIANS PLAY

1   "Moscow Olympics", Europe Branch, 12 October 1978, 69/1/3/6/19, Part 1, A1838, NAA.

2   Meeting with AOF leaders, 9 October 1978, pp. 1–3, IJLA-Jer.

3   Leibler to the AOF, 10 October 1978, IJLA-Jer.

4   Malcolm Fraser to Leibler, 29 November 1978, IJLA-Jer.

5   Outward cable, 16 November 1978, "USSR – Foreign Policy – Relations with Australia – General – Visits and Exchanges – Moscow Olympic Games (Olympic Attaché)", Part 1, 2 August – 19 March 1979, 69/1/3/6/19, A1838, NAA.

6   ibid.

7   Inward cable, 27 November 1978, 69/1/3/6/19, A1838, NAA.

8   "Confidential: Visit by Mr Isi Leibler, Executive Director of Jetset Tours, For Ambassador", Outward cable, 16 November 1978, 201/5, Part 3, A10136, NAA.

9   Isi Leibler, "Report II, Visit to Moscow 6–13 December 1978, Second 8 day visit", pp. 13–15, IJLA-Jer.

10   ibid., p. 22.

11   ibid., p. 49.

12   ibid., p. 69.

13   Inward cable, 14 December 1978, Australia – USSR Political Dissent Political and Cultural, Sep 1978 – April 79, 69/2/8/2, Part 9, A1838, NAA.

14   Rager to Leibler, 24 January 1979, IJLA-Jer. Rager served as Israeli consul in New York, working on behalf of Soviet Jewry.

15   Leibler, "Summary of Visit to Israel", pp. 43–4, IJLA-Jer.

16   John Oliver, handwritten department memo after conversation with Julius Patching, nd (late April), "USSR – Foreign Policy – Relations with Australia – General – Visits and Exchanges – Moscow Olympic Games (Olympic Attaché)", Part 2, 19 March – 31 August 1979, 69/1/3/6/19, A1838, NAA.

17   Meeting with Jetset, represented by Isi Leibler and Lionel Landman, and AOF, represented by Syd Grange, David McKenzie, 23 April 1979, "Recent Developments Re Moscow Olympic Games", pp. 4–5, IJLA-Jer.

18   Leibler to Nehemiah Levanon, 24 April 1979, IJLA-Jer.

19   Meeting with Jetset, and AOF, 23 April 1979, "Recent Developments Re Moscow Olympic Games", p. 5, IJLA-Jer.

20   ibid., p. 6.

21   ibid.

22   Leibler, "Olympic Games", No 5, 8 May 1979, p. 3, IJLA-Jer.

23   Notes for Minister by C R (Robin) Ashwin, First Assistant Secretary,

Western Division, nd (late May), "USSR – Foreign Policy – Relations with Australia – General – Visits and Exchanges – Moscow Olympic Games (Olympic Attaché)", Part 2, 19 March – 31 August 1979, 69/1/3/6/19, A1838, NAA. Ashwin continued to work for DFAT. In 1982 Leibler met with him and described him as "very intelligent, sophisticated, but certainly not a friend". Leibler noted his hostility to Israel. "Meetings in Canberra", 17 March 1982, IJLA-Jer. Ashwin was later appointed Ambassador to Moscow, taking over from Edward (Ted) Pocock in 1987.

CHAPTER 16: HAWKE'S MISSION IMPOSSIBLE

1   Bob Hawke, *The Hawke Memoirs,* Port Melbourne: William Heinemann Australia, 1994, pp. 72 and 91.
2   *The Herald* (Melbourne), 14 May 1971.
3   Robert Pullan, *Bob Hawke: A Portrait,* Sydney: Methuen of Australia, 1980, p. 146.
4   Hawke interview with Sam Lipski, 2010.
5   John Hurst, *Hawke: the definitive biography*, Sydney: Angus & Robertson Publishers, 1979, p. 105.
6   Lipski interview 2010.
7   Johnson, inward cable re Hawke's Mission to Moscow to the Department of Foreign Affairs, Canberra, 27 July 1971, Department of Foreign Affairs, item 69/2/5/7, Part 9, series A1838, NAA.
8   Johnson, inward cable re Hawke's Mission to Moscow to the Department of Foreign Affairs, Canberra, 27 July 1971, Department of Foreign Affairs, item 69/2/5/7, Part 9, series A1838, NAA.
9   Blanche d'Alpuget, *Robert J. Hawke: A Biography*, East Melbourne: Schwartz Publishing Co., 1982, p. 257.
10   ibid., p. 261.
11   ibid., p. 267.
12   Hawke, *The Hawke Memoirs*, p. 78.
13   *The Herald*, Melbourne, 11 November 1974, as quoted in Pullan, *Bob Hawke*, p. 154.
14   "Briefing for Mr Bob Hawke", p. 18, late March 1979, IJLA, Jerusalem.
15   "Further Developments Re Soviet Jewry – No 6", 9 May 1979, p. 2.
16   "Further Developments Re Soviet Jewry – NO 7", 10 May 1979, p. 2.
17   "Report on Visit to Israel and Rome", p. 12. In this detailed report of day by day events, Leibler noted that it was dictated as a summary of events as they occurred, and as such was a diary and not for distribution. The Report consists of 62 pages, IJLA, Jerusalem.

CHAPTER 17: HOPE AGAINST HOPE

1   Bourchier, "Hawke Visit to Moscow", seven-page report, 12 June 1979, Additional Materials at the end of file, pp. 228–43, Part 17, 4 June 1979 to 4 January 1985, 69/2/5/7, A1838.
2   Hawke, *The Hawke Memoirs*, p. 89.
3   Bourchier, "Hawke Visit to Moscow", Part 17, 69/2/5/7, A1838.
4   ibid.
5   Sam Lipski, Interview with Hawke, 2010.
6   ibid.
7   Leibler, "Report on Visit to Israel and Rome", p. 26. In this detailed report of day by day events, Leibler noted that it was dictated as a summary of events as they occurred, and as such was a diary and not for distribution. The Report consists of 62 pages, IJLA-Jer.
8   ibid., p. 27, IJLA-Jer.
9   ibid., p. 28, IJLA-Jer.
10   Bourchier, "Hawke Visit to Moscow", Part 17, 69/2/5/7, A1838.
11   ibid.
12   Quoted from IJLA-Jer. Also in Hawke's *Memoirs*, p. 90.
13   Hawke, *The Hawke Memoirs*, p. 90.
14   Leibler, "Hawke's Mission – Background and Assessment", Address to NSW Board of Deputies, 19 June 1979, IJLA-Jer.
15   Leiber, "Report on Visit to Israel and Rome", p. 34.
16   Cable to Department of Foreign Affairs, Rome, 26 May 1979, Part 16, 69/2/5/7/, A1838, NAA.
17   ibid.
18   See *International Daily News*, 27–28 May 1979; *Daily America*, 27–28 May; "Editorial", *The Australian* 28 May 1979; "A new unexpected role for Hawke", Rome: *Daily America*; *International Herald Tribune*, 28 May 1979; On the 28 May 1979 newspapers across Australia publicised the news. There was a large advertisement in the *Australian*; photos of Vladimir Slepak and Ida Nudel and an editorial in the *Telegraph*, Brisbane 28 May 1979, stating "The Amazing Mr Hawke: Australians have become a little accustomed to the spectacle of Bob Hawke moving into a seemingly dead-locked dispute and loving it".
19   I J Leibler, President, ECAJ, to A Basov, Soviet Ambassador, 31 May 1979, Box 78, Soviet Jewry March–May 1979 File, VJBD, LaTrobe Section, SLV, Melbourne.
20   "Parliamentary Question – Soviet dissidents and Jewish emigration", transcript of parliamentary debate, 28 May 1979, cable to the Moscow Embassy, p. 196, Part 16, 69/2/5/7/, A1838, NAA.
21   Hawke, *The Hawke Memoirs*, p. 91.
22   "Report on Visit to Israel and Rome", pp. 53–4.

23 Cables to Department of Foreign Affairs, Rome, 31 May 1979, Part 16, 69/2/5/7/, A1838, NAA.
24 Hawke, *The Hawke Memoirs*, p. 91.
25 Leibler to Begin, 4 June 1979, IJLA-Jer.
26 Bourchier, "Hawke Visit to Moscow", p. 4 (p. 231), Part 17, 69/2/5/7, A1838.
27 Pullan, *Bob Hawke*, p. 161.
28 Hawke, *The Hawke Memoirs*, p. 91.
29 Sam Lipski interview with Hawke, 2010.

CHAPTER 18: SOME OF MY CLOSEST FRIENDS ARE KGB

1 Litvinoff to Leibler after reading Leibler's "Report on Visit to Singapore, 22 August 1979", 28 August 1979, IJLA-Jer.
2 inward cablegram, 28 July 1979, "USSR – Foreign Policy – Relations with Australia – General – Visits and Exchanges – Moscow Olympic Games (Olympic Attaché)", Part 2, 19 March – 31 August 1979, 69/1/3/6/19, A1838, NAA.
3 This was particularly the case with Ron Cibas, director of Sydney-based Palanga Travel, which was the Australian agent for Aeroflot. He met with the Australian embassy officials in Moscow on 7 June 1979 trying to discredit Leibler, inward cablegram, 14 June 1979, "USSR – Foreign Policy – Relations with Australia – General – Visits and Exchanges – Moscow Olympic Games (Olympic Attaché)" Part 2, 19 March – 31 August 1979, 69/1/3/6/19, A1838, NAA.
4 Recollections of Isi Leibler, 13 January 2013.
5 "Report on Visit to Singapore", 22 August 1979, IJLA-Jer.
6 ibid.
7 *The Age*, 10 September 1979.
8 Leibler, "Meeting with Yuri Pavlov, Acting Soviet Ambassador, 16 October 1979", "Soviet Jewry October 1979 File", Box 78, VJBD, LaTrobe Section, State Library of Victoria.
9 ibid.
10 Notes re telephone conversation with Ambassador Kidron, 31 October 1979, IJLA-Jer.
11 WJC Report, Chicago, 5–7 November, IJLA-Jer
12 "Meeting Thursday 25th October at the Soviet Embassy", "Soviet Jewry October 1979 File", Box 78, VJBD, LaTrobe Section, State Library of Victoria.
13 Canberra Lakeside Hotel, "Meeting with Genandy Nayanov and Yuri Pavlov", 29 November 1979, p. 8, IJLA-Jer.
14 *Australian Jewish News*, 25 January 1979, p. 4.
15 Presentation by Mr I J Leibler to Olympic Games Meeting in London,

17 January 1980, IJLA-Jer.

16 Leibler to all key international Jewish leaders, 23 January 1980, IJLA-Jer.

17 Cables 11, 12 and 19 February, and press statement 26 February, "USSR – Foreign Policy – Relations with Australia – General – Visits and Exchanges – Moscow Olympic Games (Olympic Attaché)", Part 3, 5 September 1979 – 24 April 1980, 69/1/3/6/19, A1838, NAA.

18 Tony Wright, "All-or-None Ban on Games: Patching Stalls the PM", *Border Morning Mail*, Albury, 23 January 1980, IJLA-Jer.

19 *Morning Herald*, Sydney, 15 Feb 1980.

20 *Examiner*, Launceston, 16 February 1980 and "Hawke Blasts Boycott as Absurd", *Sunday Telegraph*, 17 February 1980.

21 *The Australian Jewish Times* (*AJT*), 24 January 1980, IJLA, Jerusalem.

22 "Ballet 'Nyet' Olympics 'Da'", Editorial, *AJT*, 31 January 1980.

23 Editorial *AJT*, 28 February 1980.

24 *AJN*, 29 February 1980.

25 Leibler to Fraser, 13 February 1980, 4 pages, IJLA-Jer.

26 Dr Ian McKay telephoned Leibler on 2 March 1980, after Fraser had read the letter. "Summary of events leading to Moscow visit – March 1980", IJLA-Jer.

27 "Summary of events leading to Moscow visit – March 1980", IJLA-Jer.

28 For Mr Ashwin from P G F Henderson, 7 March 1980, "USSR – Foreign Policy – Relations with Australia – General – Visits and Exchanges – Moscow Olympic Games (Olympic Attaché)", Part 3, 5 September 1979 – 24 April 1980, 69/1/3/6/19, A1838, NAA.

29 Outward cable to Ambassador, 7 March 2010, "USSR – Foreign Policy – Relations with Australia – General – Visits and Exchanges – Moscow Olympic Games (Olympic Attaché)", Part 3, 5 September 1979 – 24 April 1980, 69/1/3/6/19, A1838, NAA.

30 "Report of Trip to Moscow, 17–21 March", 25 March 1980, p. 32, IJLA-Jer.

31 ibid.

32 Embassy Report, 24 April 1980, "USSR – Foreign Policy – Relations with Australia – General – Visits and Exchanges – Moscow Olympic Games (Olympic Attaché)", Part 3, 5 September 1979 – 24 April 1980, A1838, item 69/1/3/6/19, NAA.

33 ibid.

34 "Report of Trip to Moscow, 17–21 March", 25 March 1980, p. 31, IJLA-Jer.

35 ibid, p. 57.

36 Leibler report, April 1980, IJLA-Jer.

37 "Post Moscow Visit", London, Israel and Paris, p. 25.

38 "Olympics: Moscow Clear of Dissidents", *News*, Perth, 20 May 1980.

CHAPTER 19: IT'S ABOUT THE REFUSENIKS

1   See for example his statement: "Soviet aggression must not triumph", *The Australian*, 14 February 1980.
2   Fraser's statement, *The Age*, 24 May 1980.
3   In the telephone survey 59 per cent opposed going to Moscow and only 33 per cent supported participation, *The Age*, 5 June 1980.
4   Leibler to Dr N G Sudarikov, 29 May 1980, IJLA-Jer.
5   Leibler to Prof Ya'acov Ro'i, and to Zvi Nezer, 21 July 1980, IJLA-Jer.
6   Report of the NSW Board of Deputies debate, *Australian Jewish Times*, 28 August 1980.
7   "Post Moscow Visit", London, Israel and Paris, p. 68, IJLA-Jer.
8   Text of B'nai B'rith International Press Release, 22 July 1980, IJLA-Jer.
9   See *The Herald*, Melbourne, 23 July 1980, *The Sun*, 23 July 1980 and *The Australian Financial Review*, 24 July 1980.
10 Douglas Wilkie, "No Reason for cynicism over the Mal medal", *Sunday Press*, 27 July 1980.
11 Telex from Leibler to Jack Spitzer, JDL Chairman, 4 August 1980.
12 "Speech to B'nai B'rith International, Prime Minister, for the Media", 1/2 September 1980, p. 5, IJLA-Jer.
13 "Treatment of Jews in the Soviet Union", House of Representatives Question Time, *Hansard*, 25 February 1982.
14 ibid.
15 *Australian Jewish Times*, 20 May 1982.
16 Letter from Leibler to Rita Ekert, The Thirty-Fivers, 7 June 1982, IJLA-Jer.
17 Peter Coleman and Tony Street, Question Time, Parliamentary Debates, *Hansard*, 28 and 29 October 1982.
18 Article on the Jewish plight in the USSR quoting Sam Salcman, *The Sun*, 17 July 1980.
19 Steven Windmueller, in Murray Friedman and Albert D Chernin (eds.), *A Second Exodus,* London and Hanover: Brandeis University Press, 1999, p. 162.
20 William Nelson, Second Secretary, Australian Embassy, Moscow, 20 July 1981, "USSR Political Nationalities Jewish", Part 17, 4 June 1979 – 4 January 1985, 69/2/5/7, A1838, NAA.
21 Article on Soviet Jewry, 8 June 1982, IJLA-Jer.
22 *Australian Jewish News*, 11 September 1981.
23 Cable from Moscow, 21 October 1983, "USSR Political Nationalities Jewish", Part 17, 4 June 1979 – 4 January 1985, 69/2/5/7, A1838, NAA.
24 "Concern in Europe on Jews in USSR", *Canberra Times*, 19 June 1984.
25 "Hayden Query Riles Reds", *The Herald*, 30 May 1984. See also *The Australian*, 31 May 1984.

26   *Australian Jewish Times*, 24 September 1981.
27   ECAJ Press Release, 6 January 1981, IJLA-Jer.
28   Memo from Sam Salcman to Isi and Mark Leibler, ALP Victorian Foreign Affairs Committee, 18 June 1982, IJLA-Jer.
29   Leibler to Hawke, 23 March 1983, IJLA-Jer.
30   Tony Duboudin, Melbourne, "Australia renews Soviet ties after freeze on Afghanistan", *The Times*, London, 19 March 1983.
31   Note from telephone conversation with Hawke, 9 July 1983, IJLA-Jer.
32   Report on meeting, 27 August 1983, IJLA-Jer.
33   Memo 6 October 1983, IJLA-Jer.
34   Hayden's views about Israel became increasingly more sympathetic, so that by 1986 he addressed the Zionist Federation of Australia's 32nd Biennial Conference. Isi Leibler's brother Mark, the Zionsit Federation President, had established a close rapport with the Foreign Affairs Minister.
35   Hayden to Leibler, 18 April 1984, IJLA-Jer.

CHAPTER 20: GORBACHEV, GENEVA AND *GLASNOST*

1   Leibler to Morris Abram, 15 February 1985, IJLA-Jer.
2   In his autobiography, Abram noted that his family had not even pressured him to have a bar mitzvah. Abram, *The Day is Short*, p. 25.
3   Abram to Leibler, 3 January 1984, IJLA-Jer.
4   Fred Lazin, *The Struggle for Soviet Jewry*, pp. 27–8.
5   "Morris Abram", Editorial, *Forward*, 24 March 2000.
6   Personal diary notes, meeting of the International Council of World Conferences for Soviet Jewry, September 1985, IJLA-Jer.
7   ibid.
8   "Address by Leibler to the United States Congressional Sub-committee", 6 September 1985, IJLA-Jer.
9   Transcript of the meeting of the International Council, 30 January 1986, Jerusalem, IJLA-Jer.
10   Prime Minister's Media Release, 7 March 1986, "USSR – Political Nationalities – Jews", Part 18, 69/2/5/7, A1838, NAA.
11   In November 1983 she raised the issue in the House, *Australian Jewish News (AJN)* 25 November 1983 and addressed a rally at Caulfield Park, *AJN*, 9 December 1983.
12   Suzanne D Rutland's interview with Joan Child, Beaumaris, Melbourne, August 2009.
13   ibid.
14   Leibler report, 19 September 1986, IJLA-Jer.
15   Departmental memo re Caplan's request, 13 October 1986, referring to "several obstacles" and Bill Hayden's reply to Joan Child, 16 October 1986, Part 18, 69/2/5/7, A1838, NAA.

16   *Sun*, Melbourne, 7 March 1987. See also *Northern Territory News*, 3
      March 1987, *The Examiner*, 4 March 1987, *Canberra Times*, 4 March
      1987, *The Age*, 4 March 1987 and *Mirror*, 6 March 1987.
17   Telephone conversation between Hawke and Leibler, 4 March 1987,
      2.30pm, IJLA-Jer.
18   Mike Davis, "Sydney Dateline", *AJN*, 13 March 1987.
19   *Border Mail*, Albury, 27 February and *AJN*, 10 April 1987.

CHAPTER 21: TEN DAYS IN MOSCOW

1   Leibler's diary notes of the May 1987 visit, pp. 53–5, IJLA, Jerusalem.
2   Initially the Australian embassy in Moscow had been reluctant to
      agree to these conditions, arguing that it would be better to take a
      lower profile during Leibler's visit. Cable from Moscow, exclusive for
      Williams, Department of the Prime Minister and Cabinet, and Michael
      Costello, Department of Foreign Affairs, 17 July 1986, "USSR – Political
      Nationalities – Jews", Item 69/2/5/7, No. 18, Series A1838, NAA. But
      during a personal meeting, Hawke agreed to all of Leibler's requests.
      Mara Mustafine, Acting/Assistant Secretary, Europe Branch, to Mr M
      Costello, EANA Division Head, and Mr S. Spencer, EEU Section, 21
      July 1986, p. 179, Item 69/2/5/7, No 18, Series A1838, NAA. However,
      with the cancellation of the visas, this was no longer relevant.
3   File note, 31 August 1987, IJLA-Jer.
4   Memo, 24 December 1987, Part 22, A1838 Series 69/2/5/7/, NAA.
5   Tim MacDonald, "Diplomat Reached out to Dissidents: Ted Pocock,
      1934–2013", Obituary, *Sydney Morning Herald*, 26 April 2013, http://
      www.smh.com.au/comment/obituaries/diplomat-reached-out-to-
      dissidents-20130425-2ih18.html accessed 30 July 2013.
6   Pocock to Canberra, inward cable, 23 December 1986, "USSR –
      Political Nationalities – Jews", Item 69/2/5/7, No 19, Series A1838,
      NAA.
7   Pocock to Canberra, PM and Cabinet Department and DFAT, 7 August
      1986, pp. 191–2, "USSR – Political Nationalities – Jews", Item 69/2/5/7,
      No 18, Series A1838, NAA.
8   Four-page cable from Moscow 23 June 1987, 139–42, Item 69/2/5/7,
      No 20, Series A1838, NAA.
9   Pocock to Canberra, PM and Cabinet Department and DFAT, 7 August
      1986, pp. 191–2, "USSR – Political Nationalities – Jews", Item 69/2/5/7,
      No 18, Series A1838, NAA.
10   Isi Leibler, "Report on Visit to Moscow, 20–29 September 1987", p. 44,
      IJLA-Jer.
11   Subsequently Lipski and Leibler drafted a lengthy unpublished report
      of their visit, nicknamed "The Red Book", because of the colour of the

cover. Isi J Leibler, Soviet Jewry: Report on Visit to Moscow (20–29 September, 1987), Melbourne, Australia, October 1987, pp. 381, 764.7941, L53m, Copy 1.

12   "2.37 Melor Sturva, Political Columnist of *Izvestia* (28 September)", Soviet Jewry Report, October 1987, pp. 236–46.

13   "2.21 Yuri Reshetov, Deputy Director of Humanitarian Affairs, Foreign Ministry (23 September)", Soviet Jewry Report, pp. 133–47.

14   Leibler's diary notes of the May 1987 visit, pp. 53–5, IJLA-Jer.

15   Copy of speech at the Choral Synagogue, Moscow, IJLA-Jer.

16   "2.24 At the Home of Yosif Begun" (26 September), Soviet Jewry Report, p. 164.

17   "2.18 farewell to Felix Abramovich" Soviet Jewry Report, p. 127a.

18   "2.40 Alexander Lerner, Vladimir Slepak, Yuli Kosharovsky and Alexander Yoffe" (28 September 1987), Soviet Jewry Report, pp. 252–3.

19   2.41 meeting at the home of Andrei Sakharov and Yelena Bonner (28 September), Soviet Jewry Report, p. 54.

20   *Jerusalem Post*, 2 October 1987 and *The Australian* 12 October 1987.

21   "2.41 Tuesday Morning", Soviet Jewry Report, pp. 256–7.

22   Soviet Jewry Report.

23   Leibler first wrote to Hawke about names on the list on 23 October, suggesting that they meet to discuss his visit to Moscow in September. "Soviet Jewry", Part 21, 19 August 1987 – 3 December 1987, 69/2/5/7/, A1838, NAA. The meeting actually took place on 24 November 1987 in Canberra. "Meeting with Hawke Agenda", "Soviet Jewry", IJLA-Jer.

CHAPTER 22: THE FULL CIRCLE

1   "The World Today", Radio 2BL transcript, 2 December 1987.

2   Michelle Grattan, "Leaders tackle Human Rights", *The Age*, Melbourne, 2 December 1987.

3   Niki Savva, "Hawke Warms to Gorbachev", *The Sun*, 2 December 1987.

4   ibid.

5   D'Alpuget, *Hawke: The Prime Minister*, p. 215

6   "Refuseniks hail battler Bob", *The Sun*, 3 December 1987.

7   "Release of Refuseniks", Radio 2FC, interview with Hawke, Leibler and Pavel Abramovitch, 3 December 1987. This was one of a number of live interviews on radio and television.

8   *Jewish Telegraphic Agency (JTA)* Report, 4 December 1987.

9   Gal Beckerman, *When they come for us, we'll be gone*, p. 527.

10   See George Shultz in Yaacov Ro'i (ed.), *The Jewish Movement in the Soviet Union*, Washington DC, Woodrow Wilson Centre Press, p. 425.

11   Leibler to British historian, Martin Gilbert, 22 December 1987, IJLA-

Jer.

12 *The Age*, Melbourne, 30 January and *Sunday Observer* 31 January 1988.

13 Isi Leibler to Emanuel Litvinoff, 15 February 1988, IJLA-Jer.

14 Leibler noted that the choice of the name "Solomon Mykhoels" would have been "unthinkable" even a few months earlier, "Isi Leibler, Glasnost: Australia, the USSR and the Jews", October–November 1988, p. 4, IJLA-Jer.

15 See for example "File Note", 28 September 1988, re a meeting with DFAT officers, IJLA-Jer. Leibler was in Moscow from 16 to 25 October to finalise the agreement. He travelled with Johnny Baker from Melbourne and Steven Lewis from Sydney.

16 The contract was signed by the Ministry of Culture, making Hebrew teaching legal for the first time in 70 years.

17 Leibler interview with Sam Lipski, "A 'new peak' for Soviet Jewry", International, *Australian Jewish News*, 4 November 1988.

18 Leibler "File note", 20 March 1988, Soviet Jewry 794 1/250, IJLA-Jer.

19 Gluz first wrote to Leibler on 16 May 1988 about a visit to Melbourne. Leibler responded on 20 May 1988 that he would only support the visit if it could be a joint venture with Australian Jewish musicians going to Moscow. This opened the door for the establishment of the Centre. IJLA-Jer.

20 *Jews in the USSR*, Vol. XVII, No. 39, October 1988.

21 Interview with Simchah Dinitz, *Jerusalem Post*, 10 November 1988, where he alleged that Leibler "had hijacked the Mykhoels Centre from the World Jewish Congress". In a letter to Russian refusenik, Kosharovsky, Leibler described this interview as "outrageous". Dinitz later wrote him a three-page apology, 3 December 1988, IJLA-Jer.

22 Bartov to Leibler, 4 October 1988, IJLA-Jer.

23 Michael Danby, "No. Australian Jews should be sceptical of Moscow", *AJN*, 2 September 1988.

24 Hawke called Leibler at 4.30 pm on Friday 8 July 1988, seven-page file note, "Highly Confidential", IJLA-Jer.

25 Isi Leibler to Reuven Merhav, on his appointment as Director General, Israel Foreign Ministry, 4 January 1989.

26 Prime Minister's Press Release, 2 September 1988, IJLA-Jer.

27 See for example "File Note", 28 September 1988, re a meeting with DFAT officers, IJLA-Jer.

28 "Isi Leibler, Glasnost: Australia, the USSR and the Jews", p. 8, JILA, Jerusalem. His visit was from 16–25 October 1988. This was later published as an article entitled "Soviet Jewry – a New Debate" in the *Jerusalem Post*, 30 November 1988, p. 4; the *Jewish Chronicle*, London, entitled "Changing Realities in a Changing World", 9 December 1988,

pp. 32–3, and in an edited version, "Australian Jews blaze a trial to Moscow", *The Australian*, 14 December 1988, p. 11.

29   Leibler to Edgar Brofman, 15 November 1988, IJLA-Jer.

30   Leibler attended the WJC meeting in Mexico on 9–10 October, before his fifth visit to Moscow, 16–25 October, IJLA-Jer.

31   Leibler and Bronfman rebuilt the bridges during the meeting of the World Conference on Soviet Jewry's International Council, held in Jerusalem, 1–3 December 1988, IJLA-Jer. Some 20 years later, in 2005–07, Leibler became the WJC's most outspoken and, ultimately, its most devastating critic when he exposed scandal and fraud at the organisation's highest levels. His relentless pursuit of WJC President Edgar Bronfman and Secretary-General Israel Singer eventually forced both their resignations.

32   Elie Wiesel had visited Australia in 1988 as a guest of the Australian Institute of Jewish Affairs, headed by Leibler. When he heard about the plans for the Mykhoels Centre, he informed Leiber that he was keen to participate. The February 1989 dates were chosen to fit into Wiesel's schedule.

33   Elie Wiesel, "To my fellow Jews in Russia", republished in the *Australian Jewish News*, 17 February 1989.

34   *Jerusalem Post*, 20 February 1989.

35   Leibler had arranged with the Soviets and the Australian Department of Foreign Affairs that the two Israelis, Dudu Fisher and Yaffa Yarkoni, would be granted their visas via Australia, since full diplomatic relations had not been re-established between Israel and the Soviets. These visas, together with the visas for Isi and Naomi Leibler, were only granted at the last moment.

36   *Jerusalem Post*, 20 February 1989.

37   Shoshana Cardin to Isi Leibler, 28 February 1989, IJLA-Jer.

INDEX

A

Aarons, Eric 80, 81, 82, 84, 85–6
Aarons, Laurie 80–1, 82
Aarons, Mark 80, 81
Abbott, Tony 12
Abram, Morris 200–2, 229
Abramovich, Pavel and Marta 5, 6, 8, 213,
    214–15, 221
Adass Yisroel 42
Aharon, Ben 165
Ahuja, Rakesh 218
aliyah 15, 160, 193
All Union Council of Trade Unions of the
    USSR (AUCTU) Presidium 171–2
Allende, Salvador 101
Allon, Yigal 53
Alony, Michael 138
Andropov, Yuri 81
anti-Semitism 15, 17, 20, 22, 34, 45, 56,
    69–70, 96, 116, 158
anti-Zionist committee 194
Apple, Rabbi Raymond 185
Aptheker, Herbert 67
Arab-Israeli conflict 169
Arnold, James 49
Arzhak, Nikolay. *See* Daniel, Yuli
Ashkanasy, Maurice 24, 28, 30–1, 32
    criticised Soviet Union 88
    early life 24
    Einfeld and 25–6, 88
    letter to Goldmann 77
    letter to Menzies 65
    in 1954 federal elections 25
    praised Leibler's role 83
Ashwin, Robin 226
Aston, William 66, 96
Australian Committee for the Rescue of
    Soviet Jews 135
Australian Council of Trade Unions
    (ACTU) 163
Australian Institute of Jewish Affairs'

Human Rights Award 7
Australian Jewish Herald 39, 54, 70, 72
Australian Jewish News 41, 54
Australian Labor Party *see* Labor Party,
    Australian
Australian Olympic Federation (AOF) 146,
    155–6, 157, 160–1, 189
Australian Security Intelligence
    Organisation (ASIO) 58, 68
Avigur, Shaul 15
    contribution to Israel 16
    headed Nativ 16
    meeting with Leibler 15–16
    Golda Meir on his style 16
    report to Ben Gurion 17
    as spymaster 15
Azbel, Mark 90

B

Barkat, Reuven 95
Barnard, Lance 123
Bartov, David 225
Barwick, Garfield 33, 34, 45, 53, 57–8
Basov, Alexander 139
Baume, Peter 136
Beazley, Kim Edward 135, 139
Becher, Michael 133
Beckerman, Gal 100, 221
Begin, Menachem 169, 188
Begun, Yosef 5, 213–14
Ben Gurion, David 17, 104
Berinson, Joe 110
Berlin Wall fall, in 1989 xiii, 14
Beware Zionism (Ivanov, Yuri) 91
Bilney, Gordon 128
Birney, Jack 136
Bishop, Julie 12
Blakeney, Fred 108
B'nei Akiva youth movement 15–16, 18, 42
Bonner, Yelena 176
Borisenko, Vladimir 176
Bornstein, David 43

Bourchier, Murray 138, 156, 157, 158–9, 170–1, 173, 186–7
Bowan, John 92, 197, 219
Bowen, Nigel 112
Brailovsky, Victor 175
Branson, George 48
Brezhnev, Leonid 4, 121–2, 134
Brezniak, Haim 71, 73
Bridge, The 72, 73
Bronfman, Edgar 7, 201, 225, 228, 264
Brown, Neil 134
Brussels Presidiums 104–5, 184
Bulgakov, Gheeman Vladimirovitch 148–9
Bulletin, The 31, 44–5, 50, 70–1
Bund youth movement 30
Burg, Joseph 212
Burgos trials 101–2

C

Cadman, Alan 191
Calwell, Arthur 28, 52
Canberra, freedom ride to 133–45
Cardin, Shoshana 229
Carter, Jimmy 133, 184
Chabad 193
channels of communication 60–6
Chernenko, Konstantin 194
Child, Joan 3, 204–5, 222
Churchward, Lloyd 80
Clancy, Pat 153
Cohen Affair 26, 36, 41, 43, 47–59, 61, 63, 74, 163
Cohen, Avraham Abba 78
Cohen, Barry 124, 194
Cohen, Sam 24, 47–8
    approach on Soviet Jewry 37–8
    Council and 27–9
    early life 26–7
    joining Einfeld to protest 64
    Leibler devised "open questions" for 38–9
    preselected for second position on Victorian Senate ticket 30
    supporters 31, 38
Cohen Case, the 31
Cohen, Judith 164
Cold War 15, 32, 58, 68, 113
Coleman, Peter 44, 53, 192
Comay, Michael 55
Commonwealth Investigation Service

(CIS) 72
Communist Party of Australia (CPA, Marxist-Leninist) 32, 65, 67–8, 70, 71, 79, 82, 85
Communist Party of the Soviet Union (CPSU) 87
    Ideological Commission 69
Concert Hall event 1
Contemporary Judaism and Zionism (Mayatsky, F S) 69
Cooney, Barney 31
Cooper, F B 106, 107
Coopersmith, Yetta 107
Cormack, Sir Magnus 135
Cowen, Zelman 25, 84
Crossing the Party Line (Taft, Bernie) 68
Crown, Alan 72
Cuban missile crisis 55, 56

D

Daghestan Komunist (newspaper) 29
Daily Telegraph 31, 44, 46, 64
Dalrymple, Rawdon 125
Danby, Michael 225
Daniel, Yuli 85
Dark Years, The 192, 195
Davis, Rufus 39
de Vahl Davis, Graham 205–6
death sentences 101–2
Decter, Moshe 21–2, 59
Democratic Labor Party (DLP) 32
Dinitz, Simcha 225
Dinstein, Yoram 197
diploma tax 109–10, 121
Dissent (journal) 70
Dixon, Richard 87, 88
Dobie, James Dov Mathieson 141
Downer, Alexander 12, 55
Dragunski, Colonel 194
Dreyfus, Alfred 50
Ducker, Klaus 141
Dulzin, Aryeh 152–3
Dymshits, Mark 97, 100, 102

E

East-West Trade Relations Act 112
Edelshtein, Yuli 228
Einfeld, Marcus
    appointed to Judicial Commission 104–5

call for protest 97
convicted for perjury 96
coordinated meetings with Labor's
    Jewish MPs 96
early life 96
petition to UN 97, 98–9
Shaw and 102
Einfeld, Syd
    Ashkanasy and 25–6, 88
    division between Cohen and 48–9,
        50, 64
    early life 25
    letter to Soviet embassy, in 1962 36
    reprinted *The Bridge*'s supplement 73
    won the seat of Phillip, in 1961 elec-
        tions 24, 25
Eliav, Binyamin 19, 21
Elitzur, Michael 146–7
Erell, Moshe 125
Erell, Shlomo 108
Eshkol, Levi 75
Evans, Gareth 12
Evatt, Herbert 28, 62
"even-handed" policy 12
Executive Council of Australian Jewry
    (ECAJ) 22, 28
Exodus (Uris, Leon) novel 90

F

Falk, Gerald 96
"Father of the Refuseniks." *See* Slepak,
    Vladimir
Fedorenko, Nikolai 87–8
Fein, Benjamin 160
Fink, Mina 107
Fishman, Fitzi 106–7
Fishman, Rabbi Yakov 150
Fitzgerald, Tom 44
Fitzpatrick, Brian 80
Ford, Gerald 134
Foreign Affairs, Department of 101, 107,
    123, 135, 141, 160, 162, 197
Franta. *See* Knopfelmacher, Frank
Fraser, Malcolm 3, 132, 184, 189–91
    AOF meet 189
    criticism of Soviets 191
    Foreign Affairs advised 190
    Hawke defeated, in 1983 196
    Leibler and 190–1
    won praise in international Soviet

Jewry movement 190
Freedom Ride
    to Canberra 133–45
    objective 134
Freedom Sunday 104
Freilich, Rabbi David 132
Frydman, Mischa 88

G

Gaffney, Abe 42
Gamazeichshikov, V. 44
Garber, Michael 78
Gates of November, The (Potok, Chaim) 5,
    215
Genscher, Hans-Dietrich 194
Georgian Jews 93
Gepner, Gary 104
glasnost 199, 210
Glasser, Phyllis 107
Glazman, Semyon 136
Gluz, Michael 224, 263
Goldberg, Arthur 104
Goldberg, Ben-Zion 72
Goldbloom, Sam 29
Goldmann, Nahum 48, 64, 72, 73, 227
    and Leibler, debate of 74–8
Goldshtein, Isai 176
Gomułka, Władysław 88
Goot, Robert 110, 136, 153, 185, 195
Gorbachev, Mikhail 1, 7–8, 178, 199–200,
    220, 221, 229
Gorton, John 37, 49, 98–9, 101
Gosper, Kevan 161, 189
Gott, Ken 70
Gouttman, Rodney 62
Govrin, Joseph 147
Gramm, Boris 207
Grange, Syd 155, 161, 162, 189
Griffiths, Alan 206
Grigorenko, Pytor 143
Grivans, H G 143
Gromyko, Andrei 112, 194–5, 197, 204–5

H

Halfpenny, John 153–4
Halfpenny, Margaret 156
Hamer, David J 98, 110
Hannan, George Conrad 47, 49
Harriman, Averell 65
Hartley, Bill 167, 195–6

Havin, Reuben 41
Hawke, Bob 1–2, 170–8
    awards 7
    Bourchier and 170–1
    defeated Fraser in 1983 196
    Gorbachev and 220
    gratitude to 4, 6
    Howard's speech on 7
    involvement with Soviet Jewry 6, 7,
        163, 167–8
    Israel visit 12, 13, 163–5, 166
    Leibler and 9–10, 168, 196–7, 206
    meeting with Begin 169
    meeting with refuseniks 8, 171, 174
    Moscow visit 170
    Pimenov and 175–6
    raised Soviet Jewry issue with
        Shevardnadze 205–6
    Shelepin and 165–7
    speech on refuseniks' night 8, 13
    speechwriter and 12–13
    views on Israel-Palestinian conflict
        8–9, 11–12
Hawke, Hazel 171, 221
Haworth, William 43, 45–6, 65
Hay, David 65
Hayden, Bill 12, 189, 194, 196, 197
Hayes, Saul 78
Haylen, Leslie 50
Hearn, Margaret 80
Heinemann, Hans 113–14
Helsinki Accords 134–5, 142, 143, 144,
    145, 200, 202
        Final Act of the 1975 Helsinki
            Agreement 143
Henderson, Peter 190
Hendrickson, Bert 49–50
Herzl, Theodor 1, 50
Hill, Robert 206
Hill, Ted 71
Holding, Clyde 164
Holocaust survivors 36
Holt, Harold 28, 31, 50
Holt, Robert 53
Horne, Donald 44
Howard, John 3, 7
human rights 57, 124, 134, 136–7, 142,
    155, 200, 204
Human Rights Award 7, 190

I

International B'nai B'rith 190
International Covenant on Civil and
    Political Rights 99, 143
International Labor Organisation (ILO)
    164, 165
Intifada, 1987 9, 11
Ioffe, Alexander and Rosa 5, 8
Irving, Terence H 79
Isvestia 210
Italian Communist Party 71
"Italian liners" 81

J

Jackson, Henry "Scoop" 112, 115–22
Jackson-Vanik amendment 112–13, 120–2,
    183
Jacobi, Ralph 141
Jacobson, Nathan 38, 105
Janner, Greville 153
Jedwab, Lou 88
Jetset 146–8, 152, 155, 161–2, 168
Jewish Council to Combat Fascism and
    Anti-Semitism 27
Jewish Minorities Research 21
Jewish Unity Association (JUA) 71–2
Jews in Eastern Europe (newsletter) 21
Joint Committee on Foreign Affairs and
    Defence (JCFAD) 135, 138
Judaism Without Embellishment (Kichko,
    Trofim) 66, 67, 91

K

Kaganovich, Lazar 216
Kane, Jack 125
Katsh, Abraham I 72
Kelly, Peter 31
Kennedy, John F 45
Kennelly, Pat 48, 60
Kerr, Sir John 132
Kholmianksy, Alexander 5
Kholmyansky, Anna 5
Kichko, Trofim 66, 91
Kichko book 69, 70
Kidron, Abraham 182
Killanin, Lord 149, 160, 161, 162, 184
Killen, James 64
Kimmel, Hans 36
King, Martin Luther 67

King, Peter 144
Kirillov, Vladimir 171, 172
Kissinger, Henry 115–22
Klein, Lou 127–8
Klugman, Richard E 141
Klutznick, Phillip 182
Knopfelmacher, Frank 39–40
    public statements, emphasised issue of
        Soviet Jewry 40
Koval, Vladimir
    demands beyond AOF 155
    Leibler copied letter to 156
Kruschev, Nikita 22
Krygier, Martin 144
Kuznetsov, Edward 97, 100, 102

L

Labor Party, Australian 17, 26, 30, 32, 167,
    196, 204
Landman, Lionel 156
Leibler, Isi 1, 4
    Ashkanasy welcomed new booklet
        of 83
    Australian Olympic Federation (AOF)
        and 146, 155–6, 157, 160–2
    B'nei Akiva youth movement 15–16,
        18, 42
    Bronfman and 225, 228, 264
    channels of communication 60–6
    Cohen and 37–9
    Decter letter to 59
    early life 17–18
    ECAJ meeting 153
    establishing ACTU-Jetset 168
    Fraser and 185, 190–1
    and Goldmann, debate of 74–8
    Grange and 155, 161, 162
    Hawke and 9–10, 168, 196–7, 206
    Haworth contacted 43
    Hayden and 197
    Knopfelmacher's attack 152
    letter to Sudarikov 190
    Levanon's criticism of 182
    Lishkah's recruitment of 22
    Litvinoff and 54, 70, 86, 89, 179–80,
        222
    married Naomi Porush, in 1958 18
    meeting with Avigur 15–16, 19
    meeting with Bowen 197
    meeting with CPA leaders, in 1964

67, 68
    meeting with Eliav 19
    meeting with Eric Aarons 82–3
    meeting with Gramm 207
    meeting with Jewish communists 71
    meeting with Reagan 202
    meeting with refuseniks 150–1, 158
    meeting with Soviet officials 148–9
    meeting with Taft 78, 243
    meeting with Zoubkov, during PATA
        meeting 180–1
    Mortimer's endorsement of his book
        73, 79, 81
    Moscow visit 148, 155–8, 168, 185–6,
        207–19
    moved to Israel, in 1999 19
    Patching and 147
    Pavlov and 181–2
    printing Kichko book 69
    relationship with Abram 200–1
    relationship with WJC 227
    Shayevich's invitation 212
    Waten criticism 69–70, 87
    Wentworth and 35–6, 37
    Whitlam's approach 129
    youth movement, development of
        15–16, 18, 42
Leibler, Naomi 9, 18, 19, 148, 151, 153,
    159, 169, 207–8, 209, 215, 224
Leningrad trial 97, 100, 101–2, 104, 106,
    107, 109–10
Lerner, Alexander 5, 7, 175, 213, 216–17,
    222
"Let My People Go" 97, 104–5, 132, 221
Levanon, Nehemiah 17
    early life 20–1
Levich, Benjamin 110–11
Levin, Rabbi Yehuda 45
Liberal Party of Australia 25, 35, 43, 44,
    61, 63
Liberal/Country Party (LCP) coalition 32
Licht, Hans 41
Lilienthal, Alfred 196
Lippmann, Walter 29, 78, 164, 194
Lishkat Hakesher (The Liaison Bureau).
    See Nativ
Litvin, Zalman 149
Litvinoff, Emanuel 21, 54, 70, 75, 179–80,
    194
Lubofsky, Rabbi Ronald 159

Lucock, Phillip E 110

M

MacCallum, Mungo 35
Macklin, Michael 206
Magid, Isador 128
Malik, Adam 108
Mann, Leon 110
Marantz, Shalom 41
matzot (unleavened bread), for Passover 29, 38, 56, 92, 135–6
"McCarthyism" 22
McIntyre, Sir Laurence 99, 128
McKenzie, David 155, 161, 189
McMahon, William 100, 107, 111–12
McMullin, Alister 49–50
Medding, Peter 30
Meiman, Naum 176
Meir, Golda 16, 93–5, 101, 117–20, 163, 164–5
Mendelevich, Yosef 103
Mendes, Philip 47, 51, 62
Menzies, Robert Gordon 24, 27, 33, 65–6
Merhav, Reuven 226
Mesyatsev, Nicolai Nikolayevich 98
Mills, Stephen 12
Mills, Wilbur 112
Missen, Alan 134
Mittelberg, David 102
Molotov, Vyacheslav 94
Montiefore, Simon Sebag 94
Mortier, Paul 81
Mortimer, Rex Alfred 67–8, 70–1, 73, 79–82, 84–9
Moscow synagogue 211
  on Arkhipova Street 92
Most Favoured Nation (MFN) amendment 112, 115
Mozhayev, Vsevolod 171, 172
Mugga. *See* Kelly, Peter
Munster, George 44
Murphy, Lionel 48–9
Musin, Dimitri 112
Mykhoels, Solomon 20, 223

N

Nasser, Gamal Abdel 88
Nation, The 44
National Conference on Soviet Jewry (NCSJ) 104, 202

Nativ (Lishkat Hakesher/The Liaison Bureau) 16, 17, 20, 21, 22, 71, 94
Nayanov, Genandy 183
Netherlands embassy, The 93, 108–9, 113–14, 125
New Leader, The 21–2
Newell, Alan 152
Newman, Horace Bonham 61
Nezer, Zvi 159
Nikolaeva, T N 56
Nixon-Kissinger administration 113, 116, 118–22
Nixon, Richard 101
noshrim 131, 193
Novick, Paul 71
Novikov, Ignati 161
Novosti 45
NSW Jewish Board of Deputies 22, 25

O

Oistralisheh Yiddisheh Neyess 41
Oistralisheh Yiddisheh Post 40
Okeley, John 186
Oppenheim, Courtney 80
Orlov, Yuri 136
Oslo Accords 13
Ostrovski, Y A (Jacub) 56

P

Packer, Frank 44
Palmer, Helen 80
Panov, Valery 126
Paro, Gina 102
Parolla, Dori 111
Patching, Julius "Judy" 147, 155, 189
Patolichev, Nikolai 125
Pavlov, Yuri 181–2, 183
Peled, Natan 125
perestroika 199, 200, 210
Perle, Richard 116, 121
Petrov, Evdokia 37
Pimenov, Peter (Piotr) 149, 171, 172, 174, 175–6
Pincus, Aryeh Louis 105
Platz, Ernest 27, 39, 69
Plimsoll, James 54, 55
Plyusch, Leonid 143
Pocock, Robert Edward "Ted" 187, 208–9
Podgorny, Nikolai 102, 110
Polsky, Victor 160

Porush, Bertha 107
Potok, Chaim 5
Powys, John C 113–14
"Prague Spring" 81
Pravda 91, 142, 210
Prestin, Elena 5
Prestin, Vladimir 5, 175
Prinz, Joachim 78
Prisoners of Zion 106, 194
Protocols of the Elders of Zion, The 91
Pullan, Robert 146

Q

quiet diplomacy 36, 65, 74, 78, 94

R

rabbinical delegation 136
Rabin, Yitzhak 117, 118–19
Rafael, Gideon 108
Rager, Yitzhak 159–60
Rank and File Committee 31
ransom tax 109
Rappaport, Yeshayeh 40–1
Reagan-Gorbachev summit 203
Reagan, Ronald 200, 202
Redlich, Peter 129
referendum, constitutional 37
refuseniks 1–14, 149, 150–1, 160, 174, 184,
    186, 189–98, 208–9
Reid, Alan 64
Reshetov, Uri 210–11
Riegner, Gerhardt 78
Robertson, Malcolm 81
Roi, Yaakov 56
Rosenbess, Oscar 31
Rosh Hashanah 207
Rothfield, Norman 29
Rozin, Samuel 45
Rubinstein, Tony 41
Rubinstein, Yitzchok 41
Ruskin, Pamela 62
Russell, Bertrand 67
"Russian Spectacular" entertainment group
    132
Rutland, Suzanne 158, 170

S

Sachar, Howard M 91
Sadlier, David 109
Sakharov, Andrei 102, 121, 217–18

Salcman, Sam 194, 195–6
Same, Saul 128
samizdat, Exodus via 90
Samoteikin, Evgeni 197
Samuel, Peter 144
Sanger, Herman 29, 69
Sayn, Geoff 86
Schaffer, Monty 41
Schappes, Morris U 71
Schifter, Robert 211
Schneeweiss, Joachim 72, 152
Schwarzkopf, Norman 199
Scott, D B 141
Sendy, John 86
Shamir, Yitzhak 11, 12
Sharansky, Avital 192
Sharansky, Natan
    arrested on trumped-up charges 192
    Prisoner of Zion xiii–xiv
    release of 203–4
Sharkey, Lance 80
Shaw, Henry 102
Shayevich, Adolf Solomonovich 212
Shelepin, Alexander N 165–7
Shevardnadze, Eduard 205, 210–11
Shibaev, Aleksei 171
Shinbaum, Myrna 137
Shin Bet 17
Shipton, Roger 136
Shteinman, Diane 195
Shultz, George xiv, 210–11
Shumilin, Boris 113
Sibraa, Kerry W 141
Simon, Barry D 141
Sinyavsky, Andrei 85
Six-Day War, 1967 20, 87, 90, 119
Slansky, Rudoph 20
Slepak, Vladimir 5, 213, 215–16
Smirnov, V N 106
Smirnov, Vitaly 161
Snedden, Billy 126
Snider, Baron 38
Solzhenitsyn, Alexander 131
Soviet invasion of Czechoslovakia, 1968
    88, 89
Soviet Jewry
    Australia raising the issue at UN 34,
        45, 99–100, 111, 204
    Australian Committee for 135, 142
    Australia's involvement with 14

books relating to 19
Brezniak's failure to mention in *The Bridge*'s first issue 72
campaign xv, 2–3, 44, 62, 68, 88
challenge to movement 195
discussing with Shevardnadze about human rights and 205–6
emigration xiv, 27–8, 55, 77, 84, 92–3, 95, 96–7, 107, 108–9, 113–14, 121, 125, 126, 130, 166, 192–3
first meeting of new national body for 96
First World Conference in Brussels 104
"Freedom Ride" for 133
Hawke's involvement with 6, 7, 163
National Conference on Soviet Jewry (NCSJ) 104
The New Leader's special edition on 22
Nixon and Kissinger expressed about 118
public rally at Sydney Town Hall 97
renaissance of 203
Wentworth's interest in 37
WJC meeting on 75
Women's Campaign for 195
Soviet Jewry – A reply to Mr I. Leibler 81
"Soviet Jewry – What is the Tragic Truth?" 97
Soviet Jewry and the Australian Communist Party – Documents (Leibler, Isi) 83
Soviet Jewry and Human Rights (Leibler, Isi) 73, 74, 79, 80
Soviet Jews 4, 9, 17, 21–2, 45, 84, 90–5, 131–2
Stein, Harry 68
Stevenson, Adlai 65
Stone, Julius 72, 110
Strategic Arms Limitation Talks (SALT) 116, 137, 176
Street, Tony 192
Sturva, Melor G 210
Sudarikov, Nikolai 190
Sultanik, Rabbi Ellis "Adi" 133–5
and Alony 138
formed a group 135
"Freedom Ride" protest 133–4
visited Soviet Union 133, 138
Suslov, Mikhail 81

Suslov, V P 129, 130
Symon, Eve 185
Symons, Phil 193

T

Taft, Bernard (Bernie) 67, 68, 70, 84, 89
Tange, Arthur 55
Tekoah, Yosef 93
Terz, Abram. *See* Sinyavsky, Andrei
Thatcher, Margaret 200
Thirty-Fives Committee 195
Tinney, John 170
Tobin, Jonathan S 120
Turner, Ian 86

U

Unity (journal) 72
Universal Declaration of Human Rights 54, 92, 99, 111–12, 143
Unsworth, Barrie 206
Ur, Doron 97
U Thant 97, 101

V

Vanik, Charles 112
Vergelis, Aaron 149, 182
Vergelis, Aron 76
Victorian Jewish Board of Deputies (VJBD) 18, 26, 27, 29, 36, 69
Volkovsky, Leonid 5
Volkovsky, Ludmilla 5
Voronel, Alexander 140, 160

W

Wallace, Andy 86
Waller, Sir Keith 108
War of Attrition 118
Washington-Moscow relationship 193, 200
Waten, Hyrall 88
Waten, Judah 27, 28, 68, 69, 87
Weiss, Eugene 42
Wentworth, William (Billy) Charles 34–7, 97, 134–5
died at aged 95 35
introducing constitutional referendum 37
letter to Leibler 35–6, 37
as Minister for Social Services 37
question and Barwick's reply 34

representing Liberal Party in
    Mackellar 35
Wheeldon, John 35, 134, 141, 143–4
White, Douglas 54, 56
Whitlam, Gough 102, 123–32
Wiener, Bono 30, 168
Wiesel, Elie 228, 264
Wilkie, Douglas 191
Willesee, Don 123, 125–6
Willis, David 177
Windmueller, Steven 193
WJC 73–8, 104, 190, 225, 227–8
Wolfensohn, William (Bill) 28
Women's Campaign for Soviet Jewry 195
Wyndham, Cyril 53

Y

Yampolsky, Mark 115
Yarkoni, Yaffa 229
Yiddish speakers 36
Yom Kippur War 118, 126, 127, 167
Yuval, Moshe 19

Z

Zablud, Robert 129
Zemstov, Valeri 224
Zionism 15, 28, 91, 149, 223
Zionist movement 16, 91–2, 96, 102,
    193–4, 212
Zola, Emile 50
Zoubkov, George 179–81

www.ingramcontent.com/pod-product-compliance
Lightning Source LLC
Chambersburg PA
CBHW062201270326

41930CB00009B/1613